D0225743

The Interpretation
of Otherness

The Interpretation
of Otherness

Literature, Religion,
and the American Imagination

GILES GUNN

New York
Oxford University Press
1979

Copyright © 1979 Oxford University Press, Inc.

Library of Congress Cataloging in Publication Data
Gunn, Giles B.
The interpretation of otherness.

Includes bibliographical references and index.
1. American literature—History and criticism.
2. Religion and literature.   3. Religion in literature.   I. Title.
PS166.G8   810'.9'31   78-17870   ISBN 0-19-502453-2

Printed in the United States of America

The Interpretation
of Otherness

Literature, Religion,
and the American Imagination

GILES GUNN

New York
Oxford University Press
1979

Copyright © 1979 Oxford University Press, Inc.

Library of Congress Cataloging in Publication Data
Gunn, Giles B.
The interpretation of otherness.

Includes bibliographical references and index.
1. American literature—History and criticism.
2. Religion and literature.   3. Religion in literature.   I. Title.
PS166.G8   810'.9'31   78-17870   ISBN 0-19-502453-2

Printed in the United States of America

To
Marilyn and Robert
Caroline and Charles

Acknowledgments

During the course of writing I have received encouragement and support from a variety of friends and colleagues. To cite only the most obvious, I wish to thank Anthony C. Yu, Charles H. Long, Schubert M. Ogden, Roland A. Delattre, William A. Clebsch, Nathan A. Scott, Jr., Leo Marx, Tom F. Driver, Martin E. Marty, Robert Detweiler, Ruel W. Tyson, David Hesla, Stephen A. Marini, John H. Schutz, Preston M. Browning, Wesley Kort, Stanley Romaine Hopper, Amos Wilder, David L. Miller, James B. Wiggins, A. K. and Mali Ramanujan, John Seelye, J. Hillis Miller, Jaygook Kim, Stanley Lusby, Thomas Helm, Errol McGuire, Frank Scafella, Michael Kinnamon, James Sellers, Laura Bird Bramlett, and, most especially, my wife, Janet Varner Gunn. While none of these individuals bears any responsibility for what I have written and many would take vigorous exception to certain of my positions, they have all contributed something to my ideas, and several suggested substantial improvements in my arguments.

Without the cheerful cooperation and stylistic good sense of Ms. Victoria Bijur of Oxford University Press, the following pages would have been far less readable and the whole book delayed considerably in production. And without the enthusiastic support and discerning editorial advice of Mr. E. Allen Kelley, vice president at Oxford, and Mr. Charles W. Scott, Oxford's religious books editor, the manuscript might never have been published, at least in its present form. Their generous encouragement and constructive suggestions not only contributed to the formation and expression of certain ideas but also helped me discover what I was really driving at. Lastly, I wish to thank Charles Carmony for able assistance in the compilation of an Index.

To the four persons to whom this book is dedicated, I owe a different debt of gratitude. Their contribution has been one of faith rather than understanding. Even when they have had difficulty grasping the meaning of my work, they have continued to believe in its importance because of their belief in me. And without that belief, as only Marilyn fully knows, since she was most responsible, the work itself would never have been undertaken.

Various early drafts of some of the material included in this volume were delivered as lectures at several institutions where I invariably met with responses that added stimulus and refinement to my thinking and that occasionally compelled me to start writing all over again, among them Syracuse University, Reed College, Duke University, Oregon State University, St. Mary's College, Notre Dame, the University of Southern California, Florida State University, Eckerd College, Yale Divinity School, the University of Tennessee at Knoxville, and Bowdoin College. Fully half of this book was written on a leave made possible through the generosity of the John Simon Guggenheim Memorial Foundation, and I wish to thank that remarkable institution for permitting me to use a portion of the time originally set aside for another project to complete this one. I also wish to acknowledge the generosity of the University Research Council of the University of North Carolina at Chapel Hill which provided me with a grant to cover the cost of preparing a portion of the manuscript for publication. Finally, I wish to thank Mrs. Barbara Jenkins of Northfield, Minnesota, and particularly Mrs. Susan Jarvis of Chapel Hill, for their cheerful patience in typing and retyping successive drafts.

An earlier version of Chapter 2 was first published as "Literature and Its Relation to Religion" in the *Journal of Religion* 50 (July, 1970): 268–91, and was later expanded as the introduction to *Literature and Religion*, edited by Giles Gunn (New York: Harper and Row, 1971), pp. 1–33. An earlier version of Chapter 3 initially appeared under the title "Threading the Eye of the Needle: The Place of the Literary Critic in Religious Studies," *Journal of the American Academy of Religion* XLIII (June, 1975): 164–84. Portions of Chapter 5 were originally published simultaneously under the title "American Literature and the Imagination of Otherness" in the *Journal of Religious Ethics* 3 (Fall, 1975): 193–215, and in *Religion as Story*, edited by James B. Wiggins (New York: Harper and Row, 1975), pp. 65–92. Additional material in Chapter 5 initially appeared as a section of "F. Scott Fitzgerald's *Gatsby* and the Imagination of Wonder," *Journal of the American Academy of Religion* XLI (June, 1973): 171–83. Permission to reprint this material has been kindly granted by the editors and publishers involved.

The lines from "Corson's Inlet" are reprinted from *Collected Poems, 1951–1971*, by A. R. Ammons, with the permission of W. W. Norton & Company, Inc. Copyright © 1972 by A. R. Ammons.

The lines from "Notes Toward a Supreme Fiction," "An Ordinary Evening in New Haven," and "Of Modern Poetry" are reprinted from *The Collected Poems of Wallace Stevens*, with the permission of Alfred A. Knopf, Inc. Copyright © 1954 by Wallace Stevens.

The lines from "My period had come for Prayer" are reprinted by permission of the publishers and the Trustees of Amherst College from *The Poems of Emily Dickinson*, edited by Thomas H. Johnson, Cambridge, Mass.: The Belknap Press of Harvard University Press, Copyright © 1951, 1955 by the President and Fellows of

Harvard College. They are also reprinted by permission of Little, Brown and Company. Copyright 1929 by Martha Dickinson Bianchi. Copyright 1957 by Mary L. Hampson.

The lines from "Spring and All" ("By the Road to the Contagious Hospital") come from William Carlos Williams, *Collected Earlier Poems*. Copyright 1938 by New Directions Publishing Corporation. Reprinted by permission of New Directions Publishing Corporation.

Grateful acknowledgment is also made for the passage from "The Abyss," copyright © 1963 by Beatrice Roethke, Administratrix for the Estate of Theodore Roethke in *The Collected Poems of Theodore Roethke*. Reprinted by permission of Doubleday & Company, Inc.

"The Most of It" and the lines from "West-Running Brook" are from *The Poetry of Robert Frost*, edited by Edward Connery Lathem. Copyright 1928, © 1969 by Holt, Rinehart and Winston. Copyright 1942, © 1956 by Robert Frost. Copyright © 1970 by Lesley Frost Ballantine. Reprinted by permission of Holt, Rinehart and Winston, Publishers.

Contents

I allow myself eddies of meaning
yielding to a direction of significance
running
like a stream through the geography of my work:
    you can find
in my sayings
           swerves of action . . .
           dunes of motion . . .
           organizations of grass. . . .
but Overall is beyond me: is the sum of these events
I cannot draw, the ledger I cannot keep. . . .
                     A. R. Ammons
                     Corson's Inlet

It is the belief and not the god that counts.
                     Wallace Stevens
                     Opus Posthumous

The Interpretation
of Otherness

Introduction

As a subject of serious critical discussion, the relation between literature and religion is no longer considered, as it once was, a privileged one. While it is almost impossible to determine just when it emerged from the shadows of the cloister and began to be treated as an issue of more than merely parochial interest, there is no arguing that it now occupies a not inconspicuous place in modern literary criticism and scholarship. The evidence is all around us, not only in such seminal works as F. O. Matthiessen's *American Renaissance* (1941), Erich Auerbach's *Mimesis* (1946), J. Hillis Miller's *The Disappearance of God* (1963), and M. H. Abrams's *Natural Supernaturalism* (1971), but also in a host of studies that have appeared recently on the religious meaning of particular kinds of literature and even of specific literary properties and elements. Contemporary interest in what is religiously distinctive about particular genres can be discerned, for example, in Eric Bentley's treatment of the anatomy of drama,[1] Northrop Frye's theory of the romance,[2] and Dorothea Krook's analysis of the elements of tragedy.[3] A parallel curiosity about the religious aspects and dimensions of specific literary properties and elements can be discerned in Walter J. Ong's studies of voice and the aurality of literature,[4]

Wayne Booth's explorations of rhetorical strategies of assent,[5] Frank Kermode's analysis of temporality and the making of fictions,[6] and Edward W. Said's examination of the ontology of beginnings.[7]

Nor are these isolated examples. Even if one confines one's attention to a single tradition such as the American, one discovers an astonishing range of studies on virtually every aspect of the relationship between literary expression and religious belief or sentiment. In addition to countless essays and monographs on all manner of religious images, symbols, themes, and motifs, there is an impressive body of scholarship on everything from the "theology" of individual writers[8] to comparisons of religious and literary currents within the same period;[9] from detailed examinations of the religious character of whole epochs in American cultural life[10] to studies of the religious meaning of such distinctively American forms as the romance,[11] the Adamic poem,[12] the novel of adventure,[13] and the romantic cosmology.[14] But this is only the tip of the iceberg. Much of the scholarship which bears greatest relevance to what Henry F. May, thinking of the most decisive event for American historiography during the last generation, once referred to as "the recovery of American religious history"[15] has been concerned either with the description and analysis of particular attributes of American writing—the recourse to symbolism,[16] the prevalence of typology,[17] the cult of experience,[18] the obsession with interpretation,[19] and the exploitation of naiveté and wonder[20]—or with such perennial issues in American literature as the relation between the temporal and the eternal,[21] the conflict between actual and ideal society,[22] the dialectic between innocence and experience,[23] the problem of tragic Faustianism,[24] the symbolic meaning of the American West,[25] the preoccupation with quest journeys into the self,[26] the religious veneration of Nature,[27] the pursuit of the American Dream,[28] the attractions of pastoral idealism,[29] the fear of the prison-house of language,[30] the yearning for states of unconditioned being,[31] and the nostalgia for paradise.[32]

To detail all the factors that lie behind the development of this relatively new academic interest would require an entire book of its own and lies quite beyond the scope of either my talents or my concerns. My attention here is restricted to more manageable issues, such as the way this modern interest developed, the major forms it has taken, the implications it holds for the future study of religion as well as of literature, and certain of its broader consequences for understanding the writer's relation of culture and the oddly religious character of the American literary imagination.

Roughly half of the material comprising this book was originally composed for other occasions and published elsewhere. That portion which has been included here, however, has been extensively rewritten before being incorporated with at least an equal amount of material that is entirely new. Thus while it would be inappropriate to view the five chapters which constitute this volume as a successive series of steps in a single and unified argument, it would be equally inappropriate to view them as but another "gathering of fugitives." In their revised and expanded form, they have been consciously designed as an interlinked series of explorations of a multiple but related set of issues from what I hope is a consistent, though not inflexible, point of view. If I go on to confess that my point of view, my "method," or "perspective," is of less importance to me than the issues it seeks to illumine, I intend no false modesty. My aim is not so much to supply a technique for resolving these issues as to provide fresh ways of understanding and assessing them. I intend to do this by suggesting that discussion of the relations between literature and religion, between culture and belief, has taken a fresh turn in recent years and that it is now necessary to widen the terms in which it is conducted: to reconstitute the discussion on the plane of the hermeneutical rather than the apologetic, the anthropological rather than theological, the broadly humanistic rather than the narrowly doctrinal.

Ever since its modern inception, study of the relations between literature and religion has proceeded in a sharply divided fashion.

Moving in one direction has been a variety of literary critics and scholars working largely in isolation from one another who have tended to subsume religious meanings and problems within essentially aesthetic categories. Moving in the opposite direction has been a somewhat more visible and more unified group of religious thinkers and historians who have tended to subordinate literary works to more explicit theological concerns. Situated precariously between these two groups has been a smaller but rapidly increasing number of scholars, both in literary and in religious studies, who have tried to discover a set of categories or a mode of discourse that would overcome this artificial and, to my mind, crippling polarization. Their purpose has been to refine the ways of formulating the connections between the literary and cultural on the one side and the religious and theological on the other by exploring the putative common ground between them.

If that common ground is to be found anywhere, I maintain that it has to be located in elements literature and religion may be said to share in equal measure by virtue of their derivation from the same common substance. That substance can be none other than the substance of culture itself, of which both literature and religion may be conceived as distinct but interrelated forms. Their interrelatedness stems from the fact that they are both composed of cultural material, namely symbols; their distinctiveness derives from the somewhat different use to which they put this symbolic cultural material interpretively. Literature, as I understand it, tends to employ the symbolic materials of culture heuristically, to test the validity traditionally ascribed to them and to explore their range of governance over the always changing terrain of human experience. Religion, as I conceive it, typically uses the materials of culture paradigmatically, to preserve or construct a model of reality that simultaneously serves as a map or template of the way things "truly are" and suggests a set of interdictions and prescriptions for determining one's conduct in relation to it. Since literature and religion are both cultural forms, then, I assume that the study of each individually, as of both in conjunction, is a form of cultural studies, and that it can only be pursued according to methods which, as one historian of religion has put it, "allow no rights of sanctuary, no immunity from the demands for evidence and plausibility that are made on [students of culture] generally." [33]

In addition to those sources cited in the notes, my own methods and perspectives seem in retrospect to have been most deeply influenced by three American philosophers—Josiah Royce, William James, and John Dewey. From Royce, whose probity in this connection has yet to be appreciated or fully absorbed, I have learned that, whatever life may be, the world is no more than the totality of our interpretations of it, and that by experience we therefore refer to that process whereby life continually seeks interpretation of the problems it constantly presents to us—not all at once or as a whole, but in and through an infinite series of individual as well as collective acts of understanding and assessment. From James I have acquired a greater sensitivity to the affective qualities of experience and a predisposition to identify those qualities not only with the things to which they are explicitly attached but with the entire though indefinite field of experience which is often felt to supercede or supervene them. In this sense, James's metaphysics of relations has exerted as much pressure on my methodological procedures as on my ontological assumptions. If James is correct that the relations between things are as directly experiencable as the things themselves, then there seems every reason to suppose that the terms of greatest intellectual utility and leverage may well be found not through a definition of the things themselves—in this case, literature, culture, and religion—but in the forms, patterns, and modes of their association.

Of the three, my debt to Dewey is the most difficult to pin down. The Dewey who has been most instructive for me is less the aesthetic philosopher of *Art as Experience* than the cultural metaphysician of *Experience and Nature*—the Dewey who places art above all other cultural agencies in having as its chief function the double task of bringing to the most complete consummation the potentialities already resident in experience and of simultaneously discovering new possibilities of experience altogether; the Dewey who, in this light, views "criticism," by which he means "intelligent inquiry into the conditions and consequences" of all objects of value,[34] as something done "not for its own sake, but for the sake of instituting and perpetuating more enduring and extensive values"[35]; and, finally, the Dewey who, accordingly, defines the goal of life not as the attainment of truth—as if truth were a substance independent of our experience of it which could be grasped once and for all—but as the enrichment and increase of experience itself. If Dewey has thereby convinced me that criticism is but a species of art, he has also, along with James, helped me to see that experience needs no transempirical justification in order to be understood religiously, that experience itself, in all its myriad combinations of stability and precariousness, or uniformity and irregularity, is more various in content and more astonishing to behold than has been dreamt of in all our philosophies and theologies.

I

The Religious Use and Abuse of Literature: Notes Toward a Short History

There is really no scientific or other method by which . . . [to] steer safely between the opposite dangers of believing too little or of believing too much. To face such dangers is apparently our duty, and to hit the right channel between them is a measure of our wisdom. . . .

WILLIAM JAMES
The Will To Believe

During the past several decades, there has appeared a considerable quantity of secondary literature devoted to an exploration of everything from correlations between theology and aesthetics to patterns of religious imagery in explicitly secular poems, novels, and plays. Those responsible for this critical activity have ranged rather widely from highly sophisticated specialists in language, literature, and religion to preachers with a taste for the classics. With work in this broad area of inquiry emerging from such disparate quarters and pursuing such different ends, it is hardly surprising that much of it has been uneven in quality as well as character. But if much of this work probably remains of greater interest for what it reveals of the mixed motives of those who undertake it, some of it ranks with the most substantial and original literary and religious scholarship of our own time. Among the latter one finds considerable variation: literary criticism that attempts to define the religious meaning and significance of particular texts, writers, and movements; literary and cultural histories that examine traditions of literature and the

9

other arts for clues to the inner moral and spiritual propulsions of an entire era or epoch; comparative studies of myth and ritual that seek to relate literary and cultural traditions, or the components thereof, to larger, collective, and often more primordial, forms of human experience; and aesthetic philosophies and theologies of culture that seek to establish the grounds of a religious poetic or to develop an aesthetics of belief.

While some of this more substantial work has been produced by individuals who in one way or another were associated with the field (or subfield) which, in religious studies, goes by the name "religion and literature" and which, in literary studies, is variously referred to as "theological criticism" or the "religious approach to literature," the great bulk of it has been produced by critics and scholars who probably possessed no awareness of any such "field" (or subfield) at all. This is as it should be. "Fields of specialization," as they are now called, are mere conveniences of the mind which have a way of diminishing in intellectual usefulness in almost direct proportion to our increased dependence upon their presumed boundaries and forms of methodological protocol. All authentic humanistic research of an interdisciplinary sort is carried on for the sake of an enhanced understanding and appreciation of the subject under investigation, and this is achieved not by differentiating that subject from everything with which it might be related so as to delimit the focus of inquiry to an ever narrower and more selective aperture, but by bringing to bear upon the subject itself anything that might shed further light on it, anything that might augment its meaningfulness. There is thus a kind of loose affinity between the methods of interdisciplinary research and the methods Joseph Conrad once ascribed to the modern story teller, for whom the meaning of any narrative does not lie inside the story, like a kernel within the shell of a cracked nut, "but outside, enveloping the tale which brought it out only as a glow brings out a haze." To extend the figure only slightly, one could add that the great problem in most forms of interdisciplinary research is how to make the haze refract the glow without at the same time permitting the glow, as it comes into sharper focus, to dispel the haze.

This problem has proven unusually intractable to those interested in the relations between religion and the arts. Chief among the reasons for this, I suppose, is their somewhat greater vulnerability to the "opposite dangers" alluded to by William James, "of believing too little or [as is more likely] of believing too much." But the problem of locating "the right channel between them" is not restricted to the study of religion and the arts; it is a problem endemic to all forms of modern intellectual inquiry and is nowhere more prevalent than in literary criticism itself. In an age when the line between the disingenuous and the sincere has been forever blurred by the advent of the mass media, what must one believe in order to begin reading at all? Is it necessary to share the writer's beliefs in order to take his work seriously? How can we take his work seriously when we know that his beliefs cannot possibly be identical with our own and when in addition we are prepared to acknowledge the relativity of both? Is it necessary to believe before we can understand, or is understanding a prerequisite for belief? Is belief the same as understanding? Can belief occur without understanding? Can understanding occur without belief? How can we be sure that what we read is worth reading when the sources of supply are, to a degree unparalleled in human history, controlled by the machinations of the market place? How can we make sense of what we read when there is such a plurality of interpretive models to choose from? What are the legitimate uses to which our reading may be put when there is no accepted tradition, or set of traditions, to which we can appeal for guidance. And so the questions multiply, leading those susceptible to "believing too much" into the embrace of some system that purports to resolve them all, leaving those susceptible to "believing too little" with the cold comfort that in a democracy it is every man for himself, and that it finally doesn't make much difference anyway.

The ancients, naturally, were wiser about this. They knew that if we don't learn how to use literature, then literature will surely use or misuse us. And they also realized that the question of the use or abuse of literature was in the end a religious question. Nor was this simply due to their own metaphysics, their own *theoria;* it was pure and simply a matter of *praxis.* Plato proposed to banish the poets from the Republic because of the enormous harm they could do by virtue of their power to move people at the profoundest levels through a representation of things not real in themselves but mere copies of reality. And Aristotle managed a rebuttal to Plato's charges only by appearing through a kind of intellectual sleight-of-hand to defuse them, conceding that poetry arouses people to action only as a way of eventually reconciling them to their circumstances which literature can do because its relation to reality is not so much second or thirdhand as vicarious. But it was the later theorist Longinus who made the boldest claims for the religious use of literature, not through his concept of the sublime, but through his discussion of the poet's vision of human greatness and its consequences for the reader:

> The central message of Longinus is that, in and through the personal rediscovery of the great, we find that we need not be the passive victims of what we deterministically call 'circumstances' (social, cultural, or reductively psychological-personal), but that by linking ourselves through what Keats calls an 'immortal free-masonry' with the great, we can become freer—freer to be ourselves, to be what we most want and value; and that by caring for the kinds of things that they did we are not only 'imitating' them, in the best and most fruitful sense of the word, but also 'joining them.'[1]

This, according to Professor Bate, is the reason why Longinus meant so much to the Romantics, to Keats, Coleridge, and Wordsworth: because Longinus not only held out an ideal of spiritual excellence but also showed others how they might share in it. And from the Romantics this spiritual ideal, based upon the coalescence of the literary with the religious, was eventually passed on in diluted form to Matthew Arnold with his theory of classical touch-stones, from whom it then descended in one direction to the aestheticism of Walter Pater and George Santayana and in another to the moralism of Paul Elmer More and Irving Babbitt.

But it would be a mistake, I think, to look for the sources of current interest in the coalescence of the literary and the religious in what was left of the old Longinian tradition. What with the intervening erosion of belief, decline of values, and general confusion of standards, modern interest in the relations between literature and religion seems to have developed on much more precarious footing. Rather than reflecting the attempt to continue something merely in need of rejuvenation, this newer interest seems in retrospect to have resulted from the attempt to reconstitute something admittedly in a state of collapse on a different basis. Curiously enough, when this renewed interest in the coalescence of literature and religion finally surfaced in America at least, during the late 1920s and early 1930s, it emerged not within the Academy but outside it, in seminary classrooms in the one case and the public precincts of literary life on the other. I would go further and suggest that formal study of literature in its relations to religion, when it did not occur simply by accident, as a result of the opportunities or requirements of the subject at hand, developed in something like three successive phases, and that during each phase this interest expressed itself in a distinctive form, can be associated with a generalized mood within the culture at large, and issued in one or more characteristic methodological orientations or modes of approach.

I

The 1920s and 1930s constituted a period of considerable theological ferment in America. Center stage was occupied by the noisy clash that broke out between modernists and fundamentalists, between those who sought to apply modern methods of scholarship to the study of the Bible and, more broadly, to accommodate Christian theology to a scientifically respectable world view, and those who assumed that scripture was literally inerrant and therefore found Christianity incompatible with the whole of modern science. The showcase of this controversy was of course the Monkey trial of 1925, when Clarence Darrow confronted William Jennings Bryan over the issue of whether John Scopes should be permitted to teach the theory of evolution to the children of Tennessee when that theory was deemed contrary to the laws of the state. But the issues underlying the modernist-fundamentalist dispute were more subtlely explored by such figures as Henry Nelson Wieman and Douglas Clyde MacIntosh among the liberals and J. Gresham Machen among the conservatives. Machen put the argument for fundamentalists in unmistakable terms when he insisted, in *Christianity and Liberalism* (1923), that "modern liberalism not only is a different religion from Christianity but belongs in a totally different class of religions";[2] to which Wieman seemed to respond in *Religious Experience and Scientific Method* (1926), and, later, in *The Source of Human Good* (1946) by arguing that the two are perfectly congenial.

Behind this controversy and going well back into the nineteenth century was a debate between liberals, who sought to interpret the Christian vision of life in terms of the most lucid, compelling, and meaningful contemporary interpretations of experience, and conservatives, who insisted on trying to keep the essentials of the Christian faith from being diluted or polluted by contemporary understanding. In the 1920s and 1930s this deeper rift between liberals and conservatives, between the critical and the traditional, was lifted to a new plane of intensity by the appearance in 1918 of a short commentary by a Swiss pastor turned theologian named Karl Barth on Saint Paul's *Epistle to the Romans*, a book which in its enlarged edition of 1921 became a veritable theological bombshell. The effects of Barth's work were not immediately to be felt in America, and when they finally were, they were felt only indirectly. Barth's first readers, who were as likely as not to be introduced to him themselves secondhand, through Douglas Horton's translation of Barth's *The Word of God and the Word of Man* (1928) and Walter Lowrie's *Our Concern with the Theology of Crisis* (1932), were a handful of professors in theological seminaries who began introducing themselves as well as their students (who later transmitted it to their parishoners) to what Barth called "the strange new world of the Bible." That world seemed to be based on the Kierkegaardian axiom of an infinite qualitative difference between time and eternity, between nature and grace, which could only be understood dialectically and which could only be overcome by the free and unmerited gift of God's love. The discovery of this strange new world of the Bible therefore led Barth in his later writings to a radical restatement of the Reformation doctrine of salvation by grace alone through Jesus Christ. The Jesus Christ to whom Barth referred, however, was not the Jesus of history, the Jesus of the liberals, but the Christ of faith, the Word of God who meets man as and when He chooses to reveal Himself in scripture and in preaching.

By insisting again upon the sovereignty of God and His Word, Barth's intention was to resist all attempts to confuse the Word of God with the words of men and thus to set the claims of the Christian Gospel apart not only from all other human claims but from all other religious claims. Indeed, the good news about Jesus Christ, which was the heart of the Christian Gospel, was to be differentiated not only from all other religious claims but from any claims made about it. The Word of God was no more "contained" in Scripture, as fundamentalists supposed, than conveyed solely through preaching or ritual, as many evangelicals and Roman Catholics tended to presume. As something "wholly Other" which stands over against man, the Word of God was merely revealed in and through these forms as independent of and sovereign over them all.

Barth's theology of crisis would not have exploded on the theological world with such force if a receptive milieu had not already been created for it. But the bankruptcy of much of the liberal heritage, both cultural and theological, had been revealed by the Great War of 1914, and prophets of doom from Oswald Spengler to T. S. Eliot had soon arisen on every hand forecasting the end, or at least the demise, of Western civilization. Some radical solution was called for, and Barth's "neo-orthodox" theology, strongly buttressed by such related developments as the rise of existential philosophy, a renaissance in Biblical scholarship, renewed interest in the theology of Martin Luther, the spreading shadow of tyranny in Europe, and the Great Depression of the 1930s, seemed to provide an answer—indeed, the Christian answer. And for those who remained unconvinced, or even untouched, by the neo-orthodox revival Barth seemed to spark, there were still the sobering realities which any enduring liberalism must confront: the cracks in its optimistic view of man, contemporary history's apparent refutation of the doctrine of progress, the enormity of the problem of evil, the lack of any satisfactory metaphysic to comprehend the modern "panorama of futility and anarchy," and the continuing general remoteness of the churches from the antinomies and injustice of ordinary human existence.

It is against this background of neo-orthodox revival on the one hand and chastened liberalism on the other that the first phase of interest in the study of the relations between literature and religion occurred. Not surprisingly, it took the more limited form of an interest in Christianity and the arts generally and seems to have been activated by a set of motives largely diagnostic or prescriptive. Looking more closely at these developments, it is now apparent that this first phase was characterized by two quite different orientations, the one expressive of more liberal inclinations, the other of more conservative. The first we might define as the pastoral, the second as the apodictic or dogmatic.

The pastoral orientation is to be associated with such men as Willard Sperry of Harvard, Lynn Harold Huff of Drew, Fred Eastman of the Chicago Theological Seminary, and Halford Luccock of Yale. None of these early advocates of the study of Christianity and the arts were either theologians in the strict sense or specialists in aesthetics, but professors of liturgics, Bible, theological education, or homiletics who simply possessed an intimate knowledge of what was going on in the churches and wanted to use the insights gained from the study of literature and the other arts to correct it. Halford Luccock, in his *Contemporary American Literature and Religion* (1934), provides an indication of their concerns.

Luccock viewed literature quite simply as an important index to the times, and he believed that organized religion neglects the temper and troubles of the times at its own peril. Like other liberals of his era, Luccock shared with Harry Emerson Fosdick, their popular spokesman, the view that religion (meaning the Christian religion) had finally broken free of its procrustean bed of dogma and that, as a consequence, nothing human could be considered foreign to it. For this reason religion could not be relegated to a single corner of life, and no issues were to be dismissed out-of-hand as alien to its own interests historically considered. The study of literature and the other arts was therefore encouraged for two reasons: both because it would help acquaint the churches with the real problems of the age, its hopes and fears, its obsessions and repressions, and because it might help save the churches from the soporific of their own doctrines.

While it is easy to reject many of the ways Luccock and his colleagues sought to implement these convictions, it is hard to fault the convictions themselves. In examining contemporary American literature, Luccock was far from dismayed by the spectacle it presented of a lack of faith in organized religion, or even of a lack of interest in faith as such. This prospect presented problems only for those who continued to associate religion in the conventional way with formulated beliefs and ceremonial practices. But to Luccock religion was "an attitude and spirit which pervades the whole, a total response to life,"[3] and evidence of its presence was to be found everywhere, even in that literature which testified to the death of belief itself. Thus Luccock could see the study of contemporary literature contributing to religious understanding in at least three ways: first, by showing the "implicit religion," as he called it, in literary materials possessing no discernible relation to inherited traditions of faith; second, by serving as a gauge of the morale of a given period; and third, by challenging the church to rethink its own positions in light of renewed exposure to the arts and sensibility of its own time. In each of these ways, Luccock could conceive of literature and the other arts performing as important a "ministry" to religion as religion was called upon to perform in behalf of its own culture.

With the nation at large and laymen in particular deeply sceptical about the value of the arts, and with theologians and churchmen becoming more and more suspicious of culture, it took considerable courage for these early proponents of a kind of *rapprochement* between Christianity and the arts to speak out. Even where, as was often the case, their competence to address such issues was narrow and their formulations loose and awkward, they correctly perceived some of the real issues involved, and they served an important heuristic function for the churches by keeping the door open to such considerations at a time when many were attempting to slam it shut.

The second orientation which characterizes the first phase of interest in the study of the relations between what was then thought of as Christianity and the arts proceeded from very different impulses. Where the pastoral critics concentrated on the way literature can serve an educative function for the churches and its parishoners, for organized religion generally, what I am calling the apodictic critics and theorists focused their attention on the question of defining a Christian art or literature, or on the ancillary issue as to what kinds of art and literature are good for Christians. If the mood of critics of the first orientation was largely receptive and accommodating to art and culture, the mood of critics belonging to the second was defensive if not downright hostile. For pastoral critics, the function of the study of Christianity and the arts was primarily pedagogical; for apodictic critics, the function of such study was and remains essentially evaluative and prescriptive. The theological position of critics representative of the first orientation was flexible and open; the theological position of critics of the second was invariably rigid and closed. The latter's standard of selection and discrimination was always some form of orthodoxy, and they saw their chief aim, indeed, the aim of all criticism, as a determination of the traditions of Christian literature; or, if it was presumed that no literature can be fully Christian but Scripture itself, then the determination of those traditions of art and literature that can serve as a propaedeutic for faith. Following his celebrated conversion to classicism in literature, royalism in politics, and Anglo-Catholicism in religion, T. S. Eliot became the first great examplar of this latter orientation, and his influential essay, "Religion and Literature" (1934), its *locus classicus*.

Eliot's position is so well known that it scarcely requires repeating. What does need to be borne in mind, however, since his position is so easy to ridicule and so tempting to dismiss, is that Eliot insisted upon the necessity of theological discrimination by Christian readers because he held that there is no way of separating our reading from the rest of our experience. Whether they know it or not, Eliot maintained, writers intend to affect the whole of our being and not just some selected aspect of it, such as the aesthetic sense; and whether we recognize it or not, he went on, we in turn respond with the whole of our being even when we think our reactions are simply a matter of training or temperament. Thus Eliot based his plea for the completion of literary criticism by a criticism written from a self-conscious and defensible religious position on the assumption that the two, finally, cannot be kept apart.

This much, it seems to me, Eliot has to be granted. Either we read with the whole of ourselves or we do not, and if we do, then there is no way of completely segregating our moral and metaphysical judgments from our literary ones. But whether for most people those judgments derive from what Eliot calls "a definite ethical and theological standpoint,"[4] or whether that standpoint, even for the Christian, can be reduced, as Eliot does in "Religion and Literature," to a belief in the supernatural order, is another matter altogether. So, too, is the assumption that elicits Eliot's essay in the first place—that the whole of modern literature, with the possible exception of the works of James Joyce, is spiritually degraded; and the conclusion to which it leads—that there ought to be one literature for Christians and another for non-Christians (Eliot actually calls them "pagans"), or, failing the possibility of this, that Christians should retain a clear sense both of what they *do* like and of what they *ought* to like, so as to extract the good from what they read and to be protected from the bad. Eliot here sounds like the latter-day New England Puritan that such fellow critics as Edmund Wilson always suspected he was, under his Anglican vestments; and in *After Strange Gods: A Primer of Modern Heresy* (1934), the book in which Eliot attempted to apply a doctrinaire and discriminatory criticism based on Christian standards, he began to act like it.

A much more sophisticated version of the same position, or variant thereof, can be found in much of the occasional criticism of C. S. Lewis, but I think the most attractive and disarming example of it is to be found in the work of W. H. Auden, particularly in an essay like "Christianity and Art." Here the critic is not trying to stipulate the standards by which readers can differentiate Christian literature, or literature beneficial to Christians, from other kinds, but to argue on orthodox grounds for the impossibility of there being a Christian art or literature in the first place. For Auden at this point in his career—there is some evidence that he modified his position in later writings—it all comes down to the mysteries of the Incarnation. God's submission to human form in the guise of a servant rather than a master was simply a miracle which remains imperceptible to all but those who see with the eyes of faith. The relation between profane appearance and sacred manifestation is therefore incomprehensible either to the intellect or to the imagination. And if the relation between sacred and profane is impassable to the imagination, then the sacred, as the Christian understands it, Divine Being, cannot be portrayed in art. But even if theoretically it could be, the Christian life would still be unamenable to dramatic representation because, in contradistinction to secular life, the perfect man for Christianity is not the heroic individual who does great deeds in public but the saint who does good deeds in private, indeed, the man whose goodness is hidden not only from the world but even from himself. Thus Auden concludes that "there can no more be a Christian art than a Christian science or a Christian diet. There can only be a Christian spirit in which an artist, a scientist, works and does not work."[5] This leaves the critic who is a Christian with the task of differentiating the Christian in art and literature from all those other ideal or classic modes of being with which it might either be confused or usefully compared for purposes of contrast. Hence much of Auden's best criticism, no doubt inspired by Soren Kierkegaard's delineation of the aesthetic, the ethical, and the religious modes of existence, is concerned with differentiating among different types of heroes or images of man in Western literature: the epic, the tragic, the contemplative, the erotic, the comic, the Romantic, and the Christian.

When employed with the kind of judiciousness and tact exhibited by Auden, or even by Eliot in his reconsideration of Dante in the monograph of 1929, this orientation does possess its uses. To employ M. H. Abrams's terms in *Natural Supernaturalism* (1971), it can clarify the lines of demarcation between the "traditional" and the "revolutionary" in matters of faith, and by the sharpness of its distinctions it can enliven the discussion between believers and non-believers. At its worst, however, the apodictic orientation can become crippling to the very interests of discrimination itself, as it does in Randall Stewart's *American Literature and Christian Doctrine* (1952). The chief problem with Stewart's book is not the high-

handed way he applies Christian doctrine as an evaluative standard
to American literature but the simplistic manner in which he proceeds to limit the whole mosaic of Christian belief to the dogma of
original sin and then dispenses censure or praise in terms of an individual writer's presumed acceptance of this, as it happens, un-
Biblical nostrum. According to this crude standard, Edwards is accepted, Jefferson rejected, Hawthorne and Melville commended,
Emerson and Thoreau found wanting, Robert Penn Warren approved, Hemingway, Fitzgerald, Stevens, and Hart Crane dismissed.

It is fairly clear that both these orientations within the first phase
of interest in the study of religion and literature presented real
problems—and still do for those who continue to exhibit them.
Among those interested in evaluation and prescription, there was
always the problem, as Amos Wilder has put it, "of violating
proper method by a prior dogmatic."[6] And among those on the
other side interested in the pastoral or educative function of literary
study, there remained in some ways the more serious contrary
problem of becoming so accommodating to literature or art that one
lost all sense of ethical and theological standards. This left those
who were in any way interested in pursuing this form of study
with a dual task: first, of working out a more explicit understanding
of the relationship between method and norm, mode of approach
and theological position; and second, of adumbrating a theological
position or set of religious norms at once more supple and capa-
cious as well as precise.

Both of these undertakings were fundamentally advanced by two
theologians who were to have a decisive influence on the work of
most people who contributed to the second generation of study in
this interdisciplinary area. But by the time their influence was
thoroughly absorbed, what had in the first stage been an interest in
Christianity and the arts had become in the second a more specialized interest in theology and literature. The two theologians to
whom I refer are Reinhold Niebuhr and Paul Tillich.

2

Niebuhr's influence was felt first, and in certain ways was more pervasive if less obvious. From this distance, it is interesting to observe that Niebuhr could have encouraged fresh interest in the study of the relations between theology and literature when neither literature nor culture as such captured a major portion of his attention; when, in addition, Niebuhr could in no conventional sense be called a theologian to begin with; and when, finally, Niebuhr remained in general agreement with the neo-Reformation revival first initiated by the writings of Barth. But to whatever extent Niebuhr echoed basic neo-orthodox themes—that man is essentially sinful rather than good, that man's only hope for redemption lies in the undeserved love of God which is preeminently revealed in the Crucifixion and Resurrection, and that man's redemption will only finally be consummated beyond history rather than within it—his general theological stance was different. Where Barth sought to recover the essential components of the Christian Gospel and to restate them in a language that would permit no confusion between the realms of the sacred and the profane, of Christianity and culture, Niebuhr's work was animated by what has been called "the Protestant search for political [and one might add, social, ethical, and religious] realism," and this had the effect not of cutting one off from culture but of precipitating new contacts with culture. In this Niebuhr, like Tillich in a different way, was as much a neo-liberal theologian as a neo-orthodox (one historian associates his most original theological contribution with "a reshaped Social Gospel"),[7] and the consequences of this shift in theological outlook were to produce, as a kind of secondary effect, profound changes in the religious study of the arts. Let me suggest only the most obvious.

In the first place, Niebuhr helped change the image of the theologian, and thus opened up opportunities for a more constructive dialogue between faith and culture, theology and literature, by devoting less of his attention to criticizing, revising, and extending the traditions of theology itself, as Barth, Brunner, and the others did, than to bringing the insights of those traditions directly to bear upon issues and problems in contemporary life. Niebuhr's great themes, for the most part, were not inherited doctrines, such as creation, atonement, and eschatology, but practical concerns, such as the problem of anxiety, the international balance of power, the dangers of national pride, the immorality of society, and the dialectical relations between love and justice. Although his own position was responsibly worked out in relation to the thought of other theologians and philosophers, Niebuhr refused to spend the bulk of his time as a theologian or ethicist talking about those relations. In the best and broadest sense of the word, Niebuhr was an apologist who believed that the chief function of theology is to show how the Christian faith, in all its essentials, provides a more adequate and meaningful interpretation of the problematic aspects of human existence than any other spiritual or religious tradition.

Second, Niebuhr's success as an apologist was considerably enhanced by his method of cultural and historical analysis, a method which was used to greatest effect in the first volume of his Gifford lectures entitled *The Nature and Destiny of Man*, published in 1941. Niebuhr's method was fundamentally typological. Assuming that one could extract from the variety and complexity of human history certain basic and recurring structures of thought, certain elementary formulations of the way in which, in any given era, men and women understand the meaning of life, and that one could then deal most effecitvely with any era by penetrating to the view of life that unified it and by then setting that view of life over against others, Niebuhr simultaneously developed a method of controlling and dominating an immense diversity of historical and intellectual material and of bringing various and often opposed traditions of thought and sentiment into effective comparison and contrast with one another and with the central insights of the Christian faith.

Third, Niebuhr's view of the human problem, no less than his explanation of the way Christianity addresses it, was distinctly modern. Like most modern thinkers and writers, Niebuhr perceived man to be at war with himself, caught in a life-and-death struggle with his own best as well as worst impulses. And also like many moderns, Niebuhr found the resources to interpret this tragic paradox not primarily in the traditions of the past, whether theological or philosophical, but in the newly developing sciences of the future, such as depth psychology and the Marxist analysis of class conflicts. Niebuhr was in complete agreement with one of the central strains of Christian thinking going back to the theology of St. Augustine, that man's problem stems from the fact that he is both free and finite and that within himself he can find no way of reconciling the two. But Niebuhr departed rather dramatically from most Augustinian interpretations of the human predicament by arguing that man's finitude is not the cause of his sin but simply its occasion. Faced with a paradox he can in no way overcome on his own, man is placed in a state of anxiety he can neither endure nor relieve. It is this anxiety common to the experience of all men and women, Niebuhr asserted, that is the cause of human waywardness, because it tempts the individual either to seek a basis of security within himself, which leads to the sin of pride, or to seek a basis of security in some mutable good, some vitality of Nature, which leads to the sin of sensuality. In either case, Niebuhr reasoned, the individual turns aside from the central Christian truth that the only enduring basis of security for individuals (as for society as a whole), just as the only way of resolving the paradox of freedom and finitude, lies in giving oneself completely to that which transcends the self, in other words, to God and the neighbor. The Christian position thus makes sense, Niebuhr reasoned, because it addresses a genuine human problem—not a problem which originated *in illo tempore* at some mythological moment of "the Fall," but a problem which has been experienced as common to all people everywhere since time immemorial.

This anthropology, which from a diagnostic point of view seemed to square with what many other more secular thinkers and writers were saying, gained in credibility because of the ethical and spiritual urgency that lay behind it. For in attempting to reexamine the age-old problem of sin, Niebuhr was asking the kind of question posed by many sensitive contemporaries both outside the churches and within them. That question, which suggests the fourth way in which Niebuhr's work activated fresh interest in the theological interpretation of cultural forms, had to do with where one looks in life and history for the actual conquest of evil by good. The question itself is clearly a universal one, but it had come to acquire a terrible new actuality in the period between the two World Wars and just after. By bringing this question into the center of his own thinking, Niebuhr was joining an issue which no thoughtful individual exposed to the problematics of modern experience could really avoid, and Niebuhr therefore exhibited, if you will, a new style of theological apologetics. The Christian apologist, in this case, was not in the business of telling people *what* to think so much as of showing them *how* to think, of taking their questions with absolute seriousness and then seeing if theology has some way of responding.

This style of theological apologetics is even more closely associated with the work of the second theologian who did so much to advance interest in the theological analysis of culture, namely Paul Tillich. Tillich was as interested as Niebuhr before him in finding an appropriate language to explore the relevance of the Christian faith to an understanding of the modern situation, and, as is well known, Tillich found that language in the traditions of classical philosophy and ontology. Like Niebuhr, he also found himself asking the question about God's sovereignty in the modern way, by inquiring whether or not there is any transcendent power in life that guarantees that good will eventually overcome evil, but Tillich posed that question in a distinctive manner. In the midst of the brokenness, distortion, and alienation in life, Tillich wanted to know, where does one find "the courage to be"? Amidst a world of non-being, where do you find the principle of Being-itself? Nonetheless, Tillich's major contribution to the study of theology and literature does not lie here. It lies rather in the method he developed to apply such language to the solution of these questions, and also in the kinds of interpretation to which this method gave rise.

Tillich's method of theological analysis was correlative, in the sense that it was specifically designed to show how the existential analysis of the human dilemma ultimately finds its answer in the Christian belief about Jesus as the Christ.[8] What was distinctive about this method was its degree of reliance upon the analysis of culture, indeed, of all secular forms, as a source of theological insight. While Tillich remained very much the conventional Christian in reserving to theology alone the right to furnish answers to the problems posed by human existence, he believed that theology itself is totally dependent upon philosophy and the other human sciences, literary study included, for a correct understanding of human existence and its attendant problems. Hence, although philosophy and the other human sciences couldn't answer the questions deriving from their own analyses—how could brokenness and distortion be the answer to brokenness and distortion?—they could uncover the terms in which those questions were posed and thus determine the limits within which theology could attempt to answer them. Indeed, as Tillich conceived it, this is exactly how matters stood: insofar as the various kinds of existential analysis agreed that the fundamental problem of human existence is its incompleteness, they simultaneously pointed to the fact that the problem itself can only be resolved by that which transcends existence, by that which is included within, but not determined by, the structures of existence itself. Hence Tillich reasoned that Christianity provides the answer to the problem posed by human existence because it does not define God in terms of any aspect of existence, say, as one being among others, even if the highest, but instead defines God as the source of Being-itself. For the Christian this is made manifestly clear in the Incarnation: the "event of Jesus Christ," as Tillich referred to it, is to be understood as the one point where the structures of existence, of being, become fully transparent to their unconditional depth, where the ground of Being-itself fully manifests Itself amidst its contemporary distortions.

From these assumptions Tillich was able to show how faith and culture are related without being identical. As he put it in one of his better known formulations, religion is the substance of culture, while culture is the form of religion. Stated in a slightly different way, religion is concerned with the dimension of depth within culture, while culture represents the totality of structures within existence by means of which that depth takes on form. Thus Tillich could assert that there can be no religion without a culture in which it manifests itself, just as the goal of every culture should be to become transparent to its own ground, to become—to use another of Tillich's favorite words—"theonomous."

But Tillich's method of correlation did more than simply provide a way of defining the relation between religion and culture or suggest a procedure for analyzing that relation; his method of correlation also enabled him to develop an existential interpretation of the human condition which was to prove extremely compelling to many theological critics of modern culture. Tillich's interpretation, which is to be found in his popular book *The Courage To Be* (1955), rests upon his definition of the three types of anxiety that can be associated with the three classic periods in Western history: ontic anxiety, or the anxiety about finitude, which was most prevalent at the end of the period of ancient civilization; moral anxiety, or the anxiety about sin and guilt, which was most prevalent at the end of the medieval period; and spiritual anxiety, or the anxiety about meaning, which was—and still is—most prevalent at the end of the modern period. Tillich's interpretation of each of these three types of anxiety led him to conclude that they can only be overcome through an assertion of "the courage to be." Predicated on the philosophical assumption that being presupposes the existence of non-being, and that being is most clearly revealed in the way it takes up the threat of non-being into itself and thereby overcomes that threat, "the courage to be" possesses an ontological as well as ethical dimension, since it ultimately rests upon a kind of "absolute faith" in what Tillich designated as "the God beyond God," the God who, in contrast to the God of classical theism, is not identical with any of the structures of being but is their depth and ground.

As an exercise in theological apologetics, Tillich's *The Courage To Be* provides a classic example of the same kind of theological criticism it was to inspire, one which takes the secular analysis provided by cultural materials as diagnostically credible but then attempts to show how the questions and unresolved problems generated by such analysis both elicit and can receive convincing theological answers. Furthermore, in the hands of someone as intellectually ambidextrous as Tillich himself, the method was almost fail-safe, for it proceeded from a clearcut definition of both religion and culture, supplied a technique for exploring their correlative relationship, and provided a way of understanding the particular task of theology in interpreting that relation. Taken together with Niebuhr's work, Tillich's writing was therefore to prove extraordinarily influential in producing a second generation of scholarship devoted in this case to the study of the relations between theology and literature.

During the years of Niebuhr's and Tillich's greatest impact, from the early 1940s to the mid-1960s, it is fair to say that two somewhat different theoretical and methodological orientations developed, one showing considerably more of their imprint than the other. The orientation most clearly associated with Niebuhr and Tillich deserves to be called, in the widest sense of the words, correlative and/or apologetic, depending on whether the emphasis is placed on merely delineating and interpreting correlations between faith and culture, theology and literature, or on showing how the first term in each of these two pairs addresses and resolves existential problems refracted and expressed in the second. Further, it is now clear that theological critics associated with the correlative/apologetic orientation tended to move in one of two opposed directions, the first more continuous with neo-liberal or, as you will, post-liberal currents in theology, the second with more traditional or neo-orthodox currents.

The more liberal and familiar kind of theological criticism in the correlative or apologetic mode inevitably asks, and sometimes attempts to propose, how the study of literature, particularly modern literature, can usefully inform the understanding of faith, how an appropriation of spiritual perceptions or aspirations in the wider culture can constructively complicate, thicken, modify, or revolutionize inherited traditions of belief, feeling, and behavior. The first important exponent of this new orientation was undoubtedly the Biblical scholar, Amos Wilder, whose early books on the subject, *The Spiritual Aspects of the New Poetry* (1940) and *Modern Poetry and the Tradition* (1952), signaled this new correlative interest and exemplified the enhanced sophistication and learning that so often differentiated this generation from the one that preceded it. But the orientation itself, in both its correlative and apologetic modes, admits of a wide margin of variance, gravitating toward the apologetic in Gabriel Vahanian's *Wait Without Idols* (1964) and *The Death of God* (1967), Julian Hartt's *A Christian Critique of American Culture* (1967), and even such later works of Wilder himself as *Theology and Modern Literature* (1958), *The New Voice* (1969), and, most recently, *Theopoetic* (1976); gravitating toward the correlative in the essays collected by Stanley Romaine Hopper in *Spiritual Problems of Contemporary Literature* (1952), Roland Mushat Frye's *Perspective on Man* (1961), Cleanth Brooks's *The Hidden God* (1963), and Maurice Friedman's *Problematic Rebel* (1963). For sheer volume of production, however, and for extended definition and exploration of the issues involved, no critic is more closely associated with this orientation than Nathan A. Scott, Jr. While I think that a more substantial case can be made for regarding Scott as a harbinger of the next generation of scholarship in this "field" rather than the classic representative of this one, there is still no gainsaying the fact that Scott has done more than anyone else to give the correlative/apologetic orientation a critical as well as theological respectability it might otherwise never have attained.

From his first book of 1952, *Rehearsals of Discomposure,* to his latest, *The Poetry of Civic Virtue* (1976), Scott has been at pains to argue that an informed and responsible understanding of the Christian faith requires that one take account of and fully attempt to absorb the meanings of life proposed by the major modern writers. The motto of this more apologetic side of Scott's work is Stein's advise to Marlow in Joseph Conrad's *Lord Jim* about submitting yourself to the destructive element and by the exertions of your hands and feet in the water making the deep, deep sea keep you up. But the correlative interest in Scott's criticism is supported by the somewhat different conviction that many of our greatest writers, when understood properly against the background of the entire modern tradition in its social, political, and metaphysical as well as literary aspects, demand to be considered as themselves religious visionaries, even as theologians manqué. Hence, at the very least, Scott has held out for the importance of a sustained dialogue between the custodians and contemporary interpreters of the Christian faith and the great literary and artistic exemplars of the modern imagination, on the supposition that Christian theology has perhaps more to learn about contemporary experience from modern literature than from any other source. More typically, however, Scott has been interested in describing what he calls the "theological horizon" of the modern "literary landscape" because of his conviction that "ours has . . . been a literature that has involved itself relentlessly in those questions with which it has traditionally been the office of religious faith to deal. . . ."[9]

Up until recently Scott, like other critics and theologians of this orientation, has tended to identify what is religiously distinctive in modern literature with its largest negative testimony, with its claims about "the disappearance of God," the erosion of any center to life, our lack of a common theme, the loss of confidence in the real, and so on; but lately, in such books as *The Wild Prayer of Longing* (1971), *Three American Moralists* (1973), and the already mentioned *Poetry of Civic Virtue*, Scott has displayed fresh interest in some of the more positive assertions to be found in modern writing and has accordingly turned his attention to strategies of moral recovery and spiritual renewal in, for example, the later poetry of Roethke, Eliot, and Auden, as well as the fiction of André Malraux and Norman Mailer. Throughout Scott's career, however, and characteristic of much of the better work of other apologetic as well as correlative critics and theologians, one can discern an almost obsessive preoccupation with the notion of "boundaries," "peripheries," and "frontiers," and a consequent respect for writers and thinkers who, as David Ignatow puts it, are feeling "along the edges of life /for a way/ that will lead to open land" [10] It is here on the margins of experience, Scott would have us believe, that one finds writers and thinkers confronting the really crucial existential issues of the times; and it is also here, he has consistently asserted, that one finds life pressing with such intense immediacy as to compel even the most secular writers into surpassing themselves, as it were, into a mode of vision at least incipiently religious.

The most damaging criticism of these assumptions is one that has been offered by a writer that Scott and others of this orientation generally respect, the contemporary novelist Saul Bellow. When Bellow's Herzog rails out against those who tout the Void "as if it were so much salable real estate" and objects to that "crisis mentality" of our time that places greater faith in states of extremity than of normality, he is calling into question the very premises upon which much of Scott's criticism, and that of others like him, is based. The issue, however, is one which radiates outward to the interpretation of modernism itself.

Those who view modernism and its legacy chiefly as a reaction to the whole funded system of meaning and value that has been bequeathed to us from the past, as a quest for some unmediated form of being, are likely to set great store by extreme states of feeling and thought as the only modes of access to the existentially authentic. Those who view modernism more dialectically as an attempt to adjust the claims of what Lionel Trilling first called "the opposing self" to the equally authentic counterclaims of social, political, and cultural actuality are more likely to share Herzog's impatience with that "modern form of historicism which sees in this civilization the defeat of the best hopes of Western religion and thought, what Heidegger calls the second Fall of Man into the quotidian or ordinary." With Herzog they tend to insist that "no philosopher knows what the ordinary is, has not fallen into it deeply enough."

These two views of modernism are ultimately no more antithetical than the kinds of criticism, theological or otherwise, that they tacitly sponsor, in the one case a criticism that trusts in the expression of what appears to be unconditioned spirit, in the other case one that distrusts any expression of spirit that discounts the conditions which the actual and the ordinary typically make for it. In the best modern criticism, however, as in the best theological criticism like Scott's in either the correlative or the apologetic mode, these perceptions are not automatically regarded as mutually exclusive and self-contradictory but simply as conflicting and creatively antagonistic, and the value of this criticism is measured in large part in terms of how much of the conflict or antagonism it can absorb and carry within itself.

In the work of other critics and theologians, however, the apologetic orientation (the correlative interest here drops away) can precipitate questions of quite a different order, questions having to do with how theology, properly conceived, instead of learning from the literary imagination, can actually instruct the literary imagination as to its place within the Divine economy and its office in the affairs of man's true business of salvation and redemption. Rather than serving as an evaluative standard for literature, as in Eliot, or as an exposition of the one ideal impossible for literature to express, as in Auden, theology (and particularly Christian theology), it is here maintained, can provide the writer with a normative understanding of the nature and function of his work or with an exemplary mode of vision. This, for example, is the kind of argument that is put negatively in Denis de Rougement's *Love in the Western World* (1956) but that is asserted positively in the series of articles Father William Lynch published on "Theology and the Imagination" in *Thought* which later became the basis of his *Christ and Apollo* (1960). Father Lynch's contention is that Christology can furnish the writer with a model for the healthy imagination. The key to his argument lies, just as it does in so many modern theological critics, in Lynch's interpretation of the Incarnation. As the most sublime example of how the Divine penetrates fully into the human, of how the Eternal has submitted Itself to all the levels of concrete, historical existence, the Incarnation, Father Lynch maintains, demonstrates that the path to the infinite always lies through the finite and not around it or over it. Underlying this argument is the neo-Thomist assumption that the Christic imagination is essentially analogical and integrative, whereas the modern imagination is typically Manichaean and divisive. What the analogical imagination perceives as multiple but somehow one and therefore capable of unification within the same image, the Manichaean or modern imagination sees as dissociated and opposite and therefore incapable of reintegration in any form, symbolic or otherwise.

So long as Father Lynch remains on the theoretical or analytical levels, his argument possesses a certain cogency, a cogency which is nicely illustrated by the way it helps him account for the nobility of someone like Oedipus Rex in the same terms that an Auden might dismiss that nobility. According to the logic of Father Lynch's argument, Oedipus is ennobled not because he has somehow managed to evade or transcend the human condition but precisely because of the depth with which he has confronted and submitted himself to it. But when Father Lynch turns his argument in

an evaluative or prescriptive direction, by following Allen Tate in
The Forlorn Demon (1953) and rejecting as "angelic" much of modern
literature, since it prefers the visionary to the vernacular and the
particular, we are suddenly back with Eliot in the realm of apodictic criticism, worrying about the kinds of writing that are injurious
to belief and treating matters of faith as though they were self-
evident and indisputable.

Even with the best of intentions, then, it must be said that both
kinds of apologetic and/or correlative criticism run the risk of theological imperialism. All too often literature's value seems to exist in
direct proportion to the "correctness" of its assertions, the usefulness of its testimony, or the paradigmatic significance of its gestures, leaving to someone else the question of what literature is in
and of itself, or what it can do given what it is. This appears to be
less of a problem for critics who exhibit the second orientation that
gained some prominence during the period from the early 1940s to
the mid-1960s, but appearances in this instance can be deceiving.
Although less directly influenced by the methods or concerns of a
Niebuhr or a Tillich, these critics and theologians still responded
to many of the themes, issues, and ideas their work brought into
view. For want of a better term, I will call this kind of criticism
"traditional" in orientation. The question the "traditional" critic
poses is how to make intellectual and religious sense of the great variety of texts, figures, and genres that constitute the literature of
the West, and the tactic he or she employs is to use any one or
more of the distinctive beliefs, assumptions, or motifs of the Ju-
diac-Christian heritage as a kind of hermeneutical key to unlock the
meaning within.

Criticism operating in this fashion usually proceeds in any one of
four ways: either by interpreting individual works, writers, genres,
or traditions in terms of some theological concept or doctrine (say,
the doctrine of Providence in *Samson Agonistes*, or Kierkegaard's notion of "the teleological suspension of the ethical" as a key to the
moral dialectic in Dostoevsky); or by interpreting them in terms of

some theologian or theological system (the "Augustinian strain of piety" in New England colonial literature, or Calvinistic echoes in the fiction of Herman Melville); or by interpreting them in terms of some more or less discrete religious movement (New England Transcendentalism in the work of Henry David Thoreau, Ignatian traditions of spiritual meditation in the poetry of the English metaphysicals); or by interpreting them in terms of some particular theological issue or religious archetype (the nature of evil in *Othello*, the relation between doubt and belief in the poetry of T. S. Eliot, guilt and forgiveness in the fiction of Graham Greene, images of the Fall in the novels of Franz Kafka, the myth of the Great Mother in D. H. Lawrence).

Like the poor, one might say, this kind of "traditional" criticism, or criticism in terms of the "tradition," will be always with us. Its merits have solely to do with how well it is done. Its chief problem is a variant of theological imperialism and takes the form of historical or religious reductionism of the sort one finds in so many studies of Christ-figures in American literature, or of alienation in modern faction, or of atonement and redemption in modern drama. Its great achievement, however, is a restoration of literary works and writers to certain of the religious and ethical traditions which inform them and which constitute a portion of their meaning, as is exemplified, say, in Perry Miller's *The New England Mind* (1939–1953), Douglas Bush's *English Literature of the Earlier Seventeenth Century* (1945), Louis L. Martz's *The Poetry of Meditation* (1954), and D. W. Robertson's *A Preface to Chaucer* (1963).

3

Mention of these admirable instances of what I am calling "traditional criticism," studies with no theological axe to grind which were conceived, researched, and composed with the sole purpose of attempting to mediate the relationship between text and context, between the individual talent and the tradition, already moves us into the third generation of scholarship in this area, a generation partially created by the discovery and assimilation of historical works just such as these. But this is to anticipate a narrative that becomes increasingly complex as we reach the present. To recapitulate, let me point out that thus far I have attempted to suggest a connection, albeit subtle and often attenuated, between certain shifts in the theological climate of opinion in America, particularly within Protestantism, and the development of at least two phases of interest in the study of the relations between religion and literature—the first where this interest was formulated in terms of the relations between Christianity and the arts generally, the second where this interest was reformulated in terms of the more specific relations between theology and literature. In the third and most recent phase, this interest has clearly been reformulated again—or is being reformulated—as an interest in the relations between religion and letters as a whole, and this reformulation involves considerable expansion both of the things being related and of the terms by which their relationship can be understood. In addition, neither the reasons for this reformulation nor the forms it has taken can be accounted for, much less explained, simply by reference to another shift in theological outlook.

That an impressive shift in theological method and point of view recently has taken place, and that it appears to be at least as consequential for the future of both Protestant and Roman Catholic theology as any associated with earlier phases of this narrative, is clearly undeniable. It would be scarcely an exaggeration to say that the whole neo-orthodox edifice has been dismantled in Protestant theology, and that in its place there are at best only a contending, and often contentious, set of conceptual and methodological options—process theology; the new analytic theology generated by the language philosophy of A. J. Ayer, Ludwig Wittgenstein, and others; a revival of interest in theological phenomenology and anthropology; the new hermeneutics; and the various theologies of liberation, which take in everything from the theology of hope,

Black theology, feminist theology, the theology of play, and the Marxist-Christian dialogue to the Death-of-God or radical theology and the new polytheism. But in addition to these theological developments—some new, some old—there have been other developments equally as important to the emergence of a new generation of scholarship devoted to the study of religion and letters. Although not necessarily appearing in this order of occurrence or exhibiting this order of importance, I would describe them as follows.

First, there has been the slow but steady discovery throughout much of the period with which we have been concerned, from the early 1940s into the present decade, of an immense body of research and scholarship, mostly academic in origin, which has already been devoted to an understanding of the religious aspects of literature and of literary traditions. I refer in this case to the works of E. R. Curtius and Eric Auerbach on the literature of the late Middle Ages, to the studies by Douglas Bush and E. M. W. Tillyard on the English Renaissance and the Elizabethan world picture, to Basic Willey's work on the seventeenth century background, to Walter Jackson Bate's numerous monographs on the Age of Johnson, to John Livingstone Lowes's monumental study of Coleridge, to Charles Feidelson's treatment of the nineteenth-century American symbolists, to Walter Houghton's anatomy of the Victorian frame of mind, to Edmund Wilson's interpretation of the metaphysics of the early moderns—all of these works representing scholarship of the highest order which, while often deeply sympathetic to their subject and even engaged, are never ideologically biased or intellectually reductive. The appearance and later discovery of this always expanding body of scholarship seems to have had a double effect upon those more directly concerned with the study of religion and literature. First, it has demonstrated to the skeptic that the study of religious aspects of literature is often a necessary as well as fruitful form of intellectual inquiry which can be conducted in a manner wholly consistent with the most respected canons of critical theory and historical method. Second, it has shown the adherent that what many still regard as a distinct "field" of religion and literature is considerably wider than anyone's previous conception of it, involving as it now so obviously does not only those who have consciously identified themselves with such an enterprise but also those who can in any way or for whatever reasons be said to have contributed to it.

The second discovery responsible for an alteration of focus in this area or "field" has involved a confrontation with, and progressive absorption of, a different tradition of scholarship which is equally as venerable as the first but devoted in this later instance to the study of the history and morphology of religion rather than of literature. Long since an area of scholarship in its own right, "the history of religions," as it is now called, broke into American programs of graduate study in religion as well as theology no earlier than the late 1940s and early 1950s, where its first task was to displace the study of what was then designated "comparative religions." "Comparative religions" was a product of the late Victorian era which had been rather recently imported into the curriculums of theological seminaries and a smattering of religion departments generally under the guise of helping prepare students for overseas missionary work or to encourage the study of foreign missions, and more often than not it carried with it all the prejudices of the British raj. By contrast, historians of religion were not interested in comparison at all, except for the purpose of displaying structural similarities and dissimilarities between and among different religions and families of religion; their real interest was the history of religions *in their traditions* in order better to understand the nature of religion itself as a manifestation of the human. Hence the development of the study of "the history of religions" did several things simultaneously. For one, it refocused attention on religion as a human rather than a superhuman phenomenon. For another, it introduced whole new worlds of material, together with new concepts and methods, to those seriously interested in understanding the nature of *homo religiosus*. For yet another, it brought the emergent academic discipline of religious studies itself into closer contact with such cognate and equally rapidly developing disciplines as cultural anthropology, comparative philology, sociolinguistics, folklore, sociology, psychology, ethnology, archeology, and semiotics.

It should be noted of course that the study of religious myth, ritual, and archetype had already influenced a generation of classical scholars through the impact of Sir James Frazer's *The Golden Bough* (1894) and Emile Durkheim's *The Elementary Forms of Religious Life* (1912) as early as 1912, with the publication of Jane Harrison's *Themis*, a study of the social origins of Greek religion, and that its influence was extended in Francis M. Cornford's *The Origins of Attic Comedy* (1914), A. B. Cook's *Zeus* (1914), and Jess L. Weston's *From Ritual to Romance* (1920), the latter which was in turn to have considerable significance for T. S. Eliot's *The Waste Land* (1922). And because of the subsequent response to the works of Sigmund Freud and Carl Jung, and the even later vogue of Lord Raglan's *The Hero* (1937), Joseph Campbell's *The Hero with a Thousand Faces* (1949), and Ernst Cassirer's multi-volume *The Philosophy of Symbolic Forms*, first published in English translation in 1955, this fascination with myth, ritual, and archetype was to be carried forward in the writings of such different critics and scholars as Kenneth Burke, Northrop Frye, Francis Fergusson, Maud Bodkin, Constance Rourke, Richard Chase, W. H. Auden, Philip Wheelwright, Stanley Edgar Hyman, and Edmund Wilson. But the opening up of scholarly traditions of religious study going back at least as far as Max Mueller's *The Science of Religion* (1864) was to initiate a major revolution in American religious studies, a revolution whose effects can be partially measured by the fact that such names as Max Weber, Durkheim himself, Lucien Levy-Bruhl, Rudolf Otto, Bronislaw Malinowski, E. E. Evans-Pritchard, Joachim Wach, Mircea Eliade, Victor Turner, and Mary Douglas have now become as familiar, and in some cases more familiar, than those of

Paul Tillich, Rudolph Bultmann, Reinhold Niebuhr, H. Richard Niebuhr, or even Karl Barth.

The third development I would point to is the previously mentioned collapse (or at least demise) of neo-orthodoxy, and with it the displacement of systematic theology as the "queen" of the theological sciences. Not only has theology in general lost much of its confidence and credibility, so has the old metaphysics of substance on which such a large portion of its best work, even as late as the neo-orthodox era, was based. This can be readily seen if we look briefly at one of neo-orthodoxy's boldest critics, the Death-of-God theology.

Although scarcely representing the most serious theological challenge to neo-orthodoxy, the Death-of-God or radical theological movement was one of the more symptomatic. Langdon Gilkey, the most lucid interpreter of this movement, has suggested that the radical theologians challenged neo-orthodox assumptions in several characteristic ways.[11] First, where neo-orthodox theologians of various kinds still insisted upon the reality, sovereignty, and all-sufficiency of God and man's consequent dependence upon Him, the radical theologians found all talk about God irrelevant, all appeal to a personal relation with Him meaningless, and all assertions about His traditional attributes incomprehensible in the face of such events as the holocaust. Second, where neo-orthodox theologians assumed that man apart from God is lost and full of sin, and that, as a consequence, secular concepts and norms deriving from man's alienated and fallen condition lack any positive theological value, the radical theologians asserted, to the contrary, that the only meaningful environment is the secular, and that the criteria the secular world recognizes as normative for all forms of inquiry must also be accepted as valid for theology. Third, where neo-orthodox theologians relied on Scripture and tradition to provide the essential material out of which theology unfolds, namely, the revelation of God in Jesus Christ, the radical dissenters perceived

Jesus as but one exemplary figure or saint among others and rejected out-of-hand the acceptance of any statement as true simply
on authoritative or traditional grounds. Hence where neo-orthodox
thinkers, with some exceptions, tended to perpetuate the traditional view that theology deals with things that are ultimately hidden from sight and mysterious in character, such as "the mighty
acts of God," "the Christ of faith," or "the presence of the risen
Lord," their radical counterparts discarded all categories that dealt
with the non-visible or the suprahistorical and confined their attention to what can be experienced and verified within the world of
everyday life. In a word, revelation was "out" and a radical kind of
spiritual honesty was "in."

    If this all begins to sound a bit *de rigueur*, it should be remem-
bered that these "radical" views were scarcely new at all in the history of American religious thought. Their seeds had been sown as
long ago as the New England Transcendentalists and can easily be
found sprinkled throughout the writings of Ralph Waldo Emerson
and Theodore Parker. And the plant had already reached a kind of
premature full growth in William James's theory of radical empiricism when he announced, in the preface to *The Meaning of Truth*
(1909), that the only things discussable should be things definable
in terms drawn from ordinary experience; that the relations between things are no less a part of our experience than the things
themselves; and that the parts of experience are therefore held
together by relations that are themselves experiencable. These
same principles have been reiterated in the interim over and over
again by process thinkers following the lead of James, Dewey, and,
particularly, Alfred North Whitehead, and their metaphysical consequences have long since been explored by such philosophers and
theologians as Charles Hartshorne, Bernard Meland, Schubert M.
Ogden, and John B. Cobb. In his theory of radical empiricism
(which was actually a metaphysics of relations), James was laying
the grounds for his belief that "the directly apprehended universe
needs . . . no extraneous transempirical support"; and by the

1970s, such a conclusion seemed to enjoy wide enough assent to lead Nathan A. Scott, Jr., scarcely a radical theologian himself, to observe,

> After Feuerbach and Nietzsche and Freud and Wittgenstein, not only is the divine *pantokrator* felt to be an unmanageable piece of metaphysical lumber which is without any real 'cash value' in the human life-world; it has also been considered by many sensitive thinkers of our age to be a morally intolerable conception which invites an attitude of reverence before a frigid monstrosity.[12]

Like Stanley Romaine Hopper and others active in the study of religion and literature, Scott had been brought to this conviction by a route that lead through European existentialism and Biblical demythologization to the phenomenology of Martin Heidegger rather than through the American pragmatists and their later empirical theological offspring, but the result was pretty much the same. A sort of consensus had been reached about the impotence and irrelevance of the supernaturalist assumptions of classical theism, and a new mood of revisionary pluralism had set in among both Protestants and Roman Catholics which has been recently described with much sympathy and discernment in David Tracy's *Blessed Rage for Order* (1975).

Parallel to the collapse and attempted reconstruction of theological methods and conceptions during this period, there has occurred a similar transformation in literary theory and method. This fourth development affecting the study of religion and letters has not been unrelated to the other three. Many of the same figures or developments that have proved significant to the fresh recovery of past traditions and texts, to the expanding study of the history and structure of religions, and to theological reconception and revision, have also affected critical theory and practice. Since many of the changes in literary criticism which have occurred as a result of these related developments are discussed at considerable length in subsequent chapters, I will forego any detailed description at this point and simply confine myself to some brief remarks about the

obvious causes of this contemporary revolution in literary studies
and its implications for more specialized inquiry into the religious
aspects of literature.

Responsibility for the current revisionary impulse in literary
theory and criticism can be laid chiefly at the door of two developments, neither of which came all at once and both of which still
seem more apparent than real, whether at the general level of critical practice or at the more specific level of curriculum design. The
first involved a reaction against the intellectual narrowness and cultural elitism of Anglo-American formalism as it had been reduced
to the theory of close reading associated with the New Criticism
and then transmitted to the schools as a pedagogical devise. The
second, no doubt precipitated by the first, resulted from the influx
of new ideas and procedures which had been gaining widespread
attention on the Continent since World War II but which reached
these shores only within the last decade or so. In the case of the
first, the New Criticism was not so much rejected or abandoned as
simply outgrown. In the case of the second, far fewer American
critics actually seem to have embraced the new theories and
methods than to have been challenged and stimulated by them.
The vigorous exponents and proponents of these new approaches
and theories have clearly shaken many critics loose from the hold of
old ideas and practices without making converts out of them. The
reason for this probably has something to do with the fact that
much of the ardent discussion of these concepts and methods has
been carried on in a language intelligible only to the disciple, and
relatively few American critics seem disposed in the end to submit
to what sounds like a painful *rite de passage* only to wind up merely
having traded in an outworn method for a new metaphysics (or
anti-metaphysics).

Nevertheless, the recent appearance or reappearance of theories
and methods as different as Marxism and psychoanalysis, semiotics
and the sociology of taste, stylistics and deconstruction, has been
felt everywhere—in the development or revival of journals such as

Diacritics, Critical Inquiry, New Literary History, The Georgia Review, and *Glyph;* in the kinds of issues now attracting attention, such as the relationship between author and work, the nature of texts and textuality, the affective distinctiveness of particular genres, the question of literary impact, the relation between the spoken and the written, the grammar of individual modes of discourse, and many others; in the reorganization of the Modern Language Association; and, not incidentally, in the development of a third generation of scholarship devoted to the study of religious dimensions of literary works and traditions.

The most important consequences of these recent developments in critical theory are two. First, they have succeeded in breaking down many of the intellectual barriers that once divided those who pursued this form of inquiry from opposite sides, as it were, of the confessional fence. It now makes no more sense, for example, to think of Hans-Georg Gadamer as a Christian philosopher interested in writing about the theory of interpretation than it does to view Harold Bloom as a literary critic and historian who just happens to specialize in the English and American Romantic poets. For Gadamer's work constitutes as important a contribution to literary theory as Bloom's does to the metaphysics of the Romantic Sublime. Or again, Claude Lévi-Strauss is as much a theologian in the closing pages of *Tristes Tropiques* as Paul Ricoeur is a structural anthropologist in *The Symbolism of Evil.* The work of Mircea Eliade has proven as rich a resource to literary critics as the theories of Northrop Frye have been for historians of religion. Thus the lines differentiating one discipline from another, when they are still visible at all, no longer seem to demarcate separate and inviolate areas of specialization but to point instead to congruent and often overlapping fields of exploration.

A second consequence of these developments, I would argue, is that they have all but shattered the latent trinitarianism of the New Criticism with its neat division of literature into poetry, fiction, and drama. Critics of nearly all theoretical persuasions are now willing to consider as literature everything from autobiography to the anatomy, from historical narrative to the philosophical treatise, with all manner of verbal unit, from the myth and folktale down to the single sentence or clause, thrown in for good measure. This displacement of the traditional belletristic notion of literature by something broader and more variegated is a healthy sign, most especially if it leads, as E. D. Hirsch has recently urged,[13] to a recovery of the older notion of literature as humane letters, or *bonnes lettres* as it was once called. Such a notion repudiates the view of literature as mere verbal artifact and restores such criteria as knowledge and wisdom to a rank of equal importance with art, sentiment, and imagination in the determination of what shall be called literature and how it shall be studied.

In addition to these two consequences, which have resulted in what would have to be called a virtual dissolution of, or—depending on one's perspective—infinite extension of, the boundaries of any "field" of religion and literature, or religion and art, as formerly conceived, one can dimly discern two somewhat different orientations which characterize the best of the work that is being done by critics and scholars of the third generation. The first orientation is analytic, interpretive, and revisionary, in that it seeks to criticize and alter previous traditions of criticism and scholarship rather than to advance new theoretical models.[14] The second new orientation is equally revisionist but in a more speculative fashion, because it is devoted either to sorting out and weighing various theoretical alternatives or to seeking some new conceptual and/or methodological synthesis.[15]

Whatever else these new orientations may indicate, they clearly reveal that fresh thinking about the relations between religion and letters, no less than the new modes of critical analysis it has generated or been generated by, is not springing from one quarter alone or assuming but a single form. Structuralists are proceeding cheek-by-jowl with phenomenologists, and Marxists with neoliberal Catholics, in exploring both the conjunctions and disjunc-

tions between the sacred and the profane in literature. Many theorists, to be sure, continue to operate as though that which they were attempting to understand was something wholly different either from themselves or from the materials in and through which it is expressed, something whose existence they seem chiefly interested simply in confirming or disconfirming. Others proceed as though the object (or subject, as you will) of their inquiry were so deeply imbedded within the formal structures and codes by which it is disclosed that to describe the objective properties of the latter would be to define the essence of the former. Still others, though admittedly a smaller number, now boldly proclaim that the goal of their inquiry is coterminous with the grammar of motives that impels it, that what they seek through interpretation is nothing short of an answer to the question of what they themselves are when, like any writer, they undertake such potentially hazardous and destructive acts as interpretation itself.

Common to them all, however, both speculative and analytic critics alike, is a growing sensitivity to the complexity of the relations between text and reader. If the recent proliferation of methods, vocabularies, and theories has accomplished little more, it has deepened appreciation of their common hermeneutical plight. Living how and as we do, at some distance both temporal and critical from the circumstances of their initial articulation, most critics no longer find it possible to suppose that we can ever recover an original relation with the great symbols of the sacred once expressed in literature. The problem is not with the sacred as such, nor even with its reputed disappearance from the literature of our period; the problem, if one need call it that, is rather with ourselves. We moderns have lost our immediate relation to the Word that literature sometimes spoke (and perhaps still does) and have been left, like T. S. Eliot's speaker in "Journey of the Magi," with mere words which cry out for interpretations we can no longer supply them. In the ancient formula, one believed in order to understand: in the modern, one reinterprets for the sake of believing once again in the possibility of understanding and thereby rediscovers what it is like to believe.

As a gloss on the above, one might say that if to dissect the letter is to risk destroying its spirit, as the old saw has it, then our very modernity condemns us to the fate of potential killers. The hope that the Romantics once held out to us, of sympathetically imagining our way back into the situation of the text's first readers, or perhaps even into the mysterious interiority of the author himself, and thus of being able to re-experience to the full the text's novelty and power in the immediacy of its first articulation—this dream of historical transcendence has now been betrayed by the very techniques we have developed to accomplish it. Our methodological sophistication merely perpetuates and extends that same distantiation and alienation from the text we would have it obliterate. For the more subtle our techniques and the more refined our methods, the more they reinforce a realization that the questions we would put to the text can never be the same questions that the text once put to its initial readers, since neither those initial readers, nor even the text's author, was ever faced in quite the same way we are with overcoming the gulf, both in time and intent, that now separates us from them.

This dilemma has now led some theorists to ask if there isn't another way out: if we cannot restore the text to its pre-critical immediacy of understanding *even by abandoning interpretation*, is it possible to achieve some post-critical or secondary immediacy of understanding *through interpretation itself?* The object of understanding, in this case, would not be the text in and of itself but the experience such a text generates or produces among readers who from this distance and with these expectations seek to understand it. One of the advocates of this view of criticism, Paul de Man, admits that such interpretations represent at best a mixture of "blindness and insight." But of such ingredients, he would also contend, is the text also a mixture. Paul Ricoeur, who has formulated this way of overcoming hermeneutics through hermeneutics itself, argues that such criticism aspires to a kind of second naiveté rather than a first—not the naiveté of those who can believe without understanding or understand only what they believe, but the naiveté of those whose commitment to understand through interpretation is itself a form of belief, an act of faith. Rather than presuming to recover the integrity of the text or even the integrity of those whose experience is revealed through the text, this kind of criticism seeks through the junctions and disjunctions of the interpretive act to become an experience with an integrity of its own, one which is scarcely possible or comprehensible independent of the text that provoked it, but which aims because of that provocation at a somewhat different mode of being altogether.

To many, this may only sound like a new invitation to subjectivism which will issue in but another form of theological or religious imperialism, less self-conscious, perhaps, than those practiced by critics of the first and second generation, but no less aggressive or disfiguring for all that. To this objection the best reply may well have been the one offered by Friedrich Nietzsche in his famous essay on history where he suggests that if man doesn't learn how to use the past, then the past will use him. But Nietzsche's essay possesses a further relevance which will help us summarize this short history.

4

In *The Use and Abuse of History*, Nietzsche asserts that history is essential to the life of man in at least three distinct ways, and that these three ways correspond to the three distinct forms of history itself. That kind of history that serves man's need for action and struggle, Nietzsche defines as "the monumental," describing it as the quest for heroic models and examples from the past that can provide courage and comfort in the face of present hardships and future challenges. That kind of history that answers man's more conservative need for a sense of rootage in the present and acceptance of the future, Nietzsche terms "the antiquarian," because its chief aim is to preserve the status quo through an often indiscriminate veneration of the ordinary, as opposed to the extraordinary, circumstances of past life. That kind of history which is born out of man's suffering and his need for deliverance, Nietzsche designates as "the critical," inasmuch as its purpose, often in the name of an ideal future, is to question, to judge, even to condemn the entire historical inheritance.

It requires only a slight expansion of Nietzsche's categories to see how they correspond roughly to the three generations of criticism we have just surveyed. These correspondences would be less noteworthy, perhaps, if it were not for the fact that while one generation has been succeeded by another, their descendants, so to speak, have lingered on. Descendants of the first generation of critics, who were essentially antiquarian, can be seen not only among those who follow the early pastoral critics by indiscriminately accepting everything cultural of potentially equal religious significance, but also among their apparent opposites, the apodictic critics, who with no less zeal for conserving the continuities between past, present, and future set about differentiating orthodox inheritance from heretical accretion. Descendants of the second generation of critics, who were closer in outlook to Nietzsche's monumental perspective, can most readily be found among those who perpetuate the apologetic and correlative models by searching for a usable past to shore up the ruins of the present, but it can also be discerned among those critics with a somewhat larger interest in history for its own sake who tend to reify elements of the past in order to lend greater force or meaning to works of the present. By contrast, critics of the present generation seem to fit Nietzsche's critical category, not simply because they have exploited as their chief contribution to method what Arnold Hauser was among the first to call, thinking of Nietzsche among others, a "hermeneutics of exposure," but also because speculative and analytic critics alike have employed this method neither in the interests of preserving the past, like the antiquarian historians, nor in the interests of repossessing the past, like the monumental historians, but instead in the interests of de-idealizing and deconstructing the past.

Nietzsche was under no illusions about the adequacy of any one of these attitudes toward the past. Though each of them has its place and use, all of them involve important exclusions that seriously diminish the essential service the past can render the present and the future. The antiquarian perspective betrays its reputed claim to cherish the past by selecting and mummifying just those elements of the past that protect the present from disruption and correction. The monumental perspective uses an excessive valuation of equally selective and admittedly unrepresentative aspects of the past to cloak a hatred of the present. And the critical perspective jeopardizes the future in behalf of which it acts by dismissing in its outright rejection of both past and present those elements of each which instruct as well as victimize.

To hold these different perspectives in constructive tension with one another, Nietzsche knew that it would take more than an effort of will. But the metaphysics he believed was necessary he never found, and the search for it eventually drove him mad. To say that contemporary critics and theorists are still faced with Nietzsche's problem is not to suggest that there haven't been numerous attempts to resolve it in the interim. It is only to confess that the resolutions still seem partial and unsatisfactory, and that the problem therefore continues to vex. But perhaps we have made some advance over Nietzsche. Where he perceived his vexations as the result of a problem whose solution might remove them, many contemporaries now seem to realize that such vexations are, as Wallace Stevens said, "part of the res itself and not about it."

2

Forms of Religious Meaning in Literature

The poem refreshes life so that we share,
For a moment, the first ideal. . . . It satisfies
Belief in an immaculate beginning

And sends us, winged by an unconscious will,
To an immaculate end. We move between these points:
From that ever-early candor to its late plural

And the candor of them is the strong exhilaration
Of what we feel from what we think, of thought
Beating in the heart, as if blood newly came,

An elixir, and excitation, a pure power.
The poem, through candor, brings back a power again
That gives a candid kind to everything.

WALLACE STEVENS
"Notes Toward a Supreme Fiction"

It has now become something of a commonplace to observe that the study of literature, and with it the study of the kind of experience that literature is designed both to clarify and advance, has undergone considerable revision in recent years. Where not too many years ago literary critics tended to resist all attempts to relate individual works of literature to anything beyond their own verbal matrix, now an increasing number of scholars and critics seem interested in exploring the relations literature possesses to everything from sociology to music, from myth and history to psychology and religion.[1] Whether or not this growth of interest in the extra- or intra-mural relations of literary study signifies a thoroughgoing transformation of our conception of the nature and function of literary art, it surely points to the greater demands we have come to place upon our reading.

Just where these demands have come from is hard to say. It used to be argued that our former indifference to what a more old-fashioned generation referred to as the relations between literature and life or art and culture was due in considerable part to the enormities of recent history and the banalities of contemporary society, both of which encouraged us to dissociate our experience as readers from our existence as butchers, bakers, and munitions makers.[2] Occasionally, it was further alleged that there was a close connection between this regrettable state of affairs and the concomitant development of a literary theory in the modern period which had the effect—though by no means necessarily the intention—of establishing, as one of its critics has suggested, "an apparently impassable chasm between the facts of our existence in contemporary society and the values of art."[3] In either case, literary education was no longer thought to humanize, so the argument ran, and a good deal of the blame was attributed to the social and political indifference of modern formalist criticism. Yet this argument was, and still is, far too simple. That our society is now crowded with semi-illiterate holders of the baccalaureate degree whose reading has only deadened rather than quickened their sensibilities, is one thing; to aver that this condition, which seems scarcely unique to our own period or society, is related to the development of modern methods of literary study, is quite another.

In retrospect it seems increasingly clear that the chief aim of the early proponents of what is now called the New Criticism was simply to rescue aesthetic values from the great welter of social, historical, etymological, and philological fact in which they were then buried. The early modern critics had no other ambition than to restore the study and appreciation of literature to its rightful place within the ecology of human affairs by redefining literature in terms of purposes and principles intrinsic to its own mode of being. Their work was in a manner undone and even undercut only later, when ardent disciples carried their ideas into the academy and made a fetish of them. The result was of course deplorable. Critics became less interested in the purposes or principles of literature than in its properties, and criticism, in turn, narrowed its focus by concentrating less on any individual work's total design than on a careful explication of the structural purpose and internal design of any one of its individual parts.

This gradual contraction of critical focus was in time to produce counter-reactions [4]—of which the relatively new interest in the relations between literature and religion is certainly one—but it is important to realize that in striking ways these counter-reactions were no more than a continuation of the impulses first released by modern criticism itself. As Stanely Edgar Hyman has argued in his excellent study, what set modern criticism apart from its predecessors was neither its sponsorship of the close reading of texts—Johnson and Hazlitt were as capable of this as Brooks and Warren—nor even its treatment of literature "as literature and not another thing"—Coleridge argued for this long before T. S. Eliot—but its radical encouragement of "the organized use of non-literary techniques and bodies of knowledge to obtain insights into literature." [5] The direct consequence of this was, to be sure, a renewed appreciation of the intrinsic qualities of literature and a deepening analysis of individual works of literature, but the purpose behind it was hardly to sever "the values of art" from "the facts of contemporary society." Whether by design or default, the methods modern critics employed in effect positively forbade it. T. S. Eliot's own criticism, at least in his earliest great period, depended upon an interplay between the individual talent and the whole literary tradition and proceeded by means of an extraordinary process of association, comparison, and contrast. R. P. Blackmur, long before he began to practice an idiosyncratic form of cultural analysis, derived many of his most brilliant insights into individual poems from an application of information found in the *Oxford English Dictionary* and *Webster's Second International*. I. A. Richards drew upon the development of semantics and behavioristic psychology; William Empson relied heavily on new theories of language and, later, on everything from psychoanalytic theory to the history of literary conventions; John Crowe Ransom turned to philosophy, aesthetics, and ontology; Yvor Winters looked back to Arnold and Newman, and behind them to Sir Philip Sidney, to traditions of moral classicism; Maud Bodkin turned to Jung; Francis Fergusson to cultural anthropology; and Kenneth Burke to anything he could lay his hands on. Therefore to say that we have recently begun to place heavier demands on our reading and that, as a consequence, criticism has grown somewhat broader in reference and more eclectic in method, is but to suggest that we have finally recovered from the timorous reaction that quickly set in after the first assaults of modern criticism and that critics are now working to extend that initial modern impulse. The chief interest in contemporary criticism, both in its European and its Anglo-American branches, continues to reside in the demarcation and definition of the intrinsically literary, but the resources that have now been brought to bear upon this task have been considerably expanded, and the critical applications that have resulted from it display a new boldness and ingenuity.

Whether this amounts to the claim that criticism has in fact improved, only time will tell, but one thing is certain: criticism has grown more interesting, more supple, and more universal just insofar as it has opened itself to other disciplines, relaxed the barriers between the literary and the non-literary, taken a new interest in the meaning of reading and writing in a mass culture, complicated its view of history, and reopened the question of hermeneutics or the theory of interpretation. And this, surely, is the background against which to understand the fairly recent post-war development of interest in the relations between literature and religion. Discounting all the aberrant parochial and ecclesiastical motives which

are likely to foster such an interest in any age, those critics and
scholars who have seriously developed such an interest in our own,
no matter what their personal confessional persuasion or philosophical commitment, have generally seen themselves as belonging
to the same continuity of tradition and drawing upon the same
store of procedures and methods as their modern forbears. Hence
whether they have sought to demonstrate how certain writers are
able to intensify their rendering of the human story to the point
where, as R. W. B. Lewis suggests in reference to Henry James, it
gives off "intimations of the sacred,"[6] or instead have proposed, as
Perry Miller has in connection with Emerson and Thoreau, that
certain thinkers make what can only be called "a religious demon-
stration" by putting "their cause in the language of philosophy and
literature rather than theology,"[7] they have assumed that they
were extending modern critical practice rather than subverting it.

Yet even a rapid scansion of some of the work which has been
done in this interdisciplinary area will quickly disclose a broad
range of critical theory and method. The spectrum seems to run all
the way from those who seek to elucidate the manner in which literature can be instructed by doctrine or doctrine "fleshed out" in
literature to those who conceive of literature, as Baudelaire says
somewhere, as "a metaphysics made sensible to the heart and expressing itself in images." Between these two alternatives, however, there are a variety of positions which oblige one neither to
construe the relationship between literature and religion as a forced
marriage between incompatibles nor to view literature itself either
as a substitute for religion or as a propaedeutic for faith.

Some critics and scholars assume that literature still holds the
mirror up to nature by serving as an index to or assessment of our
modern cultural and religious distress. Others believe that in the
perfection of its formal organization and because of the greater intensity and purity of self-revelation this allows, literature offers a
kind of golden alternative to our "gong-tormented" world of brass,
one that can provide a religious stay against the confusion of values

and commitments that otherwise clutter our experience. Still others maintain that every successful work of literature, as an instance of the artist's sacrifice of himself and his own intentions to the objective requirements of his craft, presents us with the paradigmatic religious situation, a virtual re-enactment of the Crucifixion in which the artist empties himself for the sake of his materials so that their meanings may live. Yet another group of critics works on the contrary assumption: instead of emptying himself of every last vestige of his personality, his inwardness, the true artist, they argue, serves a religious function precisely to the extent that he carries the expression of his own personality, his own *humanitas*, to its uttermost extreme, thereby demonstrating that truth of a religious order is only disclosed to man under the shadow of ultimacy. A variation on this same theme is played by still another series of critics who contend that the great writer, through his capacity to penetrate beneath the superficial appearances of his age to its deepest, unspent sources of life, is a spokesman for Being itself. And by giving formal expression to life's deep-running currents, he thus helps in his writing to conserve what has survived from the past and to release what may shape the present and the future.

Nevertheless, despite the wide latitude of theory and practice exhibited by these disparate examples, it is possible to reduce the seemingly endless variety of ways critics have discussed the relations between literature and religion to several basic types.[8] No one of these types exists independently of any of the rest; each of them shades off into one or more of its neighbors just because the critics who exemplify them conceive of and then set about developing the relationship between literature and religion in more than a single manner. Yet the artificiality of such a typology does not vitiate the service it can perform in helping us to clarify what is otherwise a hopeless Babel of approaches, assumptions, and points of view. My ultimate aim, however, is not simply to adumbrate the several types of critical theory that have influenced the work already done in this interdisciplinary area; it is rather to construct, even in barest outline, a kind of composite model or type of my own which attempts to utilize the major strengths and virtues of the other types while avoiding some of their obvious limitations and deficiencies. This requires, first of all, a backward glance at the history of critical theory itself, because the very possibility of organizing current discussion of this subject along typological lines depends upon an initial investigation of the models which the history of literary criticism has already provided for it.

                                    I

The art of literary criticism in the West is an old one, probably as old as the art of literature itself, and the theories of literature which have developed as a result of its practice are legion. To a casual student of the history of criticism, nothing may be so obvious as their variety and abundance. Yet there is a sense in which, as M. H. Abrams has demonstrated, every theory of literature in the history of criticism that has sought comprehensiveness has had to take some account of at least four elements basic to the total situation of any work of art: the artist who creates the work, the work itself, the world the work creates and reveals, and the audience the work affects.[9] While none of the important theories of literature in the history of criticism has emphasized one of these elements at the expense of excluding all the others, every major theory has tended to interpret one element in the total situation of the work as the key to an understanding of the significance and status of the other three. Thus Professor Abrams has been able to distinguish four predominant kinds of critical theory in the history of criticism, each particular theory being a function of the specific element toward which the theory is basically, even if not exclusively, oriented.

   The oldest and probably most influential literary theory in the history of criticism is the theory of mimesis, which has been the basic theoretical orientation for critics from Plato and Aristotle to

Dr. Johnson and beyond, and which has also enjoyed a modest renaissance in our own time.[10] Its principal concern has been with the world revealed by the work, and its key word is *imitation*. Though Plato was its first major theorist, Aristotle was undoubtedly its most influential because of the way he implicitly challenged the strictures which Plato placed upon it.

Those strictures left Aristotle, if he was to defend a mimetic theory at all, with the task of demonstrating how literature is less the imitation of what is simply an appearance or illusion of reality than an imitation of what is essential or basic about reality itself. Aristotle was at pains to show how literature, and particularly tragedy, could be said to complete and fulfill nature, rather than merely imitate or copy it, by presenting through its formal organization the completed imitation of an action which in nature or experience is never so unified or fully realized. Aristotle's mode of procedure was to show how art appeals not, as Plato had argued, to the more inferior human faculties—to the emotions and passions instead of the intellect or soul—but rather to the natural human instinct to imitate, and that, moreover, art arouses and excites the passions, instead of merely disciplining and controlling them, only so that it may finally allay them. This was the intention of his definition of tragedy as

> an imitation of an action that is serious, complete, and of a certain magnitude; in language embellished with each kind of artistic ornament, the several kinds being found in separate parts of the play; in the form of action, not of narrative; through pity and fear affecting the proper purgation of these emotions.[11]

Significantly, Aristotle understood the excitation and eventual catharsis of the emotions to be a direct result of the object imitated and the manner and means of its imitation, and thus integral to the nature and function of the work itself. Hence the aim of criticism was not restricted to an elaboration of the nature of the imitated object (or, in other terms, to the world revealed in and through the work), but was rather conceived to include an elucidation of the principle by which the entire work, understood as the imitation of a particular kind of action, was organized to effect the proper response.

But there was a problem inherent in Aristotle's theory of art as mimesis if any society or individual were to decide, out of an inordinate interest in the needs and requirements of a particular audience, to prescribe the kinds of effects art could legitimately produce. Such a situation in fact arose during the Renaissance, partly as a result of the influence of the study of rhetoric with its preoccupation with the way in which audiences can be most deeply moved, and gave rise to the second major orientation in critical theory, what Abrams calls the pragmatic theory of literature. Sir Philip Sidney was probably its most typical, though not necessarily its most important, exponent, and *instruction* was its most representative word.

Sidney wrote his *Defense of Poesie* in answer to Puritan charges that poetry was immoral and provocative. He countered these charges in at least three ways: first, by reminding his audience of the long and civilizing influence of poetry in the history of culture; second, by arguing that poetry imitates the real less than it invents and then represents the possible; and third, by insisting that the purpose of poetry is not to please the emotions but to instruct the mind, or, if to please at all, then in order finally to persuade. Poetry, and by implication all art, was thus understood to serve an explicitly heuristic, even didactic, purpose by pleasing in order to instruct. The purpose of poetry's instruction was to lead men to virtue by exhorting them to contemplate and then to imitate a different but a better world than our own, a world where virtue always prospers and vice always perishes. Thus Sidney could conclude that the poet is superior to the historian in that, unlike the latter, he is less concerned with what actually does happen in life than with what ideally should happen instead.

The importance of Sidney's theory of literature can in some

sense be measured, according to Professor Abrams, by the extent to which it represents all those critical theories from Horace to the Enlightenment which have considered literature chiefly as a means to some other end, and which have therefore tended to evaluate individual works of literature in terms of their relation to something else, such as moral insight, social consciousness, spiritual regeneration, and so on. For most theorists of the pragmatic orientation, literature's ability to serve moral ends has always been its chief aim, its ability to serve pleasurable ends a secondary aim. But from Dryden through the eighteenth century, the balance began to swing the other way: poetry imitated nature in order to instruct, but instructed primarily in order to please.

Yet inherent in the most important tendency of this orientation—the inclination to subordinate all other poetic matters to the spiritual and moral requirements of a particular audience—were the seeds of its own dissolution. For if the real purpose of poetics was to discover the means whereby certain kinds of significance might be effectively impressed upon a particular kind of audience, the most important subject of inquiry for poetics could easily become the particular training, resources, and personal qualifications required by the poet or artist to produce the desired effect. Such a transition eventually occurred toward the end of the eighteenth century when an interest in the audience gave way to an interest in the poet, turning the expression of the poet's own needs and abilities not only into the predominant cause of poetry but also into its final aim and ultimate task. The result of this major shift in emphasis, according to Abrams, was the emergence of the third critical orientation in the history of literary theory—the Romantic theory of literature. Though Wordsworth was its first major nineteenth-century exponent, Coleridge was undoubtedly its most important, and *expression* was its most representative word.

While Coleridge differed from Wordsworth and many of the other critics of the nineteenth century in believing that literature, particularly poetry, is at once inspired and contrived, at once the spontaneous expression of the assimilating power of the creative imagination and the result of a deliberate adoption of means to ends, he nonetheless revealed himself very much a man of his own age when he transformed the question of the nature of poetry into a question of the nature of the poet. Coleridge gave voice to the most characteristic assumption of all expressive theories of art when he remarked that "what is poetry? is so nearly the same question with, what is a poet? that the answer to the one is involved in the solution of the other." [12]

Coleridge defined the poet in his ideal perfection as the creature who "brings the whole soul of man into activity" by diffusing "a tone and spirit of unity, that blends, and (as it were) fuses, each into each, by that synthetic and magical power, to which we have exclusively appropriated the name of imagination. This power . . . reveals itself in the balance and reconciliation of opposite or discordant qualities." [13] In this definition Coleridge came perilously close to reducing the poet to little more than a vehicle for the expression of the creative imagination which then creates poetry by a reconciliation of opposite or discordant qualities. Nevertheless, his intention was the very opposite. By claiming for the poet the ability to utilize the creative imagination, Coleridge hoped to demonstrate that the poet, in effecting a reconciliation of opposite or discordant qualities, in fact imitates the ongoing work of creation itself. Coleridge conceived that the whole universe, both in what he called its "eternal act of creation in the infinite I AM" [14] and in its continuous repetition of that act in the process of synthesizing and recreation by individual minds, consists in the creative resolution of conflict and disparity. [15] Thus he believed that, in continuing that act in the creation of his poetry, the poet was simply participating in the most characteristic activity of life itself, an activity which was then mirrored and expressed in his poems.

The great liability of Coleridge's theory was its exalted conception of the poet, and hence of poetry itself, which, in a later, more skeptical age, might come to seem overly optimistic, if not somewhat presumptuous. This is in fact precisely what happened at the beginning of the twentieth century, when T. E. Hulme set off the modern critical reaction to nineteenth-century expressive theory by launching his attack against this side of Coleridge's thought, charging that it elevated the poet to the stature of a God with the power to create *ex nihilo*.[16] To counteract this tendency, Hulme once again called for the very kind of poetry which Coleridge had tried to overthrow, a poetry of fancy instead of imagination, and thus helped to establish the fourth theoretical orientation cited by Abrams, what we may call the modern or semantic theory of literature.

The major point of departure for modern theories of literature is neither the poet, nor his audience, nor even the world he reveals or creates, but rather the specific work of the poet considered for the most part in its own right. The major concern of this critical theory, which follows both Coleridge and T. S. Eliot at this point, is to consider works of literature as relatively autonomous, self-reflexive entities whose particular mode of being can only be understood in terms of the parts internal to them, and the most representative word of this orientation, is, perhaps, *objectivity*.

Modern critics have tended to be of one mind in seeking to define the nature and function of literature, primarily poetry, in terms that are broadly semantic.[17] Their chief interest has resided in language's capacity to generate the images and symbols by which literature is composed, and particularly in the relations between words in all their contextual specificity and the realities which they signify, indeed create, in experience by virtue of the poet's special use of them. Their assumption has been that the poet, given his ability to use language in fresh and unusual ways, is able to express certain kinds of experience in a manner no other medium can duplicate. Hence the business of the literary theorist who works out of this orientation is to define as precisely as possible the particular nature and structure of the poet's language so that his readers will not look for meanings poetry is unable to express or fail to comprehend the special kinds of meaning only poetry can convey. Even when they have shared certain basic assumptions, however, modern critics can scarcely be said to have written but one kind of criticism. For a similar conviction about the essentially semantic nature of literature has not stood in the way of Edmund Wilson's respect for Sainte-Beuve or his desire to produce criticism which is at once biographical and historical, or prevented Northrop Frye from using Frazer, Jung, and, most especially, Blake to write a criticism that is basically mythic and archetypal, or deterred Yvor Winters from employing Matthew Arnold as the model for a criticism that is decidedly moral as well as intellectual.

Amidst this considerable variation of interest and approach, R. S. Crane has been able to discern two singular points of view which characterize all those critics who share the modern predisposition to view literature as a special kind of language written in words. The first tendency, he suggests, is shared by critics and theorists like I. A. Richards, William Empson, G. Wilson Knight, John Crowe Ransom, R. P. Blackmur, Allen Tate, Cleanth Brooks, and their many imitators who view literature primarily as language in the ordinary sense of a statement in words. Their particular problem has thus been the negative one of distinguishing between the language of literature and the language of other kinds of discourse so that they may vindicate their claim that literature expresses certain things which are inexpressible in any other language. Their typical procedure has been to follow Coleridge by contrasting the language of poetry with the language of some other, more familiar mode of discourse, usually scientific discourse, in order to define by comparison the distinctive attributes, powers, and possibilities of the language of poetry. Because they have emphasized the various but special ways in which poetry communicates its meaning, they have characteristically conceived of poetry, Crane argues, as a special kind of meaningful expression.

The second tendency in modern criticism, according to Crane, is shared by such different critics and theorists as Kenneth Burke,

Maud Bodkin, Edmund Wilson, Lionel Trilling, Richard Chase, Francis Fergusson, and Northrop Frye who, instead of concentrating on the particular way in which poetry communicates its meaning, have emphasized the particular kinds of meaning poetry communicates. These critics have tended to conceive of poetry not as a special kind of meaningful expression but rather as the expression of a special kind of meaning. Their most revealing characteristic has been the reductive nature of their criticism, their inclination to interpret poetry in terms of something assumed to be far more basic and essential in human experience than poetry itself. Hence they have generally been inclined to think of poetry as a certain kind of symbolic language which, instead of being more unique and eccentric than any other, is more natural and universal than any other.[18]

2

My more particular concern, however, is with the way in which each of these orientations, when understood in its essentials, can suggest the possibilities and limitations of various typical approaches to the study of the relationship between literature and religion. If, for example, one asks what implications the modern semantic orientation possesses for imagining such a relationship, one must begin by observing that the commitment to language and language's capacity for creating new meaning, which is presupposed by this orientation, usually carries with it the assumption that man is a symbol-making animal whose ability to form images and metaphors expressive of the reality he at once rediscovers or recreates through his intensive use of them is generally regarded as, at the very least, one of the most significant elements of his humanity and, at the very most, a sign of his divine inheritance. Several possible consequences naturally follow from this assumption. For those theologically-inclined literary critics who view literature as a special kind of meaningful expression, poetry—and by implication all literature—acquires its religious character either because it represents, in its most intense metaphorical embrace, the closest approximation of which man himself is capable of that unification of opposites which is only perfectly envisioned in the Christian doctrine of the Incarnation;[19] or because it expresses, through a radically contextual language which is iconic, plurisignative, soft of focus, and paradoxical, an intimation of the archetypes or universals which are resident within the concretely particular;[20] or because, in its essential character as a word to be spoken and heard as well as formed, literature represents the attempt to communicate the "intensification of an interior" to another form of "interiority" and thus serves as the invitation of an "I" to enter into dialogue with a "Thou."[21] For those critics and scholars who view literature instead as the expression of a special kind of meaning, literature acquires its religious meaning and significance either because, like all other forms of symbolic expression, it is ultimately hierophantic, manifesting in its images and metaphors nothing less than the bond between man and the sacred;[22] or because it employs images, archetypes, and myths inherited from specific religious traditions which, at least in certain circumstances, continue to exert a religious hold over the imagination that is compelled to use them;[23] or, finally, because literature represents an extension and completion in language of a response to reality which, however unconventional in form when measured by the standards of orthodoxy, is nonetheless essentially religious in character.[24]

The difficulty this orientation can present as a model for the relationship between literature and religion is that, whether one focuses upon the particular kind of meaning literature communicates or instead upon the specific way in which literature communicates its meaning, one is still left with the problem of elaborating a theory of literature which demonstrates, on the one hand, how religious elements somehow enter into or at least help determine its character as a literary object without, on the other, so closely identifying those elements with the literary aspects of the work that they simply cease to deserve the designation "religious" at all. More concretely, how does one discuss the religious elements, motifs, or characteristics of any given work of literature without either turning literature into a surrogate for philosophy or theology, or reducing religion merely to any and every work's dimension of seriousness or depth?

This has been a special problem for critics of this orientation because of their wholly salutary concern to retain for literature those qualities and virtues which set it apart from other forms of verbal expression. Hence in their zeal to preserve the integrity of art, some have found a kind of refuge from these problems by turning their attention from a consideration of the religious elements within particular works of literature to a consideration of the potentially religious character of the creative process as such. Here T. S. Eliot—with Henry James and Flaubert in the not-too-distant background—often serves as an important model with his implicitly religious theory of the martyrdom of the poet to his poem. As Eliot puts it, in order for the poem—or any work of literature—to achieve its true character as an independent, self-referential object, the poet must sacrifice his personal desires and intentions to the formal requirements of his art. The poet as an individuated self in effect dies so that his poem as a concrete, impersonal object may live, the very gesture of poetic utterance thus becoming the representative religious act. The difficulty here is that if one locates the religious dimension of particular works in the process of their making, of their creation, instead of in the nature or function of the thing made, one can easily lose sight of the fact that literature not only represents the collaboration of the poet as craftsman with the materials of his craft but also the union of his art, in all its ramifications, with his matured vision of experience. What the artist wishes in fact to say, however much that may be conditioned by his manner of saying it, is overshadowed by the miraculous possibility of his saying anything at all.

This appears to be less of a problem for those critics and scholars

who rely more heavily upon the Romantic model of literary theory
with its attendant interest in the expressive character of art.
Whether such critics follow Wordsworth, and the eighteenth century generally, in conceiving of literature as a way of exploring and
expressing what is natural or essential in human nature and experience,[25] or instead follow Coleridge in grounding the nature and
function of literature in what is believed to be fundamental and
characteristic about the nature of reality itself,[26] they tend to demonstrate less of an interest in the thing made, or even in the process
of its making, and more in the character and point of view of its
maker. From this perspective, literature is understood to be expressive of vision—the artist's vision—which is itself very often conceived to be the result of the interaction between the artist's own
personality and the stress and pressure of his times. Hence criticism directed at religious elements in literature based upon the
Romantic model tends to open out from the individual work to the
embodied vision which informs it, and from the embodied vision
itself to all the influences—cultural, historical, religious, and theological as well as personal—which have worked to affect and enrich
it.

But again there can be problems if the critic moves too hastily
through the densely realized particulars of the work itself to the
vision which informs it, or beyond them to the *Zeitgeist* it may
reflect. An interest in the artist's represented vision can easily lead
the impatient reader to a facile or inaccurate identification of the
artist's own point of view with that of any one of his character's or
even his narrator's, when instead it is more likely to exist in the
complex points of view in their manifold relationships. Similarly,
an excessive preoccupation with the cultural matrix from which
particular poems, plays, and novels spring and to which they implicitly appeal can lead to the reductive tendency to view literature
merely as an index to the age, when again it is more likely that
every work of any historical significance not only reflects its age
but also helps to produce and shape it.

It is precisely this last insight which informs the best work of those critics and theologians who rely upon the pragmatic orientation in literary theory. Predisposed to view works of literature neither as the result of a certain technical process, nor as the expression of a particular perspective, nor even as the creation of a special kind of object, critics working from this orientation tend rather to interpret works of literature in light of their aims, goals, or purposes, whether expressed or implied, and are thus inclined to locate their religious meaning or significance in the particular functions they are designed to serve or assumed to perform in the broader realm of human experience as such. Most pragmatic critics follow Sidney in believing that literature presents an actual world less than it re-presents a possible one, and that its primary function is not simply to please or even to inform but somehow to instruct and by instructing to transform. Yet, in spite of certain assumptions common to them all, the actual practice of critics of this orientation admits of a wide margin of variance.

On the one side are those more theologically self-conscious critics who are inclined to invest literature, at least in certain of its forms, with the capacity to reify, or at any rate to clarify, the intent, import, or effect of particular religious beliefs or theological doctrines. Hence certain forms of literary expression, some argue, may even unknowingly serve a Christological function by demonstrating in their exacting explorations of the concrete and the particular how the actual and the finite can be trusted as a way into the Infinite, into God Himself.[27] Other forms of literature, different critics argue, testify to the Trinitarian character of human experience because the artist, in serving his potentially sacred mission to rekindle our love of the created world, in turn creates realities incarnate with his own inspiration.[28] Again still other critics try to maintain, following the later Heidegger, that literature, as the art of unconcealment and unveiling, is not so concerned with what is theologically distinctive and peculiar about Being itself as with what is religiously *a priori* and ultimately mysterious when

Being itself is experienced in its full immediacy, which is to say when Being is experienced less as a symbol, structure, or concept than simply as Presence.[29]

On the other side are those more purely academic critics who for any number of reasons believe that literature does, or at least can, serve a function analogous to, if not identical with, religion itself in certain of its aspects. Thus, specific forms of literature, particularly tragic literature, perform, according to one interpretation, the ancient mithridatic function by exposing the worst of our evils and the darkest of our terrors and thus releasing us from our bondage to them.[30] According to another, as the record of "communalized experience,"[31] literature not only reflects community but actually helps to create it by putting its society's most profound sense of self to the most rigorous tests and thus adumbrating the terms and conditions for its survival.[32] In yet a third, literature is viewed in Nietzschean terms as providing "the vindication of the worth and value of the world, of life and of human experience." From such a perspective, all literature, no matter how bleak its meaning, "is praise and celebration."[33]

Nevertheless, the temptation to ascribe a quasi-sacred or religious office to certain kinds of literary expression is not restricted to a small and eccentric group of critics in the modern period. In a time when all forms of traditionalism are on the wane, a great many critics with no particular ties to religion have found themselves compelled to think of literature in terms similar to those so eloquently employed by Wallace Stevens in "Of Modern Poetry," where he gave his famous definition of "The poem of the mind in the act of finding/ What will suffice." Poetry was not always invested with such awesome responsibility:

> It had not always had
> To find: the scene was set, it repeated what
> Was in the script.
>   Then the theatre was changed
> To something else. Its past was a souvenir.[34]

As a consequence critics, like writers themselves, have come to place increasingly heavy demands upon literature, asking it to perform a redemptive function once reserved for religion alone. For I. A. Richards, "Poetry is the supreme use of language, man's chief coordinating instrument, in the service of the most integral purposes of life";[35] for Philip Wheelwright, "The ground-bass of poetic truth is the truth, contextual but real, of man's possible redemption through the fullest imaginative response";[36] for Eliseo Vivas, "The poet brings forth values with which history is in the pain of labor";[37] for R. P. Blackmur, "poetry is the *nous poetikos*, that deep habit of mind, deeper than any sea of hope, calmer in its long swell than any mirror of despair, which imitates in forms and images dear to herself the life she has lived, the life she dreads to live, and the life she aspires to live."[38]

The faith is deep and the hope is high for the kind of fulfillment that literature alone can provide in these statements. Poetry is described as an instrument of redemption in one statement, as a creator of value in another. Whether it simply serves the most integral purposes of life, as for Richards, or very nearly becomes the most integral purpose of life, as for Blackmur, poetry seems to be able to do in these statements what only something akin to religious belief would have been expected to do in an earlier, more traditional period.

Observations such as these have led Richard Foster to conclude that for many of the American New Critics, poetry achieved the status of a form of metaphysics or revelation.[39] Professor Foster has supported this contention by demonstrating a shift of emphasis in the work of four modern American critics (Richards, Vivas, Blackmur, and Tate) from the idea of poetry conceived as form to the idea of poetry conceived as meaning, "from a formal-aesthetical to a moral-spiritual view of the nature and function of art."[40] Professor Foster has deemed it a significant shift of emphasis "because it shows the critics as typically 'modern' men of letters in uncertain quest of value and meaning in a world which looks to them like a chaos or a waste land."[41] He has therefore referred to them as "pilgrims in search of truth" in order to underscore "the essentially spiritual or religious motif of their seeking. . . ."[42]

As a gloss on Professor Foster's argument we might say that, having suffered the full onslaught of modern experience by their own close inspection and evaluation of modern literature, these critics, and many others like them, have attempted to produce a literary theory that establishes poetry as a source or instrument of the religious values they have discovered to be so radically threatened by recent history. Hence they have turned poetry into what is virtually a substitute for religion and thus exhibited the extent of their debt to that side of Coleridge's criticism which originally inspired their reaction against Romantic, expressive theories of literature in the first place.

Yet it is hardly necessary to go all the way back to Coleridge to explain the religious impulse behind so much modern criticism. Much nearer in time and spirit to our own situation is Matthew Arnold, one of the first great critics to experience the threat of modern science and the consequent loss of the power to believe in the face of its numerous implications. It was Arnold who first set the precedent for subsequent criticism by reacting positively rather than negatively to the crisis of belief produced by modern science, in claiming for poetry the possibility of providing a form of explicitly religious consolation. The opening paragraph of "The Study of Poetry" still rings with his fervor:

> The future of poetry is immense, because in poetry, where it is worthy of its high destinies, our race, as time goes on, will find an ever surer and surer stay. There is not a creed which is not shaken, not an accredited dogma which is not shown to be questionable, not a received tradition which does not threaten to dissolve. Our religion has materialized itself in the fact, in the supposed fact; it has attached its emotion to the fact, and now the fact is failing it. But for poetry the idea is everything; the rest is a world of illusion, of divine illusion. Poetry attaches its emotion to the idea; the idea *is* the fact. The strongest part of our religion *today* is its unconscious poetry.[43]

It is no doubt a simple matter to puncture Arnold's great optimism regarding the future of poetry. We have witnessed too much barbarity, destruction, and inhumanity in this century ever to be able to find in a poetry which so easily disposes of facts for the sake of ideas "What will suffice." Moreover, only relatively few people have actually found in poetry a substitute for "what now passes with us for religion and philosophy. . . ."[44] Instead, those who have successfully supplanted ideas and emotions only with facts, and facts thus devoid of all intellectual and moral significance, have dispensed with poetry for the same reason that they have also dispensed with religion or philosophy: because, unlike Arnold, they have had no need to turn to poetry or to anything else "to interpret life for us, to console us, to sustain us."[45] Yet this observation does not gainsay the relevance of Arnold's example; for those modern critics who have followed him in defining poetry, usually in distinction to science, as a source of value and meaning that scientific relativity cannot threaten have also shared the religious or spiritual impulse propelling Arnold's fervid, late Romantic humanism. And, like him as well, they have in the process run the risk of turning literature into something else.

Indeed, this is the great temptation for all critics who employ the pragmatic orientation in literary theory. Inclined to subordinate the design of any particular poem, novel, or play to its design upon its audience, to view the writer in terms of his capacities to produce the requisite response, and to ground the norms or canons of literary judgment and evaluation in terms of the needs or desires of a particular public, criticism of religious or theological interest following Renaissance models tends to reduce the meaning of works of literature to their supposed or intended effects and to view them simply as the means to a particular end.[46] And when one conceives of literature not as an object organized in terms of principles and aims intrinsic to its own mode of being but rather as the means to an end independently deduced for it, no matter how humanly significant or theologically meaningful that end or purpose may be, then one's critical discriminations will simply be limited by the suitability of the aim or purpose so envisaged. At worst, literature is turned into a form of propaganda or reduced to an object lesson. At best, literature often achieves a central religious or theological role in human experience only at the expense of sacrificing whatever is internal to its own nature which would thereby differentiate it from, say, religious revelation on the one hand or some form of psychological therapy on the other.

Yet it would be a serious mistake to assess the significance of this orientation as a model for the relation between religion and literature solely on the basis of certain limitations sometimes typical of it. The conception of literature as an instrument of instruction and human enrichment has characterized much of the most intelligent and surely the most valuable literary criticism from Dr. Johnson to the present; and it still remains the underlying assumption for all those critics and scholars, both within the theological circle and without, who have attempted to specify what great works of literature have to teach us and, in teaching us, to contribute to man's being as a moral and spiritual animal.

This brings us to the fourth and final orientation under consideration, that provided by the mimetic theory of literature. As the oldest critical theory in the history of criticism, mimesis has also been the most consistently misused. To many students of criticism, mimetic theory suggests the notion that literature merely imitates or reflects life, thus providing us with only a slightly distorted—or better, refracted—mirror-image of the world around us. Literature, according to this understanding, acquires its religious or theological character from the nature of the event, object, or feeling which it imitates. Hence the prevalent belief that literature, indeed all art, is most deeply religious or genuinely theological when it imitates, or is "about," such specific religious subjects as God, sin, prayer, atonement, blasphemy, paradise, and the like.

I. A. Richards gave the lie to such crude distortions of mimetic theory when he once remarked that works of literature are not about—that is, do not mean—anything at all, if by "being about" or "meaning" we intend to suggest that statements made in the work can be taken as propositions about the real world of everyday experience. Whether such statements concern man or God, sin or salvation, holy wonder or holy dread, they acquire such meaning as they possess, mimetic theory contends, only in terms of the presiding principle which orders the whole work toward some particular end. Hence the notion of imitation refers not to the recognizable objects, events, or feelings from ordinary experience which the work inevitably presents to us, but rather to the executive principle by which they are thrust into new and significantly different relationships and then expressed. The emphasis, in other words, is not upon the way everyday occurrences are seen and interpreted, but rather upon the way they are re-seen and re-interpreted in terms of the highly selective and very limited context in which the work presents them to us.

From this perspective one seeks to correlate literature with religion neither by relating the world view rendered in the one with the world view characteristic of the other, nor by comparing similar expressions of intent or patterns of implication. One looks for the distinctively religious significance of theological meaning of particular works of literature in terms of the inner movement and dramatic structure of the works themselves. Thus Christian tragedy is not to be distinguished from tragedies of other kinds either primarily in terms of its aims or of its ideas or even of its techniques (though all of these are important), but rather in terms of its action.[47] In like fashion, it is possible to differentiate meditative poetry from other kinds of religious verse not by its theology nor by its style, but rather by its characteristic dramatic strategy.[48]

Yet it is apparent that a criticism which focuses too exclusively upon the inner dynamics of any work of literature, upon the way one part unites with others to describe a certain meaningful trajectory of events and their significance, has its limitations. The tendency the mimetic orientation shares with all other formal theories of literature, the tendency to define each work in terms of laws of

its own origination, can, unless employed with great tact and sensitivity, isolate the work from the general religious and cultural situation it may be said to disclose or illumine. As a consequence, it
may also sever the work from those larger social, moral, and spiritual values whose inevitable implication in great literary texts constitutes one of the reasons we find it necessary to read at all. Finally, in laying such heavy stress upon each work's particular
design, the mimetic orientation can lead to a neglect of every
work's special design upon us, and thus fail to account for the way
every significant work of literature shapes the response of its
readers.

At this point it should be stressed that the several limitations associated with each of these orientations are in no sense always
replicated in the work of those critics and scholars whose positions
can be most readily identified with one or another of them. The
reasons for this are twofold: very few critics and scholars are
thoroughly consistent, and no one orientation is completely exclusive of the other three. The several orientations thus far discussed
simply describe significant, but by no means absolute, shifts of emphasis in the history of critical theory, and thereby provide a useful
heuristic device for distinguishing and evaluating some of the ways
in which a variety of critics and theologians have pursued the relationship between religion and literature. Further, they suggest that
no single theory or method will suffice to comprehend the full
range of experience and illumination that has resulted from the encounter of literature with religion and religion with literature. In
developing a viable critical conception of the relationship between
these two modes of awareness and expression, our best hope, it
seems to me, lies in the direction of a principled eclecticism in all
questions of theory and method. That is, we need with the moderns to respect the formal, objective character of literary expression
without overlooking the fact that, as the Romantics insisted, literature does in fact express something compelling our response; and
we need to take with full seriousness the normative significance

such expressions can have for us, as the pragmatic critics do, without forgetting that, as the neo-Aristotelians have reminded us, works of the imagination acquire such normative significance precisely because of the matter, medium, and manner in which they are expressed.

Once this is granted, several further observations follow. Whether one is examining St. Thomas Aquinas's importance to the cosmology of *The Divine Comedy* or the significance of St. Augustine's theory of mind for understanding John Donne's "Batter my heart, three person'd God," the relationship between Jonathan Edwards's "democratic" theory of the nature of Being and Herman Melville's view of the nature of creation in *Moby-Dick* or the influence of Schelling's view of spirit in Coleridge's *Aids to Reflection*, it is obvious that all such study requires an abandonment of the doctrinaire and the parochial both in theology and in literary theory. For the primary, if elemental, lesson such study yields is that when brought into contact in such texts, both literature and religion have a way of working strangely upon one another, even of transforming one another. Thus when T. S. Eliot submits a fairly orthodox theology of the Incarnation to the musical form of the *Four Quartets*, or Theodore Roethke carries a language experiment on natural processes to the point of meditation and revelation in the greenhouse poems; when Nathaniel Hawthorne submits the allegorical mode in *The Scarlet Letter* to the morally problematic universe of the nineteenth century, or Fyodor Dostoevsky adapts the tradition of first-person confessional narration in *The Underground Man* to a tale of *ressentiment*—in all such cases, one is witness to what Henry Rago once called "a wholly new making of experience into language, and of language into experience,"[49] and "the principle each time is some new identification of the authentic"[50] which does something in turn both to the language and to the experience.[51] It is this, surely, which anyone encounters in reading of Priam's secret night meeting with Achilles in Book XXIV of the *Iliad*; or in coming upon Cleopatra's sudden, striking comparison of herself to the

common maid who milks "And does the meanest chores" in Act IV
of *Antony and Cleopatra;* or in following Ishmael's miraculous discovery of the mute center of calm and joy "amid the tornadoed
Atlantic of my being" as he looks for the first time into the deep
clear pool at the center of the whirling maelstrom in "The Grand
Armada" and watches the young and newborn whales revelling in
"dalliance and delight." The names we glibly attach to such liminal
experiences suddenly grate upon the ear. Certain actions which all
at once seem inevitable and necessary fill familiar beliefs and
former ideas to the bursting point with new and unforeseen meaning. Life suddenly releases some of its unspent force, and conventional expectations and interpretations are toppled by the flood of
new insight and illumination.

Moments such as these, which are to be found in every great
work of the imagination, suggest that our understanding of religious belief must be revised; for the forms of belief, desire, and
dread we so often encounter in such moments of epiphany are at
the furthest remove from any set of dogmatic propositions and can
scarcely be reduced to their paraphrasable content without suffering unconscionable violence. Nor can we permit the varieties of
religious experience so encountered to be fixed in some rigid definition that robs these luminous moments of their power to instruct us
not only about the multifariousness of religious experience itself
but also about its inexplicability, its mystery. As literature under
the influence of religious propulsions is always tending to regress to
its primitive character as a form of action, a kind of gesture, a mode
of re-awakening and renewal, so religion when forced to submit to
the pressures and expansions of imaginative release tends to recover
something of its primordial form in "images and signs; events and
visions; parables and hard sayings; a Life." [52]

In stressing the need for flexibility and openness, whether in
theological definition or in critical theory, I am therefore setting
myself in firmest opposition both to those who would subsume our
experience of literature under some doctrinal umbrella and also to

those who would insist that literary experience bears no affinities, much less identities, with other kinds of experience. While the first turn literature to some narrowly didactic or apologetic use which is rarely if ever appropriate to it, the second seriously truncate and distort our actual experience of literature by striving to maintain the illusion of its purity. Yet it is as fallacious to assume, say, that a contextualist position in criticism inevitably enforces a distinction between the mind that reads and the individual who thinks and feels as it is to suppose that a committed believer is compelled to make his reading corroborate precisely the way he feels and thinks. Hence a greater awareness and appreciation of the actual complexities that attend every individual instance of the relationship between literature and religion should have a beneficial, retroactive effect upon the disciplines in and through which it has been, up until now, customary to study them: by enabling us to see what precisely as disciplines theology, religious studies, and criticism, whether taken singly or together, tend to leave out of account.

From this it should be apparent that at the conceptual level our need is neither for greater precision of definition nor for a more rigorous and systematic methodology, if either of these would have the effect of restricting our access to the multitude of ways literature and religion have and do become intertangled in specific works, careers, periods, or genres; or, beyond that, if they would lead us to suppose either that there is but one kind of religious meaning or significance which all works possess, or that such religious meaning or significance as any work may possess is always to be located in the same place and under the same conditions. While rigor and clarity of thought are hardly to be despised, such lucidity and discipline of mind as is possible must not be attained at the expense of simplifying and thereby distorting and diminishing the subject under investigation. So far as method is concerned, what is needed at this point is not greater narrowness but greater catholicity—a flexible definition of the literary work which will utilize the essential insights of all four theoretical orientations and

yet permit the widest variety of approach to the question of any
particular work's religious nature, meaning, and significance.

3

It is my conviction that we can move some way toward that ideal
model of the literary artifact, and at the same time overcome many,
if not most, of the limitations associated with each of the several
orientations, thus bringing them into closer relation and collaboration, if we complement our several senses of the imitative, the
pragmatic, the expressive, and the semantic character of literature
with an appreciation of its hypothetical character as well. For, as
Dorothy Van Ghent and Northrop Frye have recently reminded
us, literature is nothing if not suppositional or hypothetical. Every
work of literature argues implicitly, whether it is a poem, novel, or
play, "If you will grant me my initial premise or set of conditions,
then such and such would, or at least could, follow from them."
What the work of literature takes from life, from what is actual, to
paraphrase Miss Van Ghent, are the conditions for its hypothesis,
the terms and substance of its original premise. It starts from the
empirical data that we all generally recognize as given in experience. But then it selects, organizes, and motivates those conditions
"in a way that suggests a purely creative issue—a series of hypothetical events not 'given' at all but cogent as cause and effect from
the initial selection." [53]

Roy Harvey Pearce has provided further elaboration of this process by suggesting that the work so conceived is thus literally not
"true":

> it consists instead of a series of hypothetical situations, imaged
> and motivated in such a way that, within their confines, we can
> accept as necessary the actions and responses into which the situ-
> ations—and the imagined human beings in them—are made to
> issue. What primarily interests us in "created" situations of this

> sort is, of course, not their inevitable relevance to factuality, but
> their possibility: their resonance with our deepest sense of our-
> selves.[54]

The use of the word "true" in this case is carefully hedged. The
work is *not* "true" in the sense that it makes no pretense to conform
to the shape of our (or anyone else's) past experience, and because
it may bear very little resemblance in its details to what most people would concede to be indisputably certain or unequivocally real.
In another sense, however, the work *is* "true" precisely because, in
appealing to "our deepest sense of ourselves," it helps put us in
touch, as William James would have said, with the rest of our experience. A work of literature is "true," then, not because it reflects
what we already know, but because, by adding to the store of our
knowledge about what is at least possible if not actual, it thereby
extends the realm of the known, of what we are prepared to accept
as part of the potential field of our experience.

In asserting, as Pearce does, that it is neither our instinctive
delight in imitations, nor our curiosity about personality, nor even
our pleasure in discovering and unraveling complex linguistic patterns that permits us to "willingly suspend our ordinary disbelief in
such imagined situations and accordingly assent to them as fully as
an artist can compel us to," but rather our "interest in possibility,"[55] he is here closest to the pragmatic orientation in critical
theory. Pearce emphasizes this by stressing the fact that our assent
is necessarily an "as-if assent,"[56] since it is made to something
more on the order of a hypothetical conjecture than a verifiable
proposition. Yet the writer could not obtain our "assent" to "such
imagined situations," Pearce insists, if he did not possess to an extraordinary degree both a heightened "awareness to such possibility" and the "ability to express that possibility in language and all
the formal, constructivist means which language bears within itself."[57] Moreover, his capacity to see hidden possibilities and potentialities we never dreamed of in the realities which we all know,

would not remain convincing to us if it were not based upon his and our knowledge of what just possibly is or most probably could be the case. Hence the sequence or structure of possibility, which at its most abstract defines the form of his work,[58] must ultimately seem, if not altogether natural and inevitable, at least plausible and compelling to "our deepest sense of ourselves."

That the structure of possibility upon which his work is based can and does strike us as plausible, is owing to the fact that every writer draws from the common fund of human experience which has been bequeathed to us by history, society, and, as it were, blood. His procedure, however, is to select from that common fund some single assumption or interrelated series of assumptions about the way things are, or can be, or should be, and then order his entire work in terms of it. Yet his purpose is never merely analytical but also critical and evaluative. In choosing from the vast store of human experience some simple or complex notion about life, or one of its particular aspects, a notion which can then function for the duration of the work as one of life's ultimate truths, the writer is finally interested both in the possibilities and limitations of life when life itself is viewed in terms of this particular principle of ultimacy.

These observations should make clear that while literature, in this understanding of it, is closer to one of our four orientations than to the other three, it is not exclusive of any of them. With the imitationists it assumes that every work of literature is unified neither by the world it reflects, nor by the vision it expresses, nor by the end which it serves, but only, finally, by the presiding principle or cause which gives its various parts their ordered and meaningful coherence. With the pragmatists it asserts that, in creating a possible world instead of an actual one, literature is nothing if not critical of established values, since, as John Dewey once remarked, "the moral function of art . . . is to remove prejudice, do away with the scales that keep the eye from seeing, tear away the veils due to wont and custom, [and] perfect the power to perceive."[59]

With the expressionists it agrees that every work of literature springs from and appeals to our common sense of *humanitas*, thus attesting what is essential to or ultimately characteristic about life itself; and yet that because it is a unique, personal achievement, every work of literature also represents the creation of something new and distinctively individual which life otherwise would not possess. And, finally, with the objectivists it acknowledges that nothing in literature can be rendered but in words which, as they are selected, ordered, and bent to fit the purpose of the work itself, remain the most essential concrete element in every poem, novel, or play.

From this perspective, literature is neither totally immersed in the world of everyday experience nor completely divorced from it. Ontologically it belongs to the realm of hypothesis and not of actual fact. But there is, as Stevens's poem suggests, a beautiful circuit of belief and desire between them:

> We move between these points:
> From that ever-early candor to its late plural
>
> And the candor of them is the strong exhilaration
> Of what we feel from what we think, of thought
> Beating in the heart, as if blood newly came,
>
> An elixir, an excitation, a pure power.
> The poem, through candor, brings back a power again
> That gives a candid kind to everything.[60]

The tendency of all great literature, then, is to take the known, the empirically given in experience, and, as Dorothy Van Ghent has remarked in specific reference to the novel, "push it into the dimension of the unknown,"[61] into the dimension of the merely potential. From this it seems to follow that literature's value and significance for us "lies less in confirming and interpreting the known" than in compelling us to suppose, indeed at least for a time to believe, *"that something else might be the case."*[62] Hence our purpose in the study of literature cannot, in any conventional sense, be to extend our knowledge of ourselves. "It is rather," as J. V. Cunningham echoing Stevens has so trenchantly reminded us, "to enable us to think and feel otherwise than as we do. It is to erect a larger context of experience within which we may define and understand our own by attending to the disparity between it and the experience of others." [63]

Observations such as these, while protecting the integrity of art without severing it from its connections either with the artist or with the traditions and experiences upon which he draws and the society to which he addresses himself, leave quite open the variety of approaches which may be possible or appropriate to an investigation of the religious nature, meaning, or significance of particular texts. Yet they also raise further questions about whether there is not something intrinsically religious about this conception of literature itself. It is my conviction that there are at least several ways in which this theory or model involves religious and not merely philosophical assumptions. As a consequence of this, there are several ways in which this theory or model not only encourages us to investigate the religious components of any work of literature but in fact compels it, and this quite apart from the critic's own religious persuasion or lack thereof. By this, however, I do not mean that every work of literature should be interpreted solely, or even largely, in religious terms as opposed, let us say, to social, psychological, or political terms. I am simply arguing that the religious meaning of any individual work of literature is the spiritual corollary of its social, psychological, or political meaning, and that it deserves to be accorded similar respect in any interpretation that aims at completeness. But in what sense is it possible to say that every work of literature is in some sense religious, that every work of literature contains a spiritual component?

First, every work of literature, insofar as it is a hypothetical creation, presupposes for its very existence a belief in what Roy Harvey Pearce calls, borrowing a phrase from Americo Castro, a "commitment to vital possibility." [64] Without such a commitment the writer could not envisage the element of potentiality in all our experience of the actual, nor the reader give even tacit assent to it. A "commitment to vital possibility" thus represents that half-conscious, half-unconscious faith in all that lies beyond the range of our immediate perception, all that points to what William James designated as the element of the "More" in human experience, that experiential component which constitutes at once the substance of our hope and the ground of the imagination itself—indeed, without which we could not imagine at all. Northrop Frye has given this faith, this commitment, unusually forceful expression by stating that "the work of the imagination presents us with a vision, not of the personal greatness of the poet, but of something personal and far greater: the vision of a decisive act of spiritual freedom, the vision of the recreation of man." [65]

Second, the issue of religion is also involved in our inability to give full assent to the hypothetical situations literature imagines for us unless the conditions upon which they are based and the potential outcomes in which they are made to issue are in some often obscure but always crucial way commensurate with "our deepest sense of ourselves." This "deepest sense of ourselves," of which we are rarely conscious, determines the range of possibilities we are willing to entertain and thus delimits our capacity to respond to any work of literature. All this means is that as readers we are men and women and not machines; that we cannot be made to suspend our ordinary disbelief in the imagined situations literature presents to us, or to give even temporary assent to the hidden potentialities those situations then disclose to us, unless each work of literature, by virtue of all the formal devices through which it maintains its hold upon our attention, is able to convince us that "such and such" at least might have been the case if life possessed the coherence and pattern which in everyday experience it never does. Beyond this, however, that "sense of ourselves" is at the root formed, conditioned, and nourished by what we take, however mysteriously or darkly, to be ultimately real and meaningful. It is informed by, and informing of, whatever for us finally matters, whatever for us essentially counts. Thus in responding to every work of literature, we are—if we are bringing the whole of ourselves to that response—responding with whatever for us is the center of our being.

Yet, by the same token, our response to literature, while unavoidably dependent upon "our deepest sense of ourselves," is not absolutely determined by that sense. Indeed, it is precisely that sense which literature seeks to extend, to complicate, and ultimately to transform by suggesting "that something else might be the case." Which is only to reiterate that, at bottom, literature seeks not to confirm but to convert by extending the range of our imaginative grasp and hence "our knowledge and governance of human possibility."[66]

Third, and finally, there is in our experience of every work of literature something related to—I do not say identical with—the religious experience of reality as ultimate, where, as Joachim Wach once remarked, "we react not to any single or finite phenomenon, material or otherwise, but to what we realize as undergirding and conditioning all that constitutes our world of experiences."[67] This reaction to something we perceive as "undergirding" and "conditioning" all that constitutes the world of experience in the text results from the fact that every serious work of literature is based upon some deeply felt, even if not fully conscious, assumption about what possibly can, or just possibly does, constitute the ground of experience itself. This basic intuition or presiding assumption then becomes the organizing principle for the hypothetical structure the work turns out to be. Call it what you will—the informing assumption (Ronald S. Crane), the shaping cause (Allen Tate), the embodied vision (Wayne C. Booth), the concrete universal (William K. Wimsatt), or (as I prefer) the metaphysic—this executive principle, which is responsible for the work's coherence both in formal and in ideational terms, functions analogously to the notion of ultimacy in religious experience.[68]

For all that, however, there is a signal difference between the nature of any principle of ultimacy, or, as I am calling it, metaphysic that we encounter in works of literature and the notion of ultimacy or metaphysic as it operates in religion. In literature, as I have already mentioned, our assent to the meaning and implications of any notion of ultimacy or metaphysic is an "as-if assent" to what Pearce calls "a conditional [possibly] contrary-to-fact statement";[69] in religion our assent by contrast is supposed to be an unconditional assent to what, regardless of the facts, purports to be an absolute truth. Thus it would be fair to say, at least up to a point, that readers believe primarily in order to understand, whereas believers seek greater understanding from literature the better to believe. Or so it should be if this were the most consistent of worlds, where believers always knew what they believed and never held conflicting and even contradictory convictions, and where readers were able to remain neutral in the face of the truth-claims of all belief systems. Such, of course, is far from the way things actually are, which is why the distinction between reader and believer ultimately breaks down. Just as there is no perfectly consistent believer whose reading at every point corroborates his or her convictions, so there is no absolutely pure reader who is without his or her share of half-uttered, unuttered, or unutterable beliefs.

But the issue is a good deal more complicated than this. The conundrum of the relationship between belief and understanding is at least as old as St. Augustine and has achieved prominence again recently in the writings of the new proponents of interpretation theory. As Martin Heidegger, Hans-Georg Gadamer, Paul Ricoeur, and E. D. Hirsch have all reminded us, there is no way of obtaining understanding of other minds without an initial act of belief in the integrity and coherence of the mind we seek to understand. By the same token, such acts of belief automatically predispose us to understand some things about those minds and to disregard others, and this process of selection is only the more greatly exacerbated by the gulf which exists between our own mind and that of anyone else. Knowledge of other minds thus proceeds in a circular fashion which to some observers is distressingly closed. To understand at all requires belief, but belief cannot help but influence and delimit what we shall be able to understand.

Martin Heidegger was the first modern theorist to argue that the hermeneutical circle possesses an ontologically positive significance. Very much in the manner of the art historian E. H. Gombrich, with his model of schema and revision or making and matching, Heidegger assumed that the reader always projects a meaning onto any text as a whole as soon as some partial meaning emerges from his initial encounter with it. Indeed, no meaning would emerge at all if the reader didn't approach the text with certain expectations about its potential meaningfulness. The closer the text is read, the more the reader is obliged to revise his first projections in light of subsequent discoveries. Understanding thereby occurs as a result of this process of projection and revision, where the reader is constantly engaged in replacing his pre-understandings or fore-conceptions, as Gadamer calls them, with more suitable ones. According to this model of the relationship between text and reader, belief is necessary for meanings to emerge at all, but belief must be constantly revised in light of the emergence of new meaning from the text, thus closing the circle between reader and text as understanding increases.

Paul Ricoeur finds this model unsatisfactory beyond a certain point because it evades the question of truth. Yet the question of truth cannot be avoided, he argues, for the world of symbolic discourse is not static, as the comparativists argue, but dynamic. Every symbol is iconoclastic in relation to some other, and hence there is no way of remaining neutral to "the struggle," "the dynamics, in which the symbol itself becomes prey to a spontaneous hermeneutics that seeks to transcend it." [70] But how is one to participate in this process of symbolic transcendence when the very possibility of understanding at all is colored by one's own preconceptions? How can the symbol "give rise to thought" and lead to truth when the possibility of a perfect coincidence between the mind of the reader and the intentionality of the symbol is conceded to be a fiction?

Ricoeur's answer is carefully qualified. While we may never be able to attain a perspective that is completely free of preconceptions and, in that sense, objective, we can break out of the circularity of believing in order to understand and understanding in order to believe with the help of Pascal's notion of the wager. We wager that the process of symbolic reflection, the process of symbolic hermeneutics within the text, will lead somewhere. This wager, which is really an act of faith, "pays off" if it yields more in the way of understanding than would have been possible without it. In betting on the "indication" of symbolic thought, we are betting that our wager will be restored to us in the renewed power of perception, in greater insight not simply concerning the text itself but what the text refers to, what the text is about. In this sense, hermeneutics does not depend, as Dilthey supposed, on some sympathetic identification of the mind of the interpreter with the "particular expressions of life" he seeks to interpret: "It is not a kinship of one life with another that hermeneutics requires, but a kinship of thought with what the life aims at—in short, of thought with the thing which is in question." [71]

If this is the way understanding is increased, then the process is the same for believer and non-believer alike, and serious literature, when read correctly, should affect both equally. For no serious literature is neutral either to the question of belief or to the question of the relationship between belief and understanding. As dramatizations of what it could or would be like to experience life, or some selected aspect of it, ordered in terms of a specific principle of ultimacy, the function of all serious works of literature is to show us what various notions of ultimacy actually entail when certain of the elements of life are selectively arranged in accordance with them, or, conversely, how various notions of what is, or can be, ultimate in our experience of life accordingly vary the possible or potential constituents of our experience. In so doing they require us "to take into our purview, as a vital human possibility, all the historically definable forms of life in which that possibility is made operative."[72] In elucidating how the facts might have been otherwise, they compel us to imagine the innerness and otherness of different ways of being, thinking, and feeling than our own. Yet great works of the imagination would have little real effect upon the structure of our beliefs, little genuine impact upon the shape of our affections, if their designs upon us were not imbedded in all the concrete particulars of lived experience, in terms of what Yeats called "the fury and mire of human veins." We are disturbed and moved and even altered by what we read because the possibilities and potentialities which arise from such commitments are measured in terms of the price they exact from those who must test and suffer them on the pulses—characters in whose aspiration and travail is revealed something of our own at least dimly perceived human image.

But this leads us back again to the question of truth and to the relationship between literature and religion, art and faith. It was Joseph Conrad who allied literature with truth and truth with faith. Describing all art as a single-minded attempt to render the highest kind of justice to the visible universe, Conrad insisted that the artist makes us hear, feel, and, above all, see by bringing to light the truth underlying its every aspect, by finding in its form, colors, and shadows what is fundamental, enduring, and essential. In saying this and no more, Conrad was prepared to concede that he had not said anything unique about the artist, much less about the writer. The same single-mindedness, he believed, could be attributed to the scientist or the philosopher. Where the scientist and the philosopher differed with the artist, Conrad was convinced, is not over *what* they seek to find but *where* they look to find it and *how* they corroborate the authenticity of what they discover. If the scientist plunges into the world of facts and the philosopher into the world of ideas, Conrad believed that the artist plunges into the world of feelings, and there, in that region of stress and strife we normally keep well hidden from view, finds the terms of his appeal. His appeal, however, is not to our capacity for understanding and belief, like the scientist and philosopher, but to our capacity for wonder, delight, and pity, to our capacity for a feeling of fellowship, as Conrad calls it, "which binds together all humanity—the dead to the living and the living to the unborn."[73] Hence no matter what the artist sees, Conrad believed, whether it be a spectacle of folly or of mirth, of terror or beatitude, his purpose, as indeed his triumph, is so to present his vision of it as to awaken in the hearts of its beholders "that subtle but invincible conviction of solidarity" "in mysterious origin, in toil, in joy, in hope [and] in uncertain fate, which binds men to each other and all mankind to the visible world."[74] The basis of the relationship between literature and religion has never been grasped more firmly, or articulated with greater eloquence.

3

The Place of the Literary Critic
in Religious Studies

He is neither priest nor proctor . . .
It is a fresh spiritual that he defines. . . .

WALLACE STEVENS
"An Ordinary Evening in New Haven"

Until quite recently the issue raised in my title would have struck most readers as impertinent as well as irrelevant. To students of religion who as likely as not had been raised on a fairly strict and somewhat tedious diet of modern dialectical theology, any field of religious inquiry which presupposed an intimate relation between the world of faith and the world of culture, as they were then called, smacked of fuzzy-minded liberalism and seemed in imminent danger of overlooking, or, worse, dismissing the infinite, qualitative differences between the Word of God and the words of men. To literary critics, on the other hand, who had most probably been shaped by the cultural and formalistic assumptions of the New Criticism, any field of literary study which proposed to examine the relations between individual works of literature and realms of meaning independent of them savored of rank amateurism because it obscured, or, more dangerously, confused the structural properties and functions of various kinds of imaginative literature with those of all other forms of verbal expression. Both groups felt themselves confronted with what they took to be a kind of heresy, and, like the orthodox of every stripe, rushed to the defense of their particular faith.

In the intervening years, much has happened to change all this. Symptomatic of the widespread revisionism in theological studies is a book like Gordon D. Kaufman's *An Essay on Theological Method* (1975)—though it would be as easy to point to Schubert M. Ogden's *The Reality of God* (1966) or John B. Cobb's *A Christian Natural Theology* (1965)—which explicitly accepts the symbolic character of all religious language; concedes that all theological concepts are to be construed as imaginative models rather than as assertions of fact and are constructed with the aid of images and ideas drawn from the realm of ordinary human experience; interprets the word "God" as, in Stephen Toulmin's sense, "a limiting term" (that is, that term in a series beyond or behind which one cannot conceive or go); and views the function of theology not as the verification or explanation of certain objects with which its propositions must correspond but as a determination, in relation to those propositions, "of the kinds of activity and forms of experience they make possible."[1]

Indicative of the new attitudes and procedures which currently characterize literary scholarship are the new discussions which have broken out on everything from stylistics and structuralism to semiotics, and from linguistics, hermeneutics, and the New Historicism to anti-metaphysics. It is still to be regretted, I think, that many of these new discussions too often occur on a plane utterly removed from the general life of culture. Humanistic scholarship, of which literary studies and religious as well as theological studies are equally valid forms, exists not for the sake of creating an independent "house of intellect" but to augment our understanding and appreciation of their various kinds of subject-matter. Yet as between the rather precious explication, for example, that used to pass for literary criticism only a few years ago, and the new intellectual boldness and methodological dexterity that now characterize much critical practice, there is really no issue. Literary criticism in America, or at least that version of it which was (and often still is) practiced in the schools, had been so skittish about intellectual controversy as to have very nearly succeeded in banishing it altogether from the academic discussion of literature. Taking one of T. S. Eliot's observations about Henry James and apparently applying it across the board, American literary critics, and most of their British counterparts, often gave the appearance of having a mind so pure that no idea could violate it.

But now the temptation confronting literary critics and religious philosophers and historians alike seems to be just the opposite. In the face of the recent influx of theoretical models imported from Europe, the problem has more nearly become that of freeing the mind from the grasp of ideas, or, better, from the clutches of those larger systems of reference for which, to so many among us, they seem solely to exist, in order to make a reasonably fresh intellectual response to the material at hand. If we can never wholly escape interpretation, the problem still remains how to escape its seductions. And in this, theory alone is not likely to help us. The gravest issue confronting all forms of humanistic research, in religion no less than in literature, is not how to organize and legitimate the kinds of knowledge we already have but how to determine the way they can be applied and misapplied.[2]

There are, it must be admitted, no simple answers to this question. Yet one of the more encouraging signs that it is being taken seriously is the present trend toward the reintegration of particular disciplines and the coalescence of fields or areas, especially where, as in the humanities, the effects of former isolation have been so blighting. While it is devoutly to be hoped that such trends will continue, if only to stimulate further reflection and interchange, it is even more important to understand why they have begun to occur in the first place. So far as the interpenetration of literary and religious studies is concerned, it is difficult to escape the conclusion that this has happened largely as a result of the realization that these fields can no longer get along without each other, any more than they can get along without a good deal else. At the present moment this may be more obvious to students of religion, who are at least willing to accord the study of literature a kind of bemused toleration, than to literary critics, many of whom still find such a proposition generally meaningless. But one has only to point to the resource that myth critics have found in the work of religious historians from Sir James Frazer to Mircea Eliade to indicate something of the dependence that modern literary scholarship has exhibited toward modern scholarship in religion. And, conversely, one has only to invoke Erich Auerbach's research on medieval figuralism, or Perry Miller's studies of the American Puritans, or Albert Beguin's work on French Romanticism, to suggest how much we have learned of Western forms of spirituality from literary historians and critics.

I

Underlying both these phenomena is an assumption now widely held and almost too obvious to bear repetition, the assumption that religion in its essence cannot be dissociated from, or known apart from, religion in its various manifestations, and, further, that the various manifestations of religion are inevitably cultural and historical in character. By this is meant that, like any cultural form, religion represents a particular way of at once expressing and interpreting something—be that something an object, event, idea, or feeling—and that the terms both of expression and of interpretation are none other than those which historical and cultural experience has made available for such purposes.

It should be pointed out that this assumption is at considerable variance with the notion long associated with Paul Tillich that religion is the substance of culture, culture merely the form of religion.[3] Tillich's intention was not only to formulate an image of the relationship between culture and religion but also to articulate a theological judgment as to their relative priority and normative authority. However, both the formulation and the judgment were misleading, if not fallacious. Even if one is willing to grant that religion appeals traditionally to a realm of authority which is not culturally derived, such claims can neither be expressed nor understood except in cultural terms. Just as religion itself, then, cannot be known apart from its various manifestations in culture, so the most one can say with any assurance about a religious tradition, no matter what its intrinsic claims, is that it represents one assemblage of cultural forms among others. A religious tradition may, and for most people usually does, constitute an assemblage of cultural forms which is more normative than any other, but this does not gainsay the fact that it exists *only as* such an assemblage. More than this, as Tillich himself would have been the first to concede, religion may express itself culturally in one of two ways: either overtly, as one cultural form among others (the monastic movement in the Middle Ages, the Protestant Reformation in sixteenth-century Europe), or covertly, as a shaping element in cultural forms very different from itself (the Protestant ethic in Victorian England, antinomianism in nineteenth- and twentieth-century American poetry). H. Richard Niebuhr put the matter very nicely when, thinking of religion in America, he suggested that religious currents have often flowed in other than theological or ecclesiastical channels.[4]

Indeed, is this not the primary and most self-evident justification for the place of the literary critic in religious studies? Among those extra-theological and extra-ecclesiastical channels in which religious currents have so often flowed in Western culture, literary traditions are surely one of the widest and most prominent. How can one possibly understand the religious dimensions of the late medieval mind without coming to terms with Dante's *Divine Comedy?* What better avenue can one find into popular piety during the period just prior to the dawning of the Renaissance in England than Chaucer's *The Canterbury Tales?* How is one to comprehend the theological effects of that "new knowledge" associated with Renaissance achievement without studying Milton's *Paradise Lost* or the holy sonnets of John Donne? What text provides richer insight into the nature of Puritan spirituality than Bunyan's *Pilgrim's Progress?* And, as one drifts closer to the modern era, when the prestige and vitality of orthodox forms of authority are declining and new, often self-proclaimed custodians of traditional values are emerging on every hand, how is one even to recognize the religious disputes, much less comprehend the spiritual and intellectual resources for resolving them, without considerable knowledge of the French philosophes, the English Romantics, the great Russian novelists of the nineteenth century, Americans like Hawthorne, Melville, Dickinson, and James, and the host of modern writers from Kafka and Mann to Eliot and Stevens who have contributed so profoundly to our sense of our own age?

In citing only literary works and figures, I am not for a moment forgetting that they, too, need to be understood against a broader background. Trying to comprehend the phenomenon of literary modernism without an appreciation of contemporary movements in the other arts is as shortsighted as attempting to understand the English Romantics without sufficient grounding in German philosophical and theological idealism, or trying to come to terms with the English novelists of the Victorian age without general knowledge of related movements in the history of science and ethical theory. Nor do I intend to overlook the fact that dominant figures and works exist in a forest of lesser trees which, whether taken singly or together, often cast as interesting a shadow on the landscape as their more majestic neighbors. What better way to understand the manner in which clerical elements dominated a certain segment of English life in the nineteenth century than Anthony Trollope's Barsetshire novels? Or, where would one find a more probing study of the provincial Protestant's spiritual vulnerability to the spreading veneer of genteel culture in the Gilded Age than Harold Frederic's *The Damnation of Theron Ware*?

2

But does it not remain true, the skeptic might ask, that the student of religion thinks about his subject one way, the student of literature another? Is it not the case that the student of religion typically aspires, like the scientist or philosopher, to be as systematic and comprehensive as possible, searching out the general rule illustrated by the individual example and then striving for greater generality still by securing a coherence among as many abstractions as possible, moving from certainty to certainty, or at least from plausibility to plausibility, in an ever widening effort to extend the domain of intellectual consensus? And is it not also the case that the student of literature, like the man of letters, aspires to be as concrete and discriminating as possible, searching out the distinctive quality of the individual example and then striving for greater specificity still by saturating the distinctive with significance, moving from discrimination to discrimination in an ever-contracting, ever more concentrated effort to refine our perception of the particular? Wallace Stevens must have had something like this in mind when he noted, in somewhat different terms, that when the philosopher probes the spheres of perception, he "moves about therein like someone intent on making sure of every foot of the way," whereas the poet, in probing the same spheres, "is intent on what he sees and hears, and the sense of the certainty of the presences about him is as nothing to the presences themselves."[5]

Suggestive as this observation is, it stands in need of modification. True enough, there is more than one kind of mind just because there is more than one kind of mental operation that can be performed in the attempt to understand most anything, particularly cultural phenomena. Still, these two ways of thinking are not of necessity mutually exclusive and cannot be permitted to be so considered by those who share in common the task of comprehending forms which are essentially cultural in character. The nature of cultural forms themselves requires the utilization of both modes of thought. Just because cultural forms represent a particular way of making sense, as I have said earlier, of simultaneously expressing and interpreting something, our analysis of them requires a capacity for attending to what Stevens calls "the presences themselves."

It is the "sense" such presences make in and of themselves, and to themselves, that counts on this level of cultural analysis, and the student of such matters is therefore obliged to provide for them what Gilbert Ryle refers to as "thick description,"[6] what literary critics would call a close reading—that is, an analysis of the structures of signification by which these presences come to mean what they do and to be what they are. In literary criticism we say that we have done this when, according to whatever theoretical lexicon, we have accounted for the matter, medium, manner, and effect of the object either imitated or created in any work of art.

Yet, as the writings of all the great critics from Longinus to Lukacs attest, these exercises, indispensable as they are, hardly constitute the entirety of the critic's main "job of work." In point of fact, they belong properly not to the realm of criticism at all but rather to the domain of explication or exegesis, our current "Whore[s] of Babylon," as Geoffrey Hartman calls them, "sitting robed in Academic black on the great dragon of Criticism, and dispensing a repetitive and soporific balm from [their] pedantic cup."[7] The problem is not that modern critics have performed their explications badly; it is rather that they have forgotten that the function of explication is largely preparatory. "Explication is the end of criticism," Hartman writes, "only if we succumb to what Trotsky called the formalist's 'superstition of the word,'" only, that is, if we assume that the function of criticism is an understanding of the word in its pristine interiority, in the interiority of its first utterance. This, however, is but the initial stage of a critical act whose final aim involves the relation between the word's interiority as spoken and its interiority as heard. Hartman thus contends that there is but one way to redeem our critical response to literature: "to make it participate once more in a living concert of voices, and to raise exegesis to its former state by confronting art with experience as searchingly as if art were scripture."[8]

But how is this to be done? How is one to redeem the "said" of any given text, the word it speaks for hearing as well as for mere utterance, from our misplaced reverence for the form in which it is said, from our superstition about the words through which it does its speaking? The answer is by going beyond the sense such texts, such forms, make in and of and to themselves in order to try to understand their particular kind of sense-making. But this in turn calls for that different intellectual capacity for "making sure of every foot of the way," and is accomplished by devising and then implementing a standard of measurement both for "the presences themselves" and also for our sense of their certainty. To do any less is to trivialize such forms, to disregard the claims they make in their own behalf as among the foremost sense-makers of experience and thus to dismiss the meaning they in turn may possess as we try to appropriate their way of making sense for ourselves.

3

Nonetheless, a question remains as to whether literary and religious forms make the same kind of sense or make it in the same general way. One's initial response is to say that they do not: religious forms purport to define what truly is the case no matter how the facts may appear, while literary forms purport to suggest what might instead be the case if the facts were other than they obviously are. The first deals in what are generally assumed to be ontological givens, the second in what are rarely meant to be taken as anything more than hypothetical possibilities. Both are based upon essential ideas of order which compel belief, but each derives those ideas from different sources and asserts their authority in different ways. The ideas of order in literary forms are all inferential in character, the result of conclusions drawn from the nature of experience. The ideas of order in religious forms are all assumed to derive from something prior to experience and are therefore, as Alisdair MacIntyre has said, fundamentally paradigmatic in character. Furthermore, if literary forms exist to provide evidence of their truth, religious forms, by contrast, exist only to provide illustrations of it.[9]

Despite such important differences, however, religious and literary forms do share certain generic features. For one thing, they are both symbolic in character; for another, they frequently, though not always, contain a narrative component. They are symbolic in the sense that both depend upon terms designated not only to mediate between one sphere of existence and another but also to facilitate some sort of cognitive as well as emotional passage between them. To borrow Kenneth Burke's formulation, both employ symbols as strategies for encompassing situations;[10] and whenever representative examples of each define situations in the same way and propose similar strategies for encompassing them, the differences between them tend to diminish. Religious and literary forms are also narrative to the degree that both presuppose, in Lionel Trilling's words, that "life is susceptible of comprehension and thus of management" by virtue of our capacity for perceiving meaningful connections between beginnings and ends.[11] In this regard a beginning is not conceived of simply as the first of a series of events but rather as the originator of those that follow, and ends are viewed less as "the ultimate event, the cessation of happening" than as "a significance or at least the promise, dark or bright, of a significance."[12] To the narrative mind, Trilling continues, "the tale is not told by an idiot but by a rational consciousness which perceives in things the processes that are their reason and which derives from this perception a principle of conduct, a way of living among things."[13]

One need not share Trilling's skepticism about our ability "in this day and age" to "submit to a mode of explanation so primitive, so flagrantly Aristotelian,"[14] to perceive the grounds for arguing that religious forms and literary forms thus tend to converge at the level of myth. In this view myth is neither what works of imaginative literature "degenerate into . . . whenever they are not consciously held to be fictive," [15] nor what works of imaginative literature inevitably recall or become when they tell stories "in which some of the chief characters are gods or other beings larger in power than humanity." [16] Rather, myth is what works of the imagination *bulge toward* when they at once attempt to replenish our consciousness of and revivify our ability to cope with the entire created order by bringing, as Werner Berthoff has said so well, "the multiplicity of things that are known about, and the speech terms by which they are known, into an order in which they will continue to exist and be serviceable." [17]

Berthoff's view of myth is heavily indebted to the theories of Claude Lévi-Strauss and most especially to Lévi-Strauss's conception of myths as "constitutive units" or "classificatory schemes" whose purpose is to assist in "the ongoing business of dealing with (thinking about, or upon, or into) the perceived universe, natural and social." [18] But to this formulation Berthoff contributes an important revision:

> The purpose of this significatory classification is not merely to control or exorcize, one by one, the constituents of an impinging world of contingency. It is at least equally, and perhaps primarily, to stabilize and extend classification itself and the activity of formulaic speaking by which it is secured. That is to say, myth explains not so much what to think about events and objects but in what direction and with what degree of force to think and how precisely to situate the constituents of the thinkable. It tells what kind and degree of seriousness to attribute to the various elements of the self-constituting, self-organizing, self-maintaining world of human disclosure. [19]

In this conception of it, myth is not so much aetiological as, in the broad sense, hermeneutic. Its function is less to explain than to interpret, less to analyze or merely assert than to repossess and continue.

The signal difficulty with both Lévi-Strauss's and Berthoff's conceptions of myth is that they emphasize the cognitive dimension at the expense of the emotive and the conative. As Victor Turner has suggested in connection with the symbols and myths of the Ndembu, myths are equally evocative in "rousing, channeling, and domesticating powerful emotions, such as hate, fear, affection, and grief, [and] they are also informed with purposiveness. . . ."[20] Thus it is important to add that, in providing a set of directions for organizing and situating "the constituents of the thinkable," myth, like its cousin, ritual, ideally involves the whole person and not just the mind.

This revision of conventional notions about myth seems particularly pertinent to the study of literary forms because it illumines so helpfully the way in which individual works of literature, even when their integrity is respected, can contribute to the shaping and modification of the general life of culture.[21] The issue is whether it exhibits an equal degree of pertinence to the study of religious forms. It all seems to boil down to the question of whether religion itself can be thought of in such functional terms. Peter Berger, for one, has recently maintained that it cannot, and his argument deserves consideration.[22]

According to Berger, religion makes substantive claims which traditionally have far less to do with a different way of classifying and valuing the real than with the perception of a different notion of the real altogether. In religion, Berger maintains, one is continually confronted with a situation in which what is normally conceived of as reality is deprived of its paramount status through the sudden, felt intrusion of Something Else which is fundamentally alien and "other." It is this Something Else which then becomes the object of worship and devotion because of its capacity for displacing all other candidates as the normative, even constitutive, center of life in an absolute or ultimate sense. This argument is a familiar one and cannot be easily dismissed. The only way of dealing with it is to place it within the larger framework of discussion bearing upon the definition of religion in the hopes of gaining insight thereby not only into the nature of religious study itself but

also into the place of the critical study of imaginative literature
within it.

<h1 style="text-align:center">4</h1>

As is well known, there is little consensus concerning the meaning
of the word "religion." Some, like Berger, tend to define religion in
terms of the object that seems to elicit it and which men and
women thus attend to whenever they are, as we say, being religious.[23] Gerardus van der Leuuw, for example, defines the object
of religion, at least in its primordial form, as a "highly exceptional
and extremely expressive Other"[24] that produces initially, as the
subjective response to it, a state of amazement and wonder. Rudolf
Otto, by contrast, assuming that the objective reality in terms of
which religion must be defined can only be described by a careful
investigation of the subjective feelings which it evokes, defines the
object itself as the Holy or Mysterium Tremendum whose character he infers from the numinous quality of the experience that ac-
companies it, an experience of something awful and majestic as
well as fascinating and alluring. Jacques Maritain defines the object
of religion in still another way simply as Being, or a sense of the solidity of existence, of which, as he claims, all people in all ages
have a natural and immediate intuition because of the inexorable
chain of unconscious reasoning which leads us, first, from an
awareness of the solidity of our own existence, next, to a perception of the death and nothingness to which our own and all other
forms of existence are vulnerable, and, finally, to an intuition of the
necessity for some form of absolute existence or Being which is ultimately perdurable and in that sense transcendent.

Other theorists define religion not in terms of the object which
produces it and towards which its attention is directed, but rather
in terms of the subjective capacities and endowments of those who
in whatever manner give evidence of its existence and presence as
an experienced reality. Here, to foreshorten radically, religion is

defined either, as in Schleiermacher, in terms of some particular sense or feeling (say, the feeling of absolute dependence), or, as in Tillich, in terms of some capacity for concern and commitment (say, the capacity for being ultimately concerned in the depths of one's spiritual life), or, as in Malinowski, in terms of some particular social need (say, the need for social stability and coherence).

Still other theorists define religion neither in terms of certain attributes characteristic of the object which elicits it, nor in terms of subjective attributes which permit human beings to respond to it, but rather in terms of the particular way in which subjects and objects relate to one another in religious experience. Mircea Eliade is probably the foremost exponent of this definitional procedure because of his stress upon the unique way in which human beings have traditionally responded to that which was experienced as sacred. For Eliade, men and women respond religiously to that which is experienced as sacred through the mode of repetition whereby they attempt, in imitation of the divine acts of self-disclosure, not only to relocate themselves within the sacred sphere, but also to reactualize its power and thus to extend its dominion over the ephemeral world of the profane.

In virtually all of these instances—Eliade's definitional procedure may be the one exception—an attempt is made either to denominate some universal property of human nature as religious, or to define some universal but discrete object of human perception or some peculiar mode of human behavior as the essence of religion. Characteristically, that universal element or trait or mode of behavior which is said to be the essence of religion or the religious is isolated in one of two ways: either by differentiating religion and the religious from anything else with which it might otherwise be associated and confused (magic, superstition, philosophy, myth, poetry, folklore, legend), or by deriving the distinctive nature of religion and the religious from something assumed to be even more basic to the character of human being or human experience as such. In both cases the exercise tends to be futile, and not least because it either, on the one hand, produces definitions which so restrict the focus of inquiry that one is inevitably compelled to exclude from consideration vast bodies of material which common sense would suggest as germane, or because, on the other, in proceeding from some aprioristic notion of the real, it spawns such markedly diverse definitions of religion that there is almost no way of conceptually bridging the gaps between them.

Given this state of affairs, my own inclination is to follow the lead of certain cultural anthropologists and literary historians by proceeding more inductively and therefore asking if, even in the face of such a mass of relevant data, there is still not something distinctively characteristic about all that people do, say, feel, think, or believe when either they or someone else claims they are being religious. Instead of searching for essences, is it possible, as Clifford Geertz has urged, to look for a series of family resemblances and therefore to ask if there isn't a fairly simple way of defining conceptually a set of inexact but discernible similarities that characterize a wide variety of material?[25]

Putting the question this way I believe we can get an answer. For when we examine the various gestures, actions, utterances, intuitions, and convictions which most people are willing to accept as being in some sense or other religious, I think we find that they share in common—whether explicitly acknowledged or not—a certain way of looking at the world, a particular view of reality, which, to be sure, can be expressed in an almost limitless number of ways and in diverse forms. Viewed from the inside, from the point of view of one who sees the world in this way, I would propose that Alfred North Whitehead came closest to defining it when he suggested that "religion is the longing of the spirit that the facts of existence should find their justification in the nature of existence."[26] Viewed from the outside, on the other hand, from the point of view of one who is merely attempting in as objective a way as possible to understand the way religious people see and to articulate the particular mode of sight they possess or exhibit, I would

suggest that Geertz himself has provided the most helpful definition, by proposing that religion ultimately involves a particular
perspective on experience, and that this perspective rests upon "the
conviction that the values one holds are grounded in the inherent
structure of reality, that between the way one ought to live and the
way things really are there is an unbreakable inner connection."[27]

The chief problem with this definition, and one for which
Geertz has frequently been criticized, is that it seems too intellec-
tualistic. The alliance of religion with a particular way of viewing
things, a distinctive perspective on experience, seems to highlight
the self-conscious elements of religious experience at the expense of
the subconscious or the unconscious, and to subordinate the irratio-
nal to the rational. This is not, I believe, Geertz's intention—a
perspective or conviction, after all, need in no sense be fully conscious to be efficacious as an influence on behavior, and in addition
Geertz makes no speculations about the origins or source of such a
perspective in human experience—but the grounds of such reserva-
tions could be largely removed if one were to emphasize, more than
Geertz does, the way religious people in fact experience that bond
between such values as they hold and the structure, or, better,
character they impute to life itself.

As so many modern theorists of religion seem to agree, what
typifies religious man's experience of the sacred, of that which he
takes to be of the essence of life, is its "otherness," its differentiation (though not necessarily alienation) from his own mode of
being. Whatever else *homo religiosus* may assume, he is apparently
convinced that the "really real," or, to follow Geertz, the inherent
structure of reality in conformity with which he seeks to live, is not
something he has put there in life himself but rather something he
has found there, something, indeed, which makes a prior claim on
his existence and whose character as "other" is indissolubly related
to that claim. Emile Durkheim may be taken as the representative
spokesman for this view because of his conviction that all religions
presuppose an opposition between the sacred and the profane

which is distinctive precisely because it is absolute. While things profane can be transformed into the sacred and things sacred dissolve back into the profane, the opposition between the two realms is total and their existence in relation to one another is wholly "other."

With these emendations, what advantages can be found in this definition of religion? The first thing I would note is the way this definition dovetails so nicely with what a language philosopher like Stephen Toulmin,[28] a philosophical theologian like Schubert Ogden,[29] a metaphysical poet like Wallace Stevens,[30] and a theological critic like Nathan A. Scott[31] all agree is the primary, if not exclusive, function of religion. Using almost identical language, each assumes that the function of religion is to restore our confidence in the world, in the reality and final worth of our existence, and to help us bear up in the face of life's numerous challenges and obstacles. Religious rites, assertions, feelings, and beliefs provide us with what Toulmin calls "reassurance," with what Ogden and Stevens refer to as "confidence," with what Scott designates as "warrant" or "sanction," and they do so, as Geertz says so elegantly of sacred symbols, by formulating "an image of the world's construction and a program for human conduct that are mere reflexes of one another."[32]

Religion therefore possesses both an ethical and a metaphysical component, and the two are so conceived as to reinforce one another. The authority of its ethical component is seen to derive from the degree to which it represents a mode of life implied by the fundamental view of the world described by its metaphysics. The credibility attributed to its world view or metaphysics depends in large part upon how convincingly its ethics articulate a meaningful and compelling way to live in response to this fundamental view of things. Hence religious symbols, as Geertz maintains, are so designed as to render the world view or metaphysics of any particular person or people believable and their general style of life—what anthropologists call their ethos, what literary critics would call their

style and tone—justifiable. "The world view is believable because
the ethos, which grows out of it, is felt to be authoritative; the
ethos is justifiable because the world view, upon which it rests, is
held to be true."[33]

To anyone interested in the cultural analysis of religion, and
more particularly in an understanding of the place of literary study
within it, this formulation is immensely helpful for it specifies the
terms by which literary study makes its contribution to religious
study. Whatever else one may say about works of imaginative literature, it is generally agreed that at the very least they represent
forms designed to explore, to express, and even to criticize the relationship between what is here being called "metaphysics" on the
one hand and "ethics" on the other. One could corroborate this assertion by appealing to any number of sources.[34] I turn merely to
one which happens to be most readily accessible, a statement by
John F. Lynen:

> Whether one thinks of the content of a work as a set of ideas
> expressed and things portrayed or an experience of which these
> thoughts and objects are elements, most readers will agree that
> the subject matter is determined by the world view within which
> these elements exist. Whitman's world may be a set of actual cir-
> cumstances, but it is somewhat distinct from, say, Thoreau's
> world, for it not only has different contents, but constitutes the
> world as Whitman sees it, and its facts, though objectively true,
> have been organized in a unique way. To understand Whitman's
> meaning is to enter his world and see what the things he asserts
> or pictures mean there.[35]

This claim, which is made by a student of literature rather than
of religion, obviously bears as much, if not more, relevance to the
study of imaginative forms that are "secular" as it does to those that
are more clearly "religious." Hence it is as pertinent to the study of
Jane Austen's *Emma* as it is to St. Augustine's *Confessions*, to the
study of Choderlos de LaClos's *Les Liaisons Dangereuses* as to Edward
Taylor's *Preparatory Meditations*. Our purpose in reading such books

is ultimately to see for ourselves, to quote Professor Lynen again, "the values [or ethos] which life reveals when viewed from within this scheme of consciousness [or world view]." [36] And that works of imaginative literature provide us with insight, as Geertz says of the aesthetic perspective generally, only by suspending any overriding interest in the practical consequences thereof, is precisely their virtue. They show us what life could or would be like if, as is generally not the case, life were organized solely in terms of one or another schemes of consciousness or ideas of order. [37]

The second thing to note about this definition of religion is that it does not rule out the fact that most religious people have often believed or felt something a good deal more specific than this general conviction about the relationship between one's values and the inherent structure of reality. It simply assumes (and, I think, can quite readily show) that any more specific set of beliefs—say, that the empirical world, or our experience in it, does not exhaust the meaning of life itself; or that All Things work together for good in the economy of Divine Creation; or that Jesus Christ is the Way, the Truth, and the Life—are but individual variants of this more basic conviction. And, viewing them as such, it thus allows us to consider as at least potentially religious a great variety of ideas, actions, feelings, and so forth, that make no explicit reference either to divine beings, sacred rites, ecclesiastical institutions, or confessional traditions.

Again, the implications of this view for anyone engaged in the cultural analysis of religion are far reaching. To take but one example, the student of religion who works in the medium of literary and other cultural forms is frequently confronted with that situation Perry Miller articulated so clearly when he spoke of the necessity of having to trace continuities of experience that exist beneath the successive articulation of ideas. [38] Indeed, I would go further and say that those same continuities often persist in a culture long after the ideas in which they were first embodied lose their expressive power. Henry James, Senior, the father of William James the philosopher and Henry James the novelist, perceived something of this when he once remarked in a letter to Emerson "that a vital truth can never be transferred from one mind to another. The most one can do for another is to plant the rude formula of such truth in his memory, leaving his own spiritual chemistry to set free the germs whenever the demands of his life exact it."[39] Without pausing to contemplate the pertinence of this remark for an understanding of the relationship among the three Jameses, I would suggest that such "vital truths," and not the ideas in which they are cast, are precisely what a culture ultimately consists of, and therefore what the student of religion must attend to if he is ever to learn how religion as a cultural form can survive the disintegration of many of its distinctive theological ideas or chief institutional expressions and still get transmitted, albeit in somewhat altered shape, to subsequent generations, now less as a system of creedal affirmations or a body of dogma than as a mode of experience, a view of life, an imaginative circuit of belief and desire.

The third thing to note about this definition of religion is the way it so provocatively outlines a program for the critical study of religion and thus, by implication at least, proposes a way of organizing the sorts of knowledge such study is likely to yield. Assuming with Geertz that "the aim of the comparative study of religion is (or anyway, ought to be) the scientific [by which he means methodologically discrete and exact] characterization of this perspective," I believe as well that the study of religion can be divided into three distinct but interrelated components, which I will rephrase in my own words.[40] First, it entails a description of the wide variety of forms in which this perspective, this particular way of interpreting experience, has appeared down through history and within given cultural traditions. Here one is naturally interested both in those forms where this perspective has received explicit or overt expression (morality plays in the medieval period, metaphysical poetry in the seventeenth century), and also in those forms where it has received merely implicit or covert expression (the visionary tradition in nineteenth-century English poetry, the Catholic novel in the modern period). Second, it involves an examination both of those factors that have brought such forms into existence and contributed to their survival, and of those factors that have led either to their alteration and transformation or to their dissolution and eventual destruction. In this connection, such phenomena as the threat of barbarian invasion in late antiquity, the rise of towns in the Middle Ages, the circumnavigation of the globe during the Renaissance, the development of the scientific method in the seventeenth and eighteenth centuries, the spread of industrialism and urbanization in the nineteenth century, and the massive erosion of belief in all inherited systems of belief in the twentieth—all become crucially important data for studying the historical emergence, the full flowering, and the frequent disappearance of particular religious forms in the West. Third, it requires an assessment, insofar as this is possible, of the influence such forms have had or can have upon the life of men and women in everyday existence. To say this is to assert that a fully critical understanding of religious forms necessitates an evaluation of their function and effect *not only then*, in the circumstances of their initial efficacy, *but also now*, in light of our historical effort to repossess their significance for ourselves.

5

Of the first two tasks confronting the student of religion and the place of the literary critic in helping to fulfill them, relatively little needs to be said, not because the critic's contribution is likely to be so slight, but rather because it has already been so large. As an example of the kind of contribution the literary critic can make to the first of these tasks, a description of the forms in which the religious perspective appears, I would point to M. H. Abrams's magisterial *Natural Supernaturalism*. The purpose of his book is to analyze the way in which a diverse group of writers in the Romantic period— poets, philosophers, historians, autobiographers, and writers of romance—responded to the increasing secularization of inherited theological ideas and ways of thinking by undertaking a comprehensive reinterpretation of this entire legacy of belief and experience. Their overriding aim was to preserve traditional values by repossessing and reconstituting them in a mode of thought that would be acceptable to their own and future generations. Their method, as indicated by Abrams's title, was "to naturalize the supernatural and to humanize the divine"[41] by accommodating the great Christian themes of the fall, redemption, and paradise regained to the prevailing intellectual system of their own time, where life was perceived as bifurcated into subject and object, self and not-self, man and nature.

Abrams's way of substantiating this is as daring as it is brilliant. Taking as the age's definitive programmatic statement Wordsworth's Preface to *The Excursion*, which was designed as a description of the nature and scope of his unfinished masterpiece, *The Recluse*, Abrams has constructed his book as a sequence of explorations which set out from and then return to this central document. In the course of his movements out and back again, Abrams ranges over an immense body of material spanning almost two millennia to draw out crucial elements that related the Romantic age both to those more traditionally religious periods that preceded it and to those increasingly secular periods which followed it. While the main burden of his argument is undeniably weighted in favor of the continuities rather than discontinuities between the Romantic period and its more orthodox predecessors, he is in no way suggesting that the Romantics merely expressed in different language the central verities of the Judeo-Christian heritage. On the contrary, his argument is the more interesting from a religious point of view precisely because it is based upon the contention that, "despite their displacement from a supernatural to a natural frame of reference, . . . the ancient problems, terminology, and ways of thinking about human nature and history survived," not as counters in the same stale game, but "as the implicit distinctions and categories through which even radically secular writers saw themselves and their world, and as the presuppositions and forms of their thinking about the condition, the milieu, the essential values and aspirations, and the history and destiny of the individual and mankind."[42] In such terms as these, then, Abrams tries to show how the great plethora of themes, patterns, concepts, and forms so characteristic of Romantic philosophy and literature can be viewed as a kind of "displaced or reconstituted theology, or else a secularized form of devotional experience,"[43] whose essential goal, as in the ancient Biblical paradigm, was the articulation and poetic realization of man's possible redemption from the hell of self-division through reunification with the ground and substance of his being and the being of All That Is.

As an example of the kind of contribution the literary critic can make to the second of the three basic tasks of religious studies, an understanding of those factors which lead to the creation or destruction of religious forms, I would point to Erich Heller's *The Disinherited Mind*, and, for purposes of discussion, more particularly to his brilliant chapter entitled "The Hazard of Modern Poetry." There Heller summarizes his whole argument by showing how the experience of spiritual disinheritance he has traced in the writings of Goethe, Burckhardt, Schiller, Nietzsche, Rilke, Spengler, Kafka, and Karl Kraus was proleptically expressed in the debate between Luther and Zwingli concerning the nature of the sacrament. For Luther, the bread and wine of the sacrament were the body and blood of Christ, were, in other words, the very thing they symbolized. For Zwingli, on the contrary, the bread and wine of the sacrament were no more than mere symbols of the body and blood of Christ, were at most but representations of what in themselves they were not. To the historical theologian this dispute may signify no more than a single episode in the widening gulf between the right and left wings of the Reformation; to the cultural historian, however, it constitutes a kind of turning point in the history of the Western sensibility, a watershed which divides the mind of the Middle Ages from the mind of the modern era. At issue was man's very idea of reality, "that complex fabric of unconsciously held convictions about what is real and what is not,"[44] and its result, which would drastically change the spiritual climate of the centuries to follow, was a loss of "that unity of word and deed, of picture and thing, of the bread and the glorified body. Body [would] become merely body, and symbol merely symbol. And as for the refreshing wine, it [would] be drunk by thirsty souls only when in the very depths of their thirst they [were] quite sure it was pressed from real grapes in the mechanic way."[45]

To determine what this had to do with the career of modern poetry, and beyond that with the experience of increasing spiritual homelessness which characterizes the entire modern age, one has only to realize that this seemingly incidental dispute within the household of faith over degrees of symbolic literalness actually "deprived the language of religion as well as of art of an essential degree of reality."[46] Once the symbol becomes merely symbolic and reality merely real, man's soul, in its quest for significant truth, is left with no other alternative but to withdraw from the devalued realm of wordly experience and begin the progressive colonization of its own inwardness. But the cost is and has been great, according to Heller. Modern man, and preeminently the modern poet, has retained his soul only at the expense of reality's impoverishment, only at the cost of losing a sense that "everything that exists," as Goethe says somewhere, "is an analogy of existence itself." Thus the stage was set for "The Hazard of Modern Poetry." "Will it end with the homesickness of a defeated race?" Heller asks. "Or with the father's return to the prodigal son?"[47] The answer depends on the possibility of a radical revolution in our notion of reality, Heller would say. It is all a question of whether we can recover a sense of "the true stature of things," which depends upon their "having a meaningful place in a valuable world."[48]

This formulation is of a piece with Heller's conviction, so obviously shared by Abrams, that the literary and cultural historian

must frequently work with what might be called the understruc-
ture of beliefs, with their metaphysical substratum. If culture, in
Heller's words (to which Abrams would certainly subscribe), represents a tacit agreement among men as to what "the nature and
meaning of human existence really is," and if, further, "this unity
will then show itself to be at work beyond, or beneath, or despite
all differences of actually proclaimed beliefs and articulate opinions," [49] then the student of culture, and particularly the student
interested in those ontological foundations upon which culture is
built, must become a kind of spiritual geologist who is able to
measure the continuities and faults in the underlayers of what men
call reality.

As the writing of Heller and Abrams reveals, however, the aim
of such criticism is never simple description or analysis. Its intent
and achievement is best expressed by Gabriel Marcel's phrase "recuperative reflection." "Recuperative reflection," as Marcel conceives it, stands for "the thankless but indispensable task of remak-
ing, thread by thread, the spiritual fabric heedlessly torn by" what
Marcel calls "primary reflection," a form of thought "not only unable to distinguish the universal implications of life, but further,
and above all, obstinately opposed to gratitude and respect for
what is sacred in any order whatsoever." [50] The distinction between "recuperative reflection" and "primary reflection" parallels in
epistemological terms the difference in religion between piety and
impiety, where piety refers neither to "devotion" nor to "edification" but rather to "reverence," or "piety in knowledge, united to a
notion which really concerns the hallowing of the real." [51] To
express this somewhat differently, the critic who works in this sub-
terranean region of cultural interpretation is out in his own way to
re-sew the fabric of assumptions from which specific beliefs take
their rise, so that, at the minimum, we can once again comprehend
the integrity of the various tapestries of faith; so that, at the maximum, we can renew the arts of weaving. At the very least, then,
such criticism turns cultural history into a matter of ideas drama-

tized rather than ideas analyzed,[52] into a recreation of "the mode of experience in terms of which they are meant to seem true";[53] at the very most such criticism participates in the discovery of what Wallace Stevens called "a fresh spiritual."

This, then, begins to define the way in which criticism contributes to the third component of religious study. Criticism can and must play a role in assessing the influence which religious forms and values have upon the everyday life of men and women because literature itself, whether directly or indirectly, is so frequently concerned with just such questions. But this is stating the issue so weakly as to falsify it. Criticism at its most ambitious, which is the only criticism worth emulating or trying to preserve, is part and parcel of the assessment of established values which goes on in every generation. Its most important single attribute is not the technical analysis it performs but the kind of thinking it exhibits during the performance. Such thinking is at bottom moral, and that in several ways. It is moral, first of all, because of its scope. The best critics always exhibit an imagination of large concerns; in Lionel Trilling's words, they are inevitably inclined "to see literary situations as cultural situations and cultural situations as great elaborate fights about moral issues, and moral issues as having to do with gratuitously chosen images of personal being, and images of personal being as having something to do with literary style. . . ."[54] But the kind of thinking that goes on in the work of the best critics is moral in another sense: because it is based on the view that literature not only criticizes life but does so in a distinctive manner—not directly, as Matthew Arnold implied, by appealing to set judgment, but indirectly, as John Dewey contended, by disclosing to the imagination specific possibilities that contrast with actual conditions. "It is by a sense of possibilities opening before us," Dewey wrote, "that we become aware of the constrictions that hem us in and of burdens that oppress."[55] Finally, criticism is moral because of the nature and depth of its advocacy, its partisanship, its idealism. Whether one thinks of the criticism of

Charles Augustin Sainte-Beuve or William Hazlitt, Samuel Taylor Coleridge or T. S. Eliot, Edmund Wilson or F. O. Matthiessen, there is no getting around their shared tendency to measure what any individual work of art is striving to become in the light of some ideal notion of what man himself is always striving to become. Alfred Kazin, who has written so well about the moral dimension of criticism, refers to this as "the most valuable kind of criticism":

> It is the kind of criticism that I always think of as *histoire morale*, that sums up the spirit of the age in which we live and then asks us to transcend it, that enables us to see things in the grand perspective, and that, in the way of Marx on Greek philosophy, of Kierkegaard on Mozart, of Nietzsche on the birth of tragedy, of Shaw on Ibsen, of Lawrence on American literature, asks us—in the light not only of man's history but of his whole striving—to create a future in keeping with man's imagination.[56]

Convictions such as these rather profoundly affect both the way one thinks of criticism and the kind of thinking one does as a critic. Where other critics are likely to restrict their attention to the integrity of literature and the necessity of interrogating it only in terms that are in accordance with its own nature, Kazin's moral historians have in addition stressed the integrity of their own experience of literature and their obligation to interrogate that experience in light of its relation, admittedly subtle, indirect, and complex, with the whole of man's life and history. Or where others have been content to define the characteristic qualities of literary forms, they have emphasized as well the importance of defining the characteristic qualities of life revealed within those forms. Or, yet again, where others have settled for isolating the terms in which writers have extended the literary tradition or revised it, they have paid equal attention to the terms in which writers confront the experience of their own age and surmount it. In this, of course, they have run great risks: the risk of subjectivism, by converting what might be called the elements of any work of literature as an abject into elements of the work as an experience; the risk of impressionism, by subordinating an evaluation of the formal qualities of any individ-

ual work of literature into an evaluation of the experience in terms
of which the work's formal qualities are encountered; and the risk
of didacticism, by maintaining that the aim of criticism, as John
Lynen has asserted, has less to do with applying terms of censure
and praise than with exploring the values life discloses when
viewed from within the work's own frame of vision. Nevertheless,
all they have meant to contend is that "the value of a work *as art* is
precisely its power to reveal values far more important to our lives
than its own artistry, yet values which can only be known through
this aesthetic form—by this way of experience—in this work of
art" (italics mine).[57]

The most serious charge that has been brought against such
critics is that, in subordinating the formal analysis of literature to
an examination of its meaning and significance, they have ceased to
write criticism at all and have instead taken up something like the
history of culture or the sociology of taste. I would argue to the
contrary that they have simply resisted the temptation so common
among most Anglo-American critics of confusing individual literary texts with any of their distinguishing attributes of style, technique, or thematic content. No matter how variously they express
it, the best critics all seem to share something like Emerson's perception that the poet "uses forms according to the life, and not according to the form." Thus their goal, whether express or implied,
has always been to work their way through individual texts to the
organizing energies that propel them, hoping thereby to uncover,
and where appropriate to engage, those motive forces and powers
by which particular works, as well as entire traditions, give imaginative shape and realization not merely to themselves but also to a
significant portion of our actual or potential experience.

6

A crucial question for literary theory, and one over which many of
these same critics divide, concerns the way in which literature does
this. Some contend, after the manner of Matthew Arnold, that lit-

erature shapes and orders our experience by serving as a vehicle for the transmission of the best that was thought and said in the past. Others argue that it does this by enabling us to appropriate the alien inwardness of the author which we thus encounter, in our attempt to come to terms with the work, as a kind of "Thou" making a claim upon our "I." Still others maintain that literature does this by reuniting us with the collective and often unconscious traditions of legend, folklore, and myth from which the artist draws his substance.

My own view is to be distinguished from all three of these, at least to the degree that each assumes, as criticism so consistently has from the end of the eighteenth century to the present, that the meaning of any given literary text is to be found either behind it, in the *Sitz im Leben* of its first readers, or beneath it, in the deep-flowing currents of sentiment and belief that link the individual talent to the traditions of collective experience that surround him, or within it, in the internal configuration of its various parts. While important aspects of any work's meaning are to be located in each of these realms, I still agree with theorists otherwise as different as Dorothy Van Ghent and Paul Ricoeur, that the fullest portion of every work's meaning lies rather, to continue the awkward figure, out in front of it, in the hypothetical world—or, better, hypothetical way of looking at the world and orienting oneself within it— which the work is designed both to project and, through some alchemy of its own devising, to assess.

So conceived, literature's function is always that of mediating a form of otherness, a sense of things not quite our own, which it does by inviting us, at least for the length of its own duration, to think accordingly—or, as Paul Ricoeur has said, to follow the arrow of sense, whether masked or avowed, disclosed by its own propositions.[58] In works of literature, however, such propositions are always addressed more to the heart than to the head, or, in T. S. Eliot's formulation, to the logic of the imagination rather than the logic of concepts. Their appeal is to the affections, that realm of being wherein we learn to see feelingly. Archibald Mac-Leish has written of this capacity that "no man who comes to knowledge through a poem leaves the feel of what he knows behind, for the knowledge he comes to is the knowledge of that *feeling life* of the mind which comprehends by putting itself in the place where its thought goes—by realizing its thought in the only human realizer—the imagination."[59] And to the degree that we achieve such realization, I would add, we have initiated a new self-understanding and have thus acquired that margin of transcendence toward a fuller humanity which every serious work of literature compels us to "try out."

Ricoeur speaks of this process as appropriation. Appropriation in this sense is far removed from its usual meaning "as a way of taking hold of things," of possessing them; instead it represents a kind of dispossession in which the new modes of being projected by the work in turn afford the reader with new possibilities of self-knowledge.[60] In this process of imaginative expansion and enlargement, there is a difference between the new self, which results from understanding the work, and the old self, what Ricoeur calls "the ego," which, figuratively speaking, precedes it. Thus Ricoeur can describe the process of appropriation as one in which the text, with its capacity for disclosing alternative forms of life, "gives a self to the ego."[61]

The difficulty with these formulations is that they cut directly across the grain of certain critical assumptions which developed almost simultaneously with the rise of literary modernism and which still hold sway among most Anglo-American critics. The assumptions to which I refer, and which seemed at the time but an inevitable outgrowth of the difficulties of interpreting a non-linear, self-consciously disordered poem like *The Waste Land* or novel like *Lord Jim*, are notable chiefly because of their spatial character. They exhibit themselves, that is to say, most dramatically in the pervasive critical tendency to treat all works of literature as though they were paintings or pieces of sculpture, as discrete objects isolated in space whose primary meanings can only be inferred by examining the patterns of similarity and conflict reflected in their most concretely realized details. The structure of any particular work of literature thus becomes associated with its most vivid relational patterns of image and event, its form with an intellectualization of the idea of order implicit in its structure. Such abstractions are then used to show how the work, if it is successful, resolves its multiplicity of particulars into an organic unity and thus deserves to be regarded as a genuine object with its own mode of being. Following laws of its own origination, the work resists translation into any terms other than the ones intrinsic to itself and can therefore be regarded as immune to the general breakdown of taste and cultivation around it. In a world best described, in Ezra Pound's epithet, as "an old bitch gone in the teeth," the individual work of art helps ensure the continuity and integrity of civilization by retaining its character as a non-referential, autotelic, self-sufficient object, a kind of self-enclosed garden with no relation to the modern turbulence and confusion outside.

This description of the objective orientation in modern literary criticism is, to be sure, something of a caricature, but it still bears a close enough resemblance to the sort of argument one continues to discover in the journals and to confront in the classroom to evoke a shudder. One is struck both by the defensive character of the argument and also by the depth of misconception on which it is based. For, except in those comparatively few instances where individual works explicitly aspire to the condition of music, literature is less a spatial than a temporal art, one that aims neither to arrest nor to fix but to stimulate and set in motion. Its elements of structure therefore as often derive from sequences of tension and release, involvement and detachment, movement and delay, or sympathy and disapproval, as from any patterns of relationship visible, as it were, in its various concrete elements of action, character, scene, image, and the like.[62] For the same reason, the question of form in literature has less to do with the abstract idea of order we impute to its sequential pattern of details than to the way the author orders our response to those details, the word *form* in this case referring not to some pre-cast design the work possesses in and of itself, but rather to the shape of the response the work is designed to elicit in the reader. Hence what actually happens in an imaginative text, or to whom, or under what conditions, or in what sequence, or through what agency, or even with what result—these things matter in our experience as readers only to the extent that they affect the way in which we are made to feel about whatever is at issue in the entire representation. In all but explicitly didactic works, the writer is not out to secure rational conviction for an argument or confirmation of certain facts so much as a realignment of the affections, a reordered sense of value, a new disposition of the heart. Thus the thematic content of his work, to say nothing of its form, is to be found not in any systematic and logical exposition of the meaning of certain actions, but rather in "the pattern of aroused and redistributed sympathies" which such actions are intended to elicit.[63]

This, I would submit, is finally what the critic seeks to understand and to interpret—to understand, by grasping the plausible reasons for feeling this way rather than that about the hypothetical way of perceiving and relating to the world in which the work is made to issue; to interpret, by assessing the experiential paradigm that makes sense out of the individual work's logic and outcome against those more familiar or traditional paradigms from our larger cultural life and experience by which we otherwise do, or should, make sense to ourselves. The basic motive behind all such acts is to discover the truth, something which has less to do with external absolutes than with the integrity of individual experience, and the veracity and impact of which will gain in importance the more reality of experience it can encompass. Hence if the task of literature, to paraphrase Erich Heller, is to express the meanings things have in the world of values men and women create out of their own experience, the aim of criticism has less to do with merely rescuing what is expressed from its perishing occasions than with fixing those expressions in emotionally as well as conceptually intelligible terms so that we can appropriate them, so that we can transform what would otherwise remain but a personal statement of the "meaningful place" things have in a "valuable world" [64] into a public acquisition, into a repository of the culturally significant. [65] The critic's method is to saturate the text with meanings, meanings which, strictly speaking, the text does not contain solely within itself. Though the nature and design of the text delimits the range of possible meanings with which the critic can try to saturate it, its most interesting meanings may very often be those which the text merely attracts or suggests rather than literally discloses. A "complete criticism" of any text therefore entails an understanding of all that the text can be said to call forth by way of intelligent and sensitive response from any readers who are qualified, through the use of whatever necessary or fitting critical languages, to interpret it. [66]

But why bother, one might ask, and take the accompanying risk of misreading, of misinterpreting altogether? Because, I would answer, in attempting to assess the actual in light of its full potential for comprehension, we thereby re-enact one of the chief functions of culture, if not of religion. Man is that animal who survives, both literally and figuratively, solely because of his ability to distinguish between the appearances of reality and the reality of appearances, such that he can impose a meaning upon his experience which the raw facts alone do not convey. Indeed, it is just such behavior as this, and the reasons for it, which provide the student of literature and the student of religion with their material. All I would ask is that they both eventually realize that the critical, as opposed to merely exegetical, study of their material involves the same sort of thing.

But the last word must be cautionary. The great danger for critical as well as religious study is the substitution of intellectual formulas for experience, as if life ever quite submitted to the patterns we impose upon it. R. P. Blackmur summarized the problem for

every student of cultural forms and articulated the terms of its resolution when he noted that

> intellectual formulation is the great convenience for ordering the
> experience of the mind and, because of the imperfection of the
> mind, an even greater convenience for stepping in, in the guise of
> generalization or hypothesis, when there is not enough experi-
> ence to go round. If either art or criticism—if either imagination
> or intellect—were relatively perfect, we should have no trouble
> and no problem, and the [gl]aring inadequacies of either with re-
> spect to the other would long since have disappeared. The con-
> trary is so much the case that in practice we tend to get in litera-
> ture immature intellect tampering with imagination, and in
> criticism immature imagination tampering with intellect. . . .
> When you get maturity of imagination and intellect (I do not say
> perfection, only maturity: balance without loss of passion or vita-
> lity), you get great literature and great criticism—or, let us say,
> criticism that has become a part of literature or literature that has
> become a part of criticism.[67]

The success of criticism, then, like that of any other intellectual
operation, depends largely upon technique. It ultimately derives
from the art of the performance. The great critics of whatever subject are inevitably those who, through the disciplines of their craft
and the subtlety of their distinctions, lift perception to the level of
moral insight and transform learning into a mode of experience
whose validity is not wholly dependent upon the durability of its
formal conclusions.

4

The American Writer and the Formation of an American Mind: Literature, Culture, and Their Relation to Ultimate Values

> It is something to be able to paint a particular picture, or to carve a statue, and so to make a few objects beautiful; but it is far more glorious to carve and paint the very atmosphere and medium through which we look. . . .
>
> HENRY DAVID THOREAU
> *Walden*

One of the most persistent and vexacious questions confronting anyone interested in the relations between religion and literature concerns the writer's role in the formation of culture, and most especially his or her contribution to the development of any culture's distinctive way (or ways) of thinking, feeling, and behaving. This question is particularly pertinent to students of the American tradition because they so frequently find themselves in the presence of imaginative materials whose claims to be regarded as in any sense religious are often made in virtually identical terms with their claims to be regarded as somehow American. Obvious examples include such works as *Moby-Dick*, *Leaves of Grass*, "The American Scholar," *The Scarlet Letter*, *Walden*, *The Sound and the Fury*, *The Great Gatsby*, *Mont-Saint-Michel and Chartres*, *The Bridge*, and *The Deerslayer*, but it is no less true of works like *The Narrative of Arthur Gordon Pym*, *The Autobiography of Henry Adams*, *Miss Lonelyhearts*, *Lord Weary's Castle*, *Henderson the Rain King*, *Wings of the Dove*, *Let Us*

Now Praise Famous Men, The Mysterious Stranger, "An Ordinary Evening in New Haven," *The Autobiography of Malcolm X, Winesburg, Ohio, The Far Field, Armies of the Night, The Fire Next Time, The Crying of Lot 49,* and a host of other titles. To explore the religious meaning and import of such texts—however unconventional and idiosyncratic that religious meaning and significance may turn out to be—often amounts to the same thing as determining their status as American, and this latter task can only be accomplished by attempting to decide in what sense these texts can be viewed as culturally representative, or—to put it more fashionably—by attempting to define in what sense these texts express, disclose, or refract—call it what you will—an American frame of mind, form of sensibility, or mode of experience. I employ the terms "mind," "sensibility," and "experience" interchangeably in this case without presuming to think that they are synonymous. As I use them here, in their application to the evolution and development of cultural life, I assume that they belong to the same existential continuum even if they epitomize somewhat different aspects of it.

Yet the very notion that there may be an American frame of mind, form of sensibility, or mode of experience calls up a variety of unpleasant associations that leave one wondering if it might not be more advisable to let the whole matter drop right here. Most attempts to define such abstractions have turned out to be partial at best and self-serving at worst. Predicated on the belief that there is something peculiarly, perhaps even uniquely, American, they tend to perpetuate what has come to be called the myth of American exceptionalism, a myth which, for all its utility in the work of Alexis de Tocqueville as well as David Potter, Hector St. John de Crèvecoeur as well as Leslie Fiedler, has been responsible for many of the most dangerous cultural and political illusions to which Americans have been susceptible.

Notwithstanding this fact, the simple proposition that writers play some role in shaping the collective consciousness, sensibility, or experience of a people raises by itself issues of immense scope and complexity. The problem is not simply one of defining the parameters of the assertion—are we referring to writers in every era from the Puritan period to the present? Does the term "writer" include novelists, poets, and dramatists merely, or everyone from theologians to social critics and from cultural historians to public philosophers? How can writers possibly affect the thinking and feeling of individuals who have not shared their own experiences, or even some reasonable facsimile thereof? Nor is it even a matter of absorbing the great welter of secondary material that has already been devoted to such issues in scholarly monographs and learned journals. The primary problem is that of deciding whether, as formulated, this topic is a subject for discussion at all. Even if we agree that nations have writers who in our case deserve to be called American, is it true, or even intelligible, to claim that nations have what can be called minds, sensibilities, or experiences? And whether nations have anything analogous to minds, sensibilities, or experiences, is it reasonable to assume that any nation possesses sufficient cultural homogeneity to permit us to believe that it has but one such mind, sensibility, or experience?

Rather than plunge directly into some very tentative answers to these questions, it might be more helpful to linger initially over the questions themselves. For whatever one may think of the issue behind them, there can be no blinking the questions it raises. The one unspoken assumption shared by most American literary and cultural historians is that our writers have in fact contributed to the formation of a collective mental life, even though these same scholars are generally divided over what is meant by this, and how writers accomplish it.

I

It must be admitted from the outset that there is a sense in which the question of the writer's role in the formation of cultural consciousness is of far less interest to writers themselves than to people like us, readers and critics who need and want some way of classifying them, even of domesticating them. Moreover, as *our* topic rather than the writer's, it is one that reflects a certain measure of confusion about the question underlying it—namely, the artist's relation to culture. The state of contemporary understanding of this matter can be roughly gauged by an interview Saul Bellow gave recently to a panel of critics assembled by *Salmagundi*, one of our liveliest journals of arts and letters.

The interview began somewhat inauspiciously with a question about whether, as a writer, Mr. Bellow thought he had any "special task to perform at this point in time," to which Mr. Bellow rather diffidently replied that "if there's anything good that he can do, the writer should certainly do it at once."[1] Mr. Bellow clearly realized what the panel was fishing for—some declaration about the writer's responsibility to speak to and for his culture, especially in a time of national re-examination and renewal such as our own—but he refused to supply the anticipated response. Instead, after admitting his own ambivalence about the whole subject—"Occasionally I worry about what's happening to culture in the United States, but on other days I think there is no culture in the United States, and there's no point in worrying about it"[2]—Mr. Bellow went on to complain about the didactic moral responsibilities which are typically thrust upon the writer in America. Turning the question back upon the panelists, he asked:

> After all, we are, most of us, frail vessels: how much do we think we can do, what the devil do we think we are doing anyway? Do we really believe, in a country, a society, a civilization like this, that we can make that much difference? I don't even know how many times Shelley would have said that poets are the unacknowledged legislators of mankind if he had lived beyond the age of forty. . . .[3]

Not to be put off so easily, the *Salmagundi* critics then attempted a different approach by raising a question about whether, in a culture such as our own, it is still possible for writers and others to

generate anew what might be called "supreme values," values of
the sort people are willing to die for. "Are we ready to die for anything, do you think?" someone earnestly asked. "Ought we to be
ready?" To which Mr. Bellow quickly replied, "Well, I think lots
of people are ready to die because they can't stand life anymore." [4]
And so it went: the interviewers continuously prompting, encouraging, almost pleading with Mr. Bellow to stand and deliver; Mr.
Bellow constantly shifting, dodging, digressing, and evading in
order to maintain that right to the privacy and peculiarity of his
own ideas without which we would not have any writers in
America at all. If they are ours, so we seem to believe, then writers
ought to speak for us, represent us, help shape and form us; and
when they display any wariness about embracing this cultural as-
signment, then they leave us feeling, as Mr. Bellow so obviously
left the panel from *Salmagundi* feeling, slightly baffled, frustrated,
and testy.

That writers cannot be cast in the role of public philosophers or
cultural pundits because for them, as Mr. Bellow insisted, the
question is not whether you have ideas but whether you believe the
ones you profess; or that there is a profound difference between the
received opinions everybody pays lip service to and the inner convictions which for all but the empty-headed remain a very well
kept secret even from their wives and husbands, because, as Bellow
put it, "there's really no language for these secrets at the moment,
and very few people whom you can take into your confidence" [5]—
all this was quite lost on Bellow's companions since, with an insensibility quite untypical of *Salmagundi* but not unlike that found in
the society at large, they assumed that the writer's relation to culture is (or ought to be) a completely public one. But of course it
isn't and never has been, and the reasons are obvious. For one
thing, writing, at least imaginative writing, is a decidedly private
affair which, as Yeats once said, referring to poetry but including
all fictive forms within that term, is produced not out of our quarrel with others but out of our quarrel with ourselves. For another,

when writers have forgotten this fact and have attempted to speak for some larger collective entity, they have invariably wound up taking the high oracular road of poets like Vachel Lindsay or Carl Sandburg and have expended their whole energy merely echoing already-formed public sentiments.

Yet this only raises all over again the question of whether or not such an entity as the American mind, sensibility, or experience actually exists, what it does or doesn't have to do with supreme values, and how, if it does exist, writers have contributed, even in a critical or negative way, to its formation. Granted that most serious writers, like Mr. Bellow, would firmly deny any responsibility for its creation and maintenance, still the existence of something called an American mind or American experience is, like most articles of cultural belief, widely accepted but variously understood. One need only recall such titles as *The American Mind*, by Henry Steele Commager, *American Minds*, by Stow Persons, *The New England Mind*, by Perry Miller, and Daniel Boorstin's American trilogy on the colonial experience, the national experience, and the democratic experience to realize how deeply committed we are to the notion that there is some form (or forms) of collective mentality in our culture, even if these books exhibit little consensus as to what we mean by it. Professor Commager means that "there is a distinctive American way of thought, character, and conduct" which can be understood in terms of the ideas in which it has been expressed.[6] Professor Persons means instead that there have been distinctively different ways of thinking, being, and acting in successive periods of American history—hence several minds rather than one—and that these distinctive forms have resulted less from a shared set of ideas than from a common set of assumptions. Perry Miller is more circumspect still, resisting any attempt "to fix the personality of America in one eternal, unchangeable pattern" on the supposition that the only constant in our experience as a people has been our capacity to change our minds continuously about everything from the Deity to detergents.[7] And Professor Boorstin, in his turn, has

attempted to subvert the whole discussion by arguing rather per-
suasively that there is no national mind (or minds) in America at all
but only a common way of responding to novel conditions by rely-
ing upon the testimony of self-evidence.

The truth, if there is any, no doubt lies somewhere in between.
If there isn't an American mind or series of minds, it is clear that
we would have had to invent one just because we seem constitu-
tionally unable to imagine ourselves as a people without assuming
that we are unified by common thoughts, aspirations, and feelings.
These same books are in part an expression of this, and what they
commonly reveal is a tendency to conceive of the nation on the
analogue of an individual and therefore to view the expression of
the nation's self-conscious life, its culture, as a result and manifestation of a single, or at least a uniform, intelligence or will. Hence
whether we in fact possess a common mind in America may not be
to the point at all; the nub of the matter is that we somehow need
to think we do, and this need, rather than any collective form of
consciousness of which it is the expression, may be as close as one
can come to isolating any uniform patterns in the mental habits or
experience of most Americans.

Yet there is more to the problem than this. For if the phrase
"American mind" is permitted to stand for that abstraction we have
created out of our need to believe that there are distinctive patterns
of uniformity in our cognitive life as a people, then it becomes evident that most of the writers we might immediately think of as
capable of contributing to such patterns—Cooper, Hawthorne,
Melville, James, Frost, Hemingway, Faulkner—have, to varying
degrees, set themselves in firmest opposition to what in their time
were typically conceded to be its presumed referents. Far from either creating or reflecting what they associated with the American
mind or experience, they worked vigorously to question, to
challenge, even to undermine it; and they did so, it is clear, not
because of any shared conviction that we necessarily lack unity as a

people but because of their shared disinclination to define as the causes or chief components of that unity what seemed to them to be but mere rationalizations of it. In this case, then, it might be more accurate to say that American writers have created or at least contributed to the development of an American mind only in the limited sense of trying to criticize and change it.

But by mind just what do we mean? Do we mean, as Professor Commager seems to, a set of ideas which reveal a distinctive mode of thought, character, and behavior? Or do we mean, as Professor Persons does, a common set of assumptions—philosophical, religious, social—which provide the bases for thought and reflection in any given epoch? Perhaps, instead, we mean to associate mind neither with a set of discrete ideas nor with a set of assumptions from which they arise, but rather, as Professor Boorstin has argued, with a general frame of thinking which affects the manner in which all objects of perception are treated intellectually?

Yet these queries only lead to another set of questions concerning the level of consciousness on which such a national mental consensus is presumed to operate. Does such a consensus operate chiefly where our politicians and civil historians assume it does, on the level of publicly attested and professed beliefs? Or is it accessible only in the writings of our most perceptive thinkers and critics—a Jonathan Edwards, a Thomas Jefferson, a Walt Whitman, a William James—individuals who are blessed with the ability to express what we all dimly sense but rarely comprehend or are able to articulate? Perhaps, on the contrary, this consensus operates neither on the level of civic discourse, nor on the more rarified level of intellectual dialogue, but instead on a more subconscious level of image and myth, where concept and emotion, to echo one social historian, are fused into broad collective representations that sometimes serve—as in the case of the nineteenth century's inclination to conceive of America in the image of a great pastoral garden—to define an entire society's understanding of itself?[8]

2

These questions admit of no easy answers, and there is little point in pretending that they will be resolved to everyone's satisfaction here. By the same token the questions themselves won't disappear just by wishing they would. Quite the contrary, if we are to pursue the problem of the writer's relation to something called an or the American mind, then we must face them directly. But this is to risk venturing into that still opaque and relatively uncharted area known as the theory of mind and mind's relation to individual consciousness on the one side and cultural experience on the other. Such a prospect would appear more forbidding if it weren't for the critical work which has already been done on the subject by such different and seemingly incompatible philosophers as Gilbert Ryle, Ernst Cassirer, and John Dewey. Ryle's work has been particularly helpful in disabusing us of the notion that mind can be associated exclusively either with a special kind of object or thing, as Professors Commager and Persons imply, or with a particular kind of activity, as Mr. Boorstin suggests. Though mind certainly expresses itself in both, it is Ryle's conviction (which the others share) that mind is essentially dispositional in character, and that it is therefore best conceived as a series of capacities, propensities, tendencies, habits, or proclivities.[9]

This more functional orientation to the theory of mind can be traced back within the modern tradition to the later philosophy of John Dewey who, almost more than any of his contemporaries, struggled vigorously to dissociate the idea of mind from any notion of a self-contained entity existing solely within the head and thereby isolated from the world of persons, things, and, above all, events. Arguing that the word mind denotes an inclusive process that is at once intellectual (as when we use our mind to observe, remember, and operate on things), affectional (as when we use our mind to express solicitude or anxiety about persons and things we care about), and volitional (as when we act purposively), Dewey insisted that mind can be considered substantial, can be considered an object spatially restricted, only in an idiomatic sense. Otherwise, he preferred to talk about mind in terms of its effects, suggesting that mind comes into play in every interaction between the self and its environment. "Whenever anything is undergone in consequence of a doing," Dewey insisted, "the self is modified." [10] The point about such modifications, however, is that they always involve more than the acquisition of new aptitudes and skills; they also involve the acquisition of "attitudes and interests . . . which embody in themselves some deposit of the meaning of things done and undergone." [11] These deposits of meaning, along with the aptitudes and skills to use them, then become a part of the self, constituting the "capital," as Dewey termed it, upon which the self draws in all its future contacts with the environment. In this sense, then, Dewey was willing to grant that the mind is substantial: mind forms the "background," as it were, against which the self projects all its relations with the environment and in light of which the self is disposed to act in all its future contacts with the environment. Yet such language could be misleading, Dewey believed, unless it was remembered that this "background" is never stable and fixed but always changing, and that, "in the projection of the new upon it, there is assimilation and reconstruction of both background and of what is taken in and digested." [12]

Defining mind in these dynamic terms, as the ever-expanding "background" which is formed out of those inevitable modifications of the self that occur as a result of anything that happens to the self, anything the self either does or undergoes, Dewey was able to make some useful and important distinctions between mind and consciousness, between the whole funded system of meanings and skills that define the self's dispositional makeup and those meanings and skills of which the self is aware. Mind, he assumed, refers to the whole field of operative meanings, consciousness to the much more restricted field of apprehended meanings—which is to say, ideas. Therefore Dewey conceived of mind as "contextual" and perduring, consciousness as "focal" and intermittent. Mind he suggestively described as "a constant luminosity," consciousness as "a series of flashes of varying intensities." Mind was to be associated with that "connected whole" extending beyond any individual (or, for that matter, collective) process of consciousness conditioning its purpose and effect, very much as the narrative frame of a story lends coherence and significance to events whose meaning and import would otherwise remain a mystery to us. Consciousness he likened instead to "the occasional interception of messages continually transmitted," in the manner of "a mechanical receiving device [which] selects a few of the vibrations with which the air is filled and renders them audible." [13]

Through the use of such imagery Dewey hoped to show that mind changes only slowly, as both external circumstances and individual interest compel modifications in the organized body of meanings and aptitudes that dispose the self to respond this way rather than in the face of new experience, whereas consciousness changes rapidly, since it emerges at the point "where the formed disposition and the immediate situation touch and interact." [14] In relation to mind, consciousness "is that phase of a system of meanings which at a given time is undergoing re-direction, transitive formation." [15] In relation to consciousness, mind is that "continuum of meaning in process of formation" which binds the intermittent and discrete perceptions of which we are aware at any one time into a cognitively significant series. [16]

From this perspective Dewey believed that mind is susceptible to disruption and reorganization in a way that consciousness is not. Mind, after its fashion, is both structured and coherent. Disrupt its loose and, for the most part, unconscious "idea of order" and you immediately alter the habitual flow of thought and even the constituents of the thinkable. The same could hardly be said of consciousness. As no more than "a particular state of awareness *in its immediacy*," [17] consciousness merely records rather than directs by arresting the actual flow of events in their meaning and thus registering what Dewey described in another context as the process of "continuous readjustment of self and world in experience."[18]

How then, one might ask, does the mind assist the self in adjusting its relations to the world it experiences such that the mind both informs the self in its relations with the world and is also formed by the relations the self has with the world? How does the mind both develop and change as a result of the experiences of the self, and simultaneously shape and condition the self's capacity for new experience? The answer has to do with the way in which the mind responds to the experiences that are presented to it for disposition. And it does so, as Cassirer and Langer have shown, not initially by thinking about those experiences but by creating symbolic versions of them. In other words, the mind works by translating experiences into symbols which then provide the material for thought and the impulse for action. Referring to this activity of mind as the disposition to "symbolization," Miss Langer notes that while essential to thought and action it is equivalent to neither. Prior to both, the disposition to "symbolization" is the basis upon which the mind absorbs those deposits of meaning ingredient in the self's experiences and also disposes the self to react to those experiences. Thus Miss Langer can change the figure without altering the meaning by likening the mind not, as Dewey does in his most felicitous image of it, to an "active and eager background that lies in wait and engages whatever comes its way, so as to absorb it into its own being,"[19] but instead to a "great transformer." Of this she writes, "The current of experience that passes through it undergoes a change of character, not through the agency of the sense by which the perception entered, but by virtue of a primary use which is made of it immediately: it is sucked into the stream of symbols which constitute [the] human mind."[20]

These observations have important implications for our understanding of the relationship between mind and culture. For one thing, they demonstrate that mind operates on every level of cultural life, from the most intellectually rarified to the most subconsciously diffuse, from the elite to the popular, and that it manifests itself not only in cognitive forms but also in emotional and practical forms, looking in some instances as though it were an entity, a substantial thing, in others as though it were an expressive activity or process. As the ever-present but always changing background of which consciousness is the foreground, mind is to be associated with that continuum of meaningful symbolic activity which enables the self to manage its contacts with the environment. It accomplishes this by translating those contacts into construable signs, signs that simultaneously permit the self "to synthesize, delay and modify [its] reactions" to "the gaps and confusions of [its] experience, and by means of these 'signs' to add the experience of other people to [its] own." [21]

This leads directly to the second important implication these observations have for an understanding of the relationship between mind and culture. For if mind is to be defined as that peculiar set of dispositions which empowers individuals to seek some control over their experience by producing symbolic versions of it, culture may be viewed as that continually expanding web of symbolic versions which human beings use hermeneutically to achieve this control. Though mind and culture are not to be confused, they nevertheless constitute responses to the same general need and conspire to serve the same general function. Both exist to help man orient himself within, and adjust his relations to, a world he cannot cope with, much less survive, without understanding. As such, the existence of both is due to a deficiency within the human organism—its inability to manage its relations with the environment on the basis of the equipment with which it was genetically endowed [22]—and mind and culture compensate for this deficiency by providing the human organism with the extragenetic means and tools, respectively, to confer sense and significance upon its experiences by creating a larger context of meaning in which to interpret them.

On this reading culture is no mere supplement to mind but actually ingredient in it without being identical with it. [23] Their relationship is perhaps most easily conceived as a variant of the relationship between mind and consciousness. What culture supplies mind is that set of more or less public and approved versions of human experience which have, at least symbolically, met the test of time, and which have thus become available as part of the operative system of meanings of which the mind is a repository. What mind provides culture, on the other hand, is the machinery for constantly re-testing and modifying as well as expanding its system of operative symbolic meanings so that the self can more effectively negotiate its relations with the environment by interpreting them.

But if culture is to be distinguished from mind, so, too, it must be distinguished from society. Where the former refers to that ordered system of symbolic meaning and significance in terms of which social interaction occurs, the latter refers to the patterns of social interaction itself. Clifford Geertz, whose formulations I am following here, contrasts them as follows: "Culture is the fabric of meaning in terms of which human beings interpret their experience and guide their actions; social structure is the form that action takes, the actually existing network of social relations."[24] This distinction is useful inasmuch as it suggests the way in which culture and society interact with and affect one another. Though independently variable, as Geertz says, they are also mutually interdependent. Changes in the one influence the course of the other, but each operates according to its own principle of integration. Culture is integrated in terms of "logico-meaningful" relations, society in terms of "causal-functional" relations,[25] and this difference in their respective principles of integration goes a long way toward explaining the frequent incidence of tension between them. It also suggests, as Geertz points out, that the primary causes of social and cultural change are less likely to be found in what is continuous between them than in what is radically discontinuous and even disjunctive.

Underlying this view of social and cultural change is an assumption that culture in particular is comprised of elements of *praxis* as well as *theoria*, and that culture itself may perhaps be most helpfully understood as a kind of dialectical exchange between them. Cultural change occurs, according to this model, whenever *theoria*, or the inherited modes of interpreting experience and organizing it into hierarchies of significance, becomes dissociated from *praxis*, or the ever-changing patterns of ongoing experience itself. The increasing discontinuity between them eventually generates the search for alternative modes of interpretation which will more adequately explain, or at least "fit," the actual texture and shape of new experience.

Such a model of cultural growth and change has been ingeniously adumbrated by the Spanish philosopher, Ortega y Gasset. Ortega's reflections are particularly apt because he makes a direct connection between cultural development and religious meaning, arguing that a pragmatic theory of culture, such as this one, is not neutral to the existence of ultimate values and beliefs but in fact creative of them. Ortega's theory of culture is rooted in his epistemological conviction that reality cannot be defined either in terms of the inherent nature of things or in terms of man's consciousness but only in terms of their dialogical relation, the relation between what Ortega prefers to call the "self" and its "circumstances." The one essential given of man's experience, Ortega insists, is his problematic co-existence with a world not of his own making, and everything man does he does in response to this fact. Shipwrecked amid circumstances, as Ortega is fond of saying, and unable to live in a constant state of uncertainty, man must find some tentative solutions to this predicament, must give at least a portion of his life some stability. But as tentative solutions to the problem of reality become more stable, Ortega argues, they take on the character of what he calls *creencias*, or beliefs about an aspect of reality that carry the authority of absolute certainty. *Creencias*, says Ortega, "are not ideas which we *have*, but ideas which we *are*, . . . [not ideas] *with* which we encounter ourselves . . . [but ideas] *in* which we encounter ourselves, [ideas] which seem to be present before we think."[26] To be sure, *creencias* are not for the most part created by each individual for himself but are acquired by each individual as part of his circumstances, as part of his cultural inheritance. Having orginated as someone else's tentative solutions to the problem of reality, they eventually lose their provisional status and assume an absolute character by becoming identified with a sphere of existence that is now unquestioned. To this extent they come to represent a zone of stability in terms of which man can locate himself and out of which he can live.

Yet man is more than what he is and has for Ortega; he is also what he will do and be. Even as man lives within and out of his *creencias*, his ultimate beliefs, he lives for and because of his task. That task involves laboring continually to extend the zone of stability, of certainty, out into the realm of problematic circumstances surrounding it. At any given moment, then, life possesses a definite structure not only for the individual but also for culture. There is a firm area of *creencias*, or what we might call ultimate values, which includes the repertoire of beliefs that map the territory of understanding about which there is virtually complete certainty; and there is the more dubious area of "ideas," as Ortega calls it, associated with those dimensions of experience which are still opaque, unpredictable, and unstable. The whole of man's life is thus depicted as an attempt to discover solutions to an unending situation, where culture simply represents the totality of such solutions, some of which seem to have greater authority, permanence, and warrant than others.[27]

3

The problem with these very general and—some might add—very abstract formulations is that it is difficult to see how they apply concretely to a culture as protean and heterogeneous as the American. Reduced to its essentials, the question is how to place any credence in the existence of a common cultural mind, much less a common cultural consciousness, when we know that most Ameri-

cans, no matter how stereotyped their thinking or how standard-
ized their behavior, have not, except in the most superficial sense,
shared the same or even similar individual experiences. Critics and
historians, as we know, are forever declaiming that the American
understanding of Nature comes from Jefferson or Emerson; that
Benjamin Franklin was responsible for, or anyway gave classic
expression to, the American doctrine of self-reliance; that the
American Dream received its definitive interpretation in *The Great
Gatsby;* that the American experience is summed up, if anywhere,
in the pages of *Moby-Dick.* Yet a deeper part of ourselves wants to
resist these claims by asking in what sense such books, and others
like them, really treat anything resembling the content of the experience—mental, emotional, or material—of most Americans. How
many Americans, for example, at least before the Age of the Cam-
per, have, like Emerson, had an unmediated experience with the
Divine out in the woods? How many Americans lacking all social
and economic advantage have really gloried, as Franklin did, in the
opportunity to raise themselves up by their own bootstraps in a
fundamentally hostile world? Or how many Americans have ever
known someone who is really rich, and what common bond, as
Fitzgerald himself sometimes wondered, do the rest of us mortals
share with the rich anyway? And how many of us have taken ship
in search of answers to life's deepest questions and there confronted
an admixture of all man's nobility and all his evil in the concentrated brow of a mad old man?

Nevertheless, a moment's reflection will serve to remind us that,
as natural as such questions are, and as often as they have been
asked in recent years by anyone impatient with facile general-
izations about American uniqueness, they still betray a serious confusion about the relationship between a people's shared experience
of an event or idea and their shared experience of an interpretation
of such things. Those who ask such questions usually suppose that
these two sorts of experience—of an event or idea on the one hand,
of an interpretation of them on the other—are diametrically op-

posed in kind and therefore mutually exclusive, whereas common sense should tell us that they are different only in degree and therefore mutually inclusive. Indeed, the term "experience," as we use it colloquially, always refers to something acquired, something grasped, something interpreted, there being no experience, so to speak, in the buff. Exposure to events and participation in events does not become what we usually think of as an "experience" of them until we have, however minimally, begun to assess and appropriate their significance for ourselves, whereupon the terms of assessment and the manner of appropriation suddenly become as much a part of the substance of the experience itself as any of its other features. Thus it is fair to say that the common elements in a people's experience or mind may have very little to do with the actual substance of what each individual among them has either undergone or thought. What unifies them culturally as a people, and thereby orders their thinking into widely shared patterns of meaning and significance, is not the substantive identity of their individual experiences and ideas but the systematic relationships that exist among the various interpretations they have each employed to comprehend those ideas and experiences.

To speak of an American mind, then, as of a French or Japanese or New England mind, is not to refer to anything like a single set of experiences, mental or otherwise, but to a general family or constellation of modes of experience, affective, volitional, and cognitive in their turn, which are related as alternatives within a single but always expanding range of possibilities.[28] To understand the workings of the American mind, as of any cultural mind, thus requires something quite different from an analysis of its contents and the way those contents are related one to another. To understand the American mind involves an understanding of the experience of those contents *in their relations*, that is, an understanding of the whole implied system of alternative modes of experience of which this or that expression is but one variant. The converse of this is that writers cannot be said to contribute to the formation of an American mind simply by adding new contents to it, simply, as it were, by providing the mind with fresh material to think about. That writers do, indeed, furnish readers with fresh food for thought, I have no doubt; this is surely one of the reasons why most of us turn to them in the first place—for information, entertainment, instruction. But to contribute to the formation of mind, whether our own individual mind or some larger collective mentality, they must do something more: they must teach us new ways to think and feel about such material; in other words, they must alter our habitual modes of response to the material which is constantly presented to us for reflection by eliciting in us new ways of disposing of such material interpretively.

4

The difference between a work which merely added new contents to our collective experience by providing Americans with fresh material to think about and one which seems to have been designed to alter the way Americans organized those contents by providing new ways of culturally interpreting such material, is readily brought out by a comparison of *Uncle Tom's Cabin* and *The Adventures of Huckleberry Finn*. Of the two, Mrs. Stowe's novel was clearly the more popular in its own time, selling during its first year of publication over 300,000 copies in America and more than two-and-a-half million copies, both in English and in translation, the world over. In retrospect, of course, the astonishing success of *Uncle Tom's Cabin* was hardly an accident. Mrs. Stowe provided her readers with something new and important to think about, an extremely affecting picture of the plight of Negro slaves caught in the clutches of a vicious social system, one that destroyed the family, eroded the legal foundations of society, hardened men's hearts against God, oppressed the innocent, and brought out all the latent fear and guilt in their oppressors. The spectacle of Uncle Tom's Christian fidelity, of little Eva's pure devotion, of Simon Legree's paranoid cruelty, of George Shelby's ineffectual but well-intentioned decency, of Augustine St. Clare's elegant and tortured self-mockery, of Mrs. Byrd's firm moral rectitude, of Cassy's sense of injury and desperation, and of the narrator's hope for a brighter day to come, if not in America, then in Liberia, where the emancipated slaves, she hoped, could be deported—all these images and ideas were enormously arresting in the intensely moralistic era of abolitionism, and, like so much additional material in the book, they continue to remain moving, as Edmund Wilson remarked not too many years ago, down to the present day.[29] Mrs. Stowe exerted such broad influence on the popular sentiment of her time because she painted the horrors of the slave system and what it was doing to the South with a pen dipped in the ink of moral and religious outrage. More than this, she had a premonition of what was to come and was therefore able to register "the moment when the Civil War was looming as something already felt but not yet clearly foreseen: an ambiguous promise and menace, the fulfillment of some awful prophecy which had never quite been put into words."[30]

Considerable as these achievements are, however, the question is whether Mrs. Stowe provided her readers with a new way of thinking and feeling about such matters. For all her massive popularity and impact, did she fundamentally alter conventional modes of reflection and assessment? The scholarly consensus on this question is generally negative. The huge appeal of her book depended almost exclusively on the way she confirmed and supported the manner in which most of her readers—and not only those who, like herself, were militantly anti-slavery—already thought and felt. All she did was to supply them with a fresh field of facts, sentiments, and ideas upon which to exercise their powers of analysis and discrimination. At bottom, if we can believe a cultural historian like Cushing Strout, her anti-slavery fervor derived from a mixture of elements her readers generally shared—sentimental piety, associated with the Christianity of the Sermon on the Mount and un-

dergirded by a militant commitment to the Victorian cult of home
and family; millenialistic hope, expressed in the late Edwardian
belief in a new Golden Age that was to precede the Second Coming of Christ and which had been given fresh currency by Charles
Grandison Finney's preaching about the possibility of instant salvation; romantic racism, based on the view that the slave was in truth
a kind of a noble savage undaunted by adversity and ennobled by
suffering who deserved the white man's respect and understanding
less than his solicitous protection and assistance; and political con-
servatism, which was expressed in her advocacy of racial division
on the ground that blacks could never achieve the rights to which
they were entitled unless they were separated permanently from
whites and resettled in their own country.[31] For all its prescience,
then, Mrs. Stowe's novel serves as a Baedeker to the ideological
confusion and moral ambiguity of her own age. Idealizing the cults
of home, love, and instant conversion which by mid-century had
turned American Protestantism into a kind of culture religion, as
Strout points out, Mrs. Stowe struck out sharply and effectively at
the two contemporary practices which most ruthlessly violated
them, miscegenation and slave-holding. But despite her abhorrence
of these practices and their effects, all she could propose as an antidote was the strangely unChristian notion, shared for some time
by no less an important Northern contemporary than Lincoln himself, of racial separatism and African resettlement for the emancipated slaves.

Compare this with Mark Twain's novel. Not only did he repudi-
ate the idea of racial separation—albeit an easier thing to do *after*
the Civil War than *before* it—but he attacked all the props which
supported Mrs. Stowe's culture religion, all the assumptions which
undergirded her criticism of contemporary social life. Sentimental
piety, so intimately related to the Victorian cult of home and family, he exposed as a mask for monstrous self-pity which inevitably
led to the senseless slaughter of the Sheperdson-Grangerford feud
and to Colonel Sherburn's brutal murder of the drunken, pathetic

Boggs. Millennialistic hope he associated with a debased and fraud-
ulent Calvinism particularly attractive to social status-seekers such
as the late Peter Wilk's fellow townsmen whose religious shal-
lowness was revealed for what it was in their susceptibility to being
gulled by the King's sermonette of "soul-butter and hogwash."
Romantic racism he indicted as a thinly disguised attempt to recover a lost sense of self-importance by turning the Negro and his
plight, as Tom Sawyer does at the Phelps plantation, into a source
of entertainment and adventure, thereby relating Tom to the Duke
and the Dauphin, who merely carry to the extreme Tom's own inclination to exploit others for his own benefit. Political conserva-
tism Twain depicted as a repressive creed which united the civilization of the Widow Douglas and Miss Watson on the one side with
the degradation of Pap Finn and the savagery down river on the
other.

   Significant as these reversals are, however, they do not account
for the chief difference between Mark Twain's book and Mrs.
Stowe's. Taken alone, all they demonstrate is that Mark Twain
was able to bring forward new evidence to challenge the presiding
assumptions that informed Mrs. Stowe's criticism of slavery. Mark
Twain's real achievement, however, was to force his readers to
think about these matters in a fundamentally different and novel
way, and this he accomplished by using as the protagonist and
first-person narrator of his story a vernacular hero initially susceptible to every kind of social prejudice, particularly about the Negro,
who is obliged in the course of his adventures with an escaped slave
to relinquish these prior attitudes in order to remain true to the
new, spontaneous, and uncoerced sense of life they have experienced together during their flight down river toward freedom.[32] By
making Huck's own emerging sense of values, which develops
chiefly as a result of his exposure to Jim's innate integrity as a
human being, and of the way Huck and others violate it, both the
counterforce to, and the lens through which we see and assess the
prevailing system of values in society, Mark Twain is able to make

us think differently not only about the horrors of slavery but also about the source of values in life. We think differently about the horrors of slavery because we are forced to associate them with the condition of whites and blacks alike, and because we are obliged to measure their effects upon two individuals we have finally come to respect neither as black nor as white but essentially as persons who need and love each other. We think differently about the source of values in life because, through a boy's experience of disillusionment and discovery, we have been compelled to realize how inimical society is to the interests of the individual self, and how, simultaneously, the deepest and most natural impulses of the self, when disencumbered of social conventions and prejudices, can provide a genuine basis for human community.

Implicit in this contrast between what must be judged a minor work, since it merely provided countless Americans with something new to think about, and a major work, because it adumbrated, albeit initially for a much smaller audience, a new way of thinking and feeling in America, is the assumption that serious literature, like all serious art, does more than reflect what is already there in reality prior to our experience of it. In the hands of a major artist like Mark Twain, literature becomes, as Henry James once said, a vicarious form of learning in which the writer is able to examine inherited modes of comprehending and evaluating experience by submitting them to various tests of social, political, aesthetic, ethical, or even metaphysical adequacy. The aim of such learning, to paraphrase Stuart Hampshire, is to strip experience of its false overlay of approved interpretation and get back to what is considered its essential substance.[33] And the effect of such learning is not so much to change the contents of our experience as to articulate new and different combinations in which those contents can be plausibly organized. From this perspective, literature does not, as Melville had it, present us with "another world, yet one to which we feel the tie," but presents us instead with a new relationship to the world we have inherited from the past. "The ques-

tion behind every work of literature," as Hayden White has said in
another context, "is not 'What is reality?' but rather 'What would
reality be like if the relationship between consciousness and experience were viewed like *this?*' This is what makes every genuine work
of art a revolutionary gesture." [34]

5

Among those modern critical theorists who have discussed the revolutionary implications art has for culture, none has been more discerning than the art historian E. H. Gombrich. To explain how art
at once reflects cultural perception and also changes it, Gombrich
has invoked the now common psychological notion of *mental set.*
Applying the term to that shared set of perceptions, or "horizon of
expectation[s]" as he calls it at one point,[35] Gombrich believes that
all art, like all communication, is based upon the interplay between
anticipation and observation, projection and corroboration. All perception involves the matching of the framework or "schema" of
meanings on which we provisionally rely (what was earlier called
"mind") with the actualities of our own ongoing experience. The
process of learning therefore entails the falsification of our premises
or expectations and their continuous revision to fit the "facts."

This same rule applies to art, which Gombrich depicts as a
dialectic between making and matching, where the aim is not "to
see the object as in itself it really is," as the familiar Arnoldian
expression puts it, but to adjust the schema with which we see to
the things it permits us to see. We cannot "see" at all, Gombrich
assumes, without some initial schema, some set of expectations, to
arrest and organize the flux of our perceptions: "Without
categories, we could not sort our impressions." [36] Therefore the artist does not so much paint what he sees as see what he paints.[37]
And the truly creative artist is the one whose painting not only
presents us with new things to see but provides us with a new way
of seeing, whose painting adumbrates possibilities for imaging,

comprehending, and evaluating reality which transcend the schema or mental set currently employed for that purpose. Authentic artistic innovations occur, then, whenever the artist successfully challenges his culture's mental set by breaking through the conventional hierarchies of significance in which experience is presently ordered to a new vision of things which previously existed only as a perceptual possibility. The history of art, Gombrich therefore concludes, is no more and no less than in fine the history of violated mental sets.

Many of Gombrich's ideas have been given fuller application to problems of literary and cultural history by the German critical theorist, Hans Robert Jauss. Jauss is interested in reconciling the opposed claims of Marxists and formalists by bringing into the center of critical discussion again what both schools tend to leave out of account, namely, the reader and his reactions. In the case of the first, the reader tends to be regarded as little more than a member of a specific social class whose role in the aesthetic transaction can be sufficiently accounted for by describing his place within the structure of society. In reference to the second, the reader's social station is as nothing compared to the importance of his linguistic endowment which qualifies him to follow the directions laid down by the text to decipher its particular mode of encoding. In both cases, however, the reader who is affected by what he reads and carries traces of those affects out into the world with him, there to influence how he behaves as a social and cultural animal—this reader is largely neglected or dismissed outright. As a consequence, neither theory has a way of talking about the constructive dimension of literary experience and, particularly, about literature's role in helping to create the social and cultural world it presupposes for its existence. To correct this imbalance, Jauss is inclined to define literature in terms of its function and to identify its function with its social and cultural subversiveness. The artist's role, Jauss asserts, is to challenge and, if possible, to displace those accretions of interpretation that have become ritualized into fixed modes of response in the artist's own time, which he does by exploring forms of thought and action as yet untested, seeking answers to questions still unformulated, and imagining new possibilities of experience altogether. To miss this critical and constructive dimension in all serious works of literature, Jauss insists, is to subordinate their "virtual meaning and productive function in the process of experience" to their imitative or reproductive function.[38] Thus in his view, as in Gombrich's and Hampshire's, the history of literature becomes part of the larger history of changes in a culture's fundamental modes of perception and evaluation, of its mind set.

Jauss places himself squarely within the tradition of Vico, who was the first to propose that genuine knowledge of anything requires an understanding of it in its original otherness as a new presence in the world. Therefore central to Jauss's theory is an assumption going all the way back through Herder to Vico, but revived for modern critics by R. G. Collingwood and Hans-Georg Gadamer, that the only way of understanding a literary text is by attempting to recover the question to which the text was originally framed as an answer, or—as in the case of the *nouveau roman* and other post-modern traditions—by attempting to decipher the answer the text implies when there are no discernible questions to which it is directed.[39] Whichever the text is presumed to be— "either a question put to reality which demands an answer from the reader, or an answer to a question which the reader must himself provide," as Hayden White has rephrased it—serious works of literature are produced "at the point where our apprehension of the world outstrips our capacities for comprehending it, or conversely, where canonized modes of comprehension have closed off our capacities for new experience."[40] In both instances the reader is active rather than passive. To understand the text he must use whatever clues the text provides to reconstruct the question it presupposes. Yet complete historical retrieval of the context in which the text's question was asked is never possible because, as Gadamer has demonstrated and Jauss accepts, the context we reconstruct for any text is inevitably colored by the very different context out of which we seek to interrogate it. Thus understanding does not, because it cannot, depend on a perfect retrieval and repossession of the original context of the text itself but involves instead as complete a fusion as possible between the reconstructed context of the text and the different context, not always readily apparent to us, of our attempts to effect that retrieval and repossession.[41]

Jauss speaks of this process of constant interaction between text and reader, between past and present, in Heideggerian terms, as an interaction between the horizon of expectations presupposed and projected by the text and the horizon of expectations that define, as Gombrich would say, the mental set of the reader. When the distance between these two is great, as in the case of *The Adventures of Huckleberry Finn*, then the text demands a "horizon change" on the part of the reader and can be said to have large cultural influence. When the distance between them is slight, as in the case of *Uncle Tom's Cabin*, then the text approaches the level of what Jauss calls "culinary" or light reading where, instead of altering expectations, the text actually proceeds to fulfill them and thus has only minimal cultural influence.

But cultural influence should not be confused with historical impact. A novel like *Uncle Tom's Cabin*, whose contemporary popularity rested on what it did to confirm rather than to challenge or to change the horizon of expectations of its first readers, had immense historical consequences, while a work like *The Adventures of Huckleberry Finn*, which was intended up to a point as a frontal assault upon the mental set of its initial readers, had, in the short run at least, virtually none. Yet Twain's novel is clearly conceded to have been more influential culturally, even though it did not, as in the case of Mrs. Stowe's novel, make anything "happen." W. H. Auden was correct: great art makes nothing "happen," if by that we mean occur in a material sense. But great art does make things "happen" in other and often more profound ways, at least insofar as it alters the web of culturally created and historically transmitted meanings which influence our thoughts, shape our feelings, and guide our actions. However, to say for this reason that Mark Twain's novel exerted greater cultural influence than Mrs. Stowe's is, as Leo Marx has noted in another connection, somewhat inaccurate. *The Adventures of Huckleberry Finn* contributed to the formation of an American mind in a way that *Uncle Tom's Cabin* did not because in time it virtually became the culture that produced it. That is to say, Mark Twain's novel, along with works of similar stature, has come to comprise "a greater and greater portion of the consciousness of nineteenth-century America that remains effectively alive in the present."[42]

One of the lessons to be drawn from this, as has already been noted, is that mind, in its cultural no less than its individual manifestations, changes very slowly, and it does so only when habitual modes of thought and feeling are disrupted and displaced, only when the familiar, to use Victor Shklovsky's word, is "defamiliarized."[43] Paradoxically, the function of such strategies, at least as they operate in art, is to enable us to "see" what was potentially there all along, to discern possible aspects of our experience which established and assured habits of perception and interpretation had hidden from view.[44] But the familiar in this deeper sense, as the element of potentiality in all our experience, "does not consciously appear, save in an unexpected, novel, situation, where the familiar presents itself in a new light and is therefore not wholly familiar."[45] In time, of course, the techniques of defamiliarization themselves become familiar and eventually wind up obscuring once again the very things they were meant to disclose; but not before they have provided the mind with new meanings and thereby added to the store of potential symbolic resources we have at our disposal to adjust our relations with the environment.

This distinction between the kinds of works that simply confirm our horizon of expectations and those which challenge or displace them is integral to any theory which, like Jauss's and Gombrich's, assumes that art is constitutive of culture. The problem for most people who might otherwise be disposed to sympathize with it is that this proposition sounds overly cognitive. The notion that art shares common ground with science, politics, and metaphysics in comprising the implicit frame of reference or horizon of expectations—what Ortega called *creencias*—in terms of which a culture does its thinking, willing, and feeling seems to run counter to much recent aesthetic theory, which defines art in isolation from the larger cultural experience either by viewing it as a self-constituting form that evolves out of its own history or as a mimetic device that imitates what cannot be known through any other medium. In either case, the integrity of art is presumably preserved only at the risk of maintaining that individual works, like whole artistic traditions, are, and should remain, essentially ineffectual as determinants of thought and conduct. But even if in some cases it might be preferable that they were, who can suppose that Puritan piety remained unaffected by the appearance of *Pilgrim's Progress*, or that the nineteenth-century glorification of Nature had nothing to do with the reading of such works as *The Prelude* and Emerson's essays, or that the shape of twentieth-century belief remained unchanged after the publication of *The Waste Land?* That these works were not ineffectual is owing to the fact that the literary experience of many people exerted powerful pressure on their general horizon of expectations, not only affecting the interpretations they made of the world, but also influencing the way they determined to conduct themselves in light of those interpretations. Any texts which play such a role in culture have acquired what deserves to be called canonical status within that culture. Thus to answer the question of how the writer contributes to the formation of culture, it finally becomes necessary to define what we mean by a classic.

6

As Frank Kermode has recently demonstrated, there is no area of literary inquiry in which the effects of change in our own horizon of cultural assumptions, indeed, of the instability of the whole cultural inheritance, are more vividly apparent than in our modern conception of the classic.[46] Where the classic was once regarded as a self-authenticating form comprised of more or less absolute truths which communicated themselves in the same way to successive generations and could yield but one correct reading, we now realize that texts denominated as classics can be read in very different ways in different ages, and that what one age deems a classic another age may dismiss as a boring antique.[47] This inevitably raises two interrelated questions: what determines the selection of a classic in any given age? and what, if anything, distinguishes those texts which have the potential to become classics from those which do not?

As to the first, the historical mutability of so many classics, together with the historical relativity of our interpretations of all classics, leaves us with no other alternative but to suppose that the one factor which overrides all others in the selection of any classic is simply the decision which successive generations make to regard it as such, to accept this text as a valid, if not definitive, approach to the problem of conceiving and comprehending reality, of defining the relationship between consciousness and experience. As to the second, it has now become increasingly apparent that the only thing which differentiates classic texts from others is their greater plurality and opacity of meaning. Thus instead of being regarded as "a repository of certain, unchanging truths" which admit of but one interpretation,[48] the classic is now perceived to contain what, in another context, Claude Lévi-Strauss calls a "surplus of signifier," an excess of meaning, if you will, which permits it to remain so rich in content and so complex in import that no single age, and certainly no single reading, can ever completely exhaust it. The classic survives, when it does, because its plurality of signification together with its interpretive elusiveness enable succeeding generations to keep rereading it as a convincing answer to the differing questions each of them respectively asks.

In this de-idealized or "democratized" notion of the classic, in which the elevation of texts to the rank of the classic and their ability to maintain that rank is something over which the people, as it were, the common reader, and not a mysterious entity called The Tradition, exerts chief authority, we are frequently confronted with a paradox. For in the last analysis, texts both attain and retain classical status not because they strike us as strange but because they strike us as familiar. Indeed, their canonical function stems precisely from their ability to keep effectively alive in the present that portion of the past that is still meaningful to us, that portion of the past that continues to order the way we think and feel now.[49] However alien they may have appeared to their first readers, and however disruptive they may have proved to the mental set currently in use at the time of their initial appearance, by the time they have become classics the questions for which they provide answers have become one of the alternative modes of experience which is accepted as a possible component of our cultural endowment. "They are familiar to us," as Hayden White has said, "because we have chosen them; *we* are a realization of *their* potentialities for conceptualizing a world."[50] And the history of such choices, White goes on, is what we mean by tradition, which simply represents the continuity of thought and feeling, of mind, from one generation to the next.[51]

In this view the classic is not regarded, to use Gadamer's useful formulation, as "a suprahistorical concept of value" but as "a notable mode of being historical."[52] What Benjamin Lee Wharf said of language generally can be equally applied to works of art, of which the classic is but the preeminent example: their purpose is not so much to give a name to pre-existing things or concepts as to articulate the world, or at least a portion of the world, of our experience.[53] What sets the classic apart from all other works with a similar ambition is that the duration of its power to articulate such a world seems potentially limitless. But limited it inevitably is by all those factors, material as well as spiritual, social as well as psychological, which predispose us to experience one way today, another tomorrow. All I am contending is that the classic itself is one of those factors.

There can be no doubt that classics articulate the world of experience in a variety of ways. To adapt Lascelles Abercrombie's definition of the epic, some seem to do so simply by expressing what seems to be the unconscious metaphysic of their age. Others place that metaphysic under severe pressure and even seek to supplant it with another.[54] In the first instance, it must be conceded, the classic appears less interested in challenging or revising the mind, after the fashion, say, of Kafka's *The Castle* or even *Paradise Lost*, than in legitimating, virtually reifying, its essential structures, say, in the manner of Virgil's *Aeneid*. Yet even the *Aeneid* does more than this. While Aeneas' sense of historical destiny, which is but a reflection of Rome's own sense of destiny in the Augustan age, is never in doubt, its contemporary meaning is given added complication through its contrast with the more classically heroic and self-assertive virtues represented by Dido and Turnus, and his sense of destiny is tested and found wanting not only in his relations with Dido but also at the Sack of Troy and during the burning of his ships in Sicily. On each of these occasions, Aeneas' failures of character throw into bold relief a good deal more than his own imperfections; they also dramatize what Virgil thought was at stake in the history of the age. Far from simply expressing the contemporary assumption that the meaning of the whole of history was to be found in Rome's emergence as a world power dedicated to peace, Virgil intended for Aeneas' development to show that the "pietas" of Augustus had been the instrument by which the destiny of Rome had entered its greatest and final phase, and that the salvation of every Roman citizen now depended upon subordinating all other interests, as Aeneas had done, to the service of the empire. Thus even where its main object is to express and confirm the unconscious metaphysic or mental set of its first readers, the classic refines, revises, and reformulates that metaphysic or mental set in the process of articulating it.

This dialectic of representation and reconstruction, of legitima-
tion and displacement, is naturally even more apparent in modern
classics like *Moby-Dick*, because of the more widespread instability
and erosion of values and beliefs in the period we refer to as the
"modern." But Melville's great work is also instructive in another
way. As a text whose recognition as a classic was delayed for
nearly a century, *Moby-Dick* serves as a perfect illustration of the
thesis that no text can become a classic until it is perceived as such,
until a particular generation of readers decides that this text provides a normative model of the way reality is (or can be) constituted
and of how one can (or should) relate to it.

Such clearly was not the case at the time *Moby-Dick* was first
published. To judge from the books they bought, most readers in
mid-nineteenth century America were interested solely in what
Henry Nash Smith calls "the cosmic success story,"[55] and it would
be close to another century before a new generation of readers was
prepared to consider as a classic any text which didn't accentuate,
as William Dean Howells termed it, the more smiling aspects of
American life. But by the time such a generation appeared, *Moby-
Dick*'s belated acceptance as a classic was so quick to occur and so
universal in scope as to raise a very real question about whether the
book eventually found its audience or rather created one. The answer, of course, is both, which only confirms all over again what I
have said previously about the classic's curious relation to history.
Even though it reflects a world whose meanings are historically
possible, the classic must create the formal conditions under which
they can be accepted as potentially true, whereupon the form in
which those meanings are ordered and expressed becomes more or
less indistinguishable from the plausible truth they are felt to possess, becomes, in fact, the only mode by which those meanings in
all their existential probability can survive the vicissitudes of time
and remain contemporary, which is to say, timeless.

Moby-Dick seems to present an ideal example of this. A work
deeply informed by the mind of its age, which mind operated on

every level of cultural life, Melville's masterpiece nevertheless sought to subvert important components of that mind and reconstitute them in light of an altered understanding of the relationship between consciousness and experience. That the book failed to strike any responsive chord among Melville's first readers is owing chiefly to the fact that even where, as was infrequent, his readers could accept as historically possible the deficiencies of the contemporary understanding of this relationship, they could make little sense of the form in which Melville had attempted to portray the plausibility of those deficiencies or propose an alternative to them. Thus to understand the way Melville attempted to reconceive the relations between consciousness and experience, it is necessary to understand the form in which this reconceived relationship was meant to be accepted as credible. But to concede the credibility of the formal conditions in terms of which Melville reconceived the relationship between consciousness and experience is already to read him with the mind he helped to create rather than with the one he displaced.

7

In arguing that *Moby-Dick* simultaneously expressed the unconscious metaphysic, or, if you prefer, mental set, of its age and also submitted that mental set or metaphysic to extreme critical pressure, what concretely do I mean? I mean in the first instance that *Moby-Dick* gave expression to the nineteenth century's dream of power and plentitude, its absorption with fact, its love of adventure and daredeviltry, its veneration of Nature, its trust in moments of vision, its obsession with extreme states of emotion, its sense of moral self-righteousness, its love of the exotic, and, not least, its paradoxical fascination with the heroic, isolated individual and its sentimental glorification of the common man. But I mean as well that *Moby-Dick* exposed the common man's capacity for self-deception and moral cowardice; gave the lie to the view that the extraordinary individual can cut himself off from his fellows and place himself above every moral law without in the process becoming dead to feeling and an egomaniac; portrayed the exotic as nearly synonymous with the savage; found moral self-righteousness to be a seed bed for self-glorification; discovered extreme states of emotion to be a frequent indication of mental and spiritual imbalance; showed how visionary instants can blind one to the light of the commonplace; brought out the disparity between Nature's benign appearance and its sharkish reality; dramatized the pursuit of adventure as, among other things, an escape from intellectual torpor and psychological depression; perceived the trust in empirical fact to be a feeble substitute for metaphysical certainty; and suggested that the dream of power and dominion is no more than a mask for the expression of tyrannical self-assertion. Yet *Moby-Dick* did considerably more than this. In relation to its age, the book also adumbrated a new way to think about and understand such matters.

Like Hawthorne before him but in a much more radical fashion, Melville sought to displace an essentially allegorical theory of truth with one that more nearly deserves to be called symbolic. The allegorical theory, inherited somewhat indirectly from the Puritans and essentially monistic in character, posited a series of correspondences—Ahab called them "linked analogies"—between matter and mind, Nature and Spirit, on the basis of which, so it was assumed, man could confidently determine the nature of the real. The symbolic theory, on the one hand, stemming from more secular traditions and essentially pluralistic in outlook, was based on the inherent multiplicity and openness of experience, and therefore ironically undercut all pretensions to absolute certitude about the relation between subjects and objects or mind and Nature, as John Seelye has shown,[56] without completely undermining the possibility that there exists a realm of being that transcends all of man's attempts to ferret it out and comprehend its nature, as Daniel Hoffman and, before him, Newton Arvin[57] have shown.

The possible existence of this realm of being, which includes but is not exhausted by every individual attempt to define it, is attested in those parts of the novel that deserve to be called an anatomy. The anatomy, as Northrop Frye defines it,[58] is that form of fiction descended from Menippean satire which, at its purest, orders experience in terms of a single intellectual pattern or community of ideas, and there is little doubt that the anatomical elements of *Moby-Dick* constitute a large portion of the book's meaning. Indeed, Frye's four categories of prose fiction are so germane to an understanding of *Moby-Dick* that it comes as a surprise to discover that no one, to my knowledge, has discerned their pertinence.

Frye differentiates among the novel, the romance, the confession, and the anatomy. The main difference between the novel, the romance, and the confession, according to Frye, is their conception of character. Where the novel deals with characters defined against a carefully articulated social background and finds in their individual responses to a central situation or issue the clue to the quality of their souls, the romance abandons any attempt to create "real" people in favor of exploring individual personifications of ideal qualities or types which have little or no relation to a densely realized world of social particulars. As Frye puts it rather too neatly, "the romance, which deals with heroes, is intermediate between the novel, which deals with men, and the myth, which deals with gods."[59] Distinct from both the novel and the romance, at least until the modern period, is the third form of fiction which Frye calls the autobiography or confession. Here the interest is again in character but this time in the character of the writer himself and those details of his own life which, when interpreted, yield an integrated pattern. The one form which is organized in terms of something altogether unrelated to character is the anatomy, whose definition constitutes Frye's most significant and original contribution to the theory of fiction.

In the book from which it derives its name, Robert Burton's *Anatomy of Melancholy*, the anatomy is closely associated with such intellectual activities as dissection and analysis. In its characteristic form, such as that employed by Burton himself or by Izaak Walton in *The Compleat Angler*, the anatomy submits an entire society to intellectual examination either by amassing an enormous amount of information about a particular theme or by overwhelming the book's pedantic subjects with their own learning. In either case the creative element is to be found in the exhaustive play of erudition in behalf of a specific idea that is assumed to illumine an entire social world; and the form can be found stretching all the way back through Castiglione's *Book of the Courtier* and Rabelais's *Gargantua and Pantagruel* to *The Golden Ass of Apuleius*, Petronius's *Satyricon*, and Lucian's satires, and reaching forward from Swift's *Gulliver's Travels*, Voltaire's *Candide*, and Rousseau's *Emile* to Carlyle's *Sartor Resartus*, Huxley's *Brave New World*, Henry Adams's *Mont-Saint-Michel and Chartres*, and even Thomas Pynchon's *Gravity's Rainbow*.

It is Frye's conviction that no work of fiction perfectly embodies any one of these forms. Just as the forms themselves, considered historically, merge into each other through a process of subtle gradations, so every work of fiction is likely to represent a combination or amalgam of more than one of them. This last observation does a good deal more than facilitate the job of literary classification so that we can assess and evaluate particular works of literature according to standards which are appropriate to their kind. As we will see with respect to *Moby-Dick*, it also helps to determine where one looks for meaning in any particular work, and in many instances, of which *Moby-Dick* is a prominent example, considerably expands the meanings one finds there. Frye maintains that *Moby-Dick* includes elements of the romance as well as the anatomy, but I would suggest that the book also contains important elements of confession. Viewing the book schematically, one can in fact see it shifting from one form to another as it progresses, even though elements of each reappear throughout the narrative and eventually modulate the impact of the others.

The first twenty-two chapters, which include Ishmael's introduction of himself and his developing relation to Queequeg, are almost pure confession—the book begins with the words "Call me Ishmael"—and our interest lies in following Ishmael's development from his initial experience of the doldrums to his meeting with Queequeg, on through their adventures in New Bedford and Nantucket to their signing on the Pequod, and then to the fateful embarkation on Christmas Day. Throughout this confessional section there are numerous foreshadowings of what is later to come when the book turns into a romance—introduced at the very beginning with Ishmael's admission of heartsickness and the expression of his obsession with the "grand hooded phantom" that looms before his imagination as a symbol of all life's mysteries and dangers, all its enigmas and promise; renewed by the painting Ishmael discovers at Peter Coffin's Spouter Inn which, upon closer inspection, turns out to represent a huge whale in the act of impaling itself on the masts of a sailing vessel foundering during a great storm; lent added significance in the disarming descriptions of Ahab by Captain Peleg; and given a new twist during the strange interview Ishmael and Queequeg share with the prophet Elijah just before they board the ship for the voyage—but the mood in this first section is predominantly comic interspersed with the macabre, and our curiosity is centered around whether Ishmael's alternating combination of inexperience, gullibility, pluck, foolishness, wit, decency, impressionability, diffidence, and common sense will enable him to overcome the variety of obstacles that seem almost preternaturally placed in his way.

The book changes to a romance even before Ahab steps to the front "with a crucifixion in his face" and the expression of "an infinity of firmest fortitude" in his glance, during the somber meditation evoked by the image of the ethereal Bulkington in "The Lee Shore" (Chapter 23). And from then on until the diabolical sacrament on the quarterdeck (Chapter 36) and the brace of chapters that speculate on what the white whale means to Ahab and then to Ishmael (Chapters 41 and 42), the book is dominated by Ahab's presence—"a grand ungodly, godlike man," as Captain Peleg describes him, whose patrimony on the one side goes back to such demigods as Perseus, Prometheus, Hercules, and St. George, on the other to King Ahab of old, Faustus, and even Lucifer.

Nevertheless, for all his imposing scale and force, Ahab does not hold center stage past the several chapters that reflect in decending order the aftershock of the quarterdeck scene where the crew seals its pledge to join Ahab in his covenant of revenge. As early as "The Advocate" (Chapter 24), and with increasing frequency after "The Affidavit" (Chapter 45), the book begins to shift its attention both from Ishmael's development as a character and from Ahab's epic conflict with the elements to a consideration of the business of the Pequod and the industry of whaling. During the course of this section, which takes up the great bulk of the book (from "The Affidavit" to "Does the Whale Diminish" [Chapter 105]), the discussion of whales and whaling becomes a kind of extended trope for exploring what there is to know about life as a whole, and how, and with what degree of certitude, one can know it. As is typical of anatomies, much of the discussion is fanciful as well as learned, parodistic as well as speculative, but the chief purpose of this section is to transform "this whaling world" that Melville has evoked in his book into a paradigm or model of the entire human situation.

Throughout the anatomy, elements of confession and romance recur. Such chapters as "The First Lowering" (Chapter 48), "The Hyena" (Chapter 49), "The Monkey-rope" (Chapter 72), "The Fountain" (Chapter 85), "A Squeeze of the Hand" (Chapter 94), and "The Try-Works" (Chapter 96) serve to keep alive our interest in Ishmael's development and show him slowly overcoming the transcendental euphoria that first revealed itself as his chief affliction as early as "The Mast-Head" (Chapter 35), and eventually withdrawing from Ahab's diabolic quest altogether when he discovers that "there is a wisdom that is woe, but there is a woe that is madness," and thereupon realizes anew that man must learn to lower, or at least to shift, his conception of attainable felicity. Similarly, there are a variety of chapters, most especially those treating the "gams" (the meetings with other ships), which drama-tize the progress of Ahab's monomania and show him assuming in-creasingly more rigid postures of defiance. But even when Ahab takes the book over again in the chapter on his leg (Chapter 106) and *Moby-Dick* reverts back to a romance, the preceding section has done its work. Far from simply serving as ballast to keep Melville's "whale of a book" afloat, the long section of anatomy has changed the book's character both as a confession and as a romance, and the anatomy has accomplished this by setting up in counterpoint to all the views of whales and whaling that can be inferred from Ish-mael's or Ahab's stories a variety of different views or perspectives which serve to complement and even undercut them. Where the tone of the confession, as I previously noted, is essentially comic, vacillating between the extremes of farce ("The Carpet-Bag," "Chowder") and the grotesque or absurd ("The Spouter-Inn," "The Ship," "The Try-Works"), and the tone of the romance tends toward the tragic, moving between the poles of melodrama ("Sun-set," "Hark!" "The Deck, Ahab and the Carpenter") and blasphe-mous Timonism ("The Quarter-Deck," "The Candles," "The Chase. Third Day"), the tone of the anatomy is generally philo-sophic and circumspect, though lightened with numerous, playful asides, and essentially serves to cast doubt on every attempt to fathom the whale's nature—not because the whale, like everything else in life, is ultimately unknowable, but rather because, like all things living, the whale transcends in its fullness and vitality every endeavor to fix its identity in a single image. And just as the whale continually eludes every attempt to stabilize its identity in a single image, so must the imagery which Melville uses to explore the whale's general significance keep changing as well.

Among the most important of such images are those associated with lines and ropes that do double duty in *Moby-Dick*, serving both as instruments essential to the business of whaling, where their meaning is thematic, and as ligatures which bind together various components of the narrative, where their meaning and function is more directly formal. The act of binding, in fact, possesses an importance that far exceeds the splicing of lines and mending of sails and becomes one of the major symbolic activities of the entire voyage. As narrator, Ishmael is constantly involved in weaving and reweaving the book's diverse threads of meaning into a significant pattern, and this interpretive activity receives enlarged metaphorical expression on four separate occasions. The first occurs in the chapter entitled "The Mat-Maker" (Chapter 47). Here, as Ishmael is employed with Queequeg in weaving a sword-mat to be wound round the spars and rigging to keep them from chafing, he imagines himself sitting before the Loom of Time weaving a tapestry out of the basic components of life itself— Chance, Free Will, and Necessity—each of them representing terms which can be (and are) used to interpret the actions of Moby Dick during the course of the narrative. The fixed threads of the warp Ishmael likens to Necessity, which at various intervals submit to the crosswise interblending of other threads cast from the shuttle Ishmael throws at will; but the fabric itself is not completed until the woof is hit haphazardly by Queequeg's sword, which sometimes chances to strike a glancing blow, and at other times, no less accidental, meets the woof squarely. The image seems to work perfectly, with Fate, Free Will, and Chance "no wise incompatible—all interweavingly working together"—until the cry "Thar she blows!" suddenly rings out from the crow's nest and the ball of free will drops from Ishmael's hand as he rushes off to his "first lowering."

The second time this imagery receives systematic articulation is in "The Monkey-rope" (Chapter 72) when Ishmael finds himself bound to Queequeg's waist as the latter flounders below him on a dead whale's back. Queequeg, who is assisting with the cutting in and stripping operation, is simultaneously endangered on the one side by the sharks who have been drawn to this butchery and on the other by the flashing spades of Tashtego and Daggoo who are suspended above him trying to fend them off. As Ishmael meditates on the single "hempen bond" which links them together and which dictates that if Queequeg were to sink and rise no more Ishmael would be obliged to share his fate, he slowly comes to realize that the precarious situation they share in common by virtue of their "Siamese connexion" is but a symbol of the condition of all men. Ishmael's individuality has been merged into "a joint stock company of two" which can be metaphorically expanded indefinitely, uniting Christians and cannibals, civilized and primitive, in a single but multiform common destiny. Each bears the image of all, and therefore none can escape the "dangerous liabilities of that hempen bond" that, in Joseph Conrad's words, "binds men to each other and all mankind to the visible world."

The third time this imagery receives explicit formulation, and no doubt the most important, is in "A Bower in the Arsacides" (Chapter 102). Ishmael has now determined to set the whale before the reader "in his ultimatum," "his unconditional skeleton"; but Ishmael will delay performing this anatomical exercise until the following chapter when, after considerable effort, he will reluctantly concede that the attempt is futile, since "the skeleton of the whale is by no means the mould of his invested form," and "only in the heart of quickest perils; only when within the eddyings of his angry flukes; only on the profound unbounded sea, can the fully invested whale be truly and livingly found out." In the interim Ishmael tells of the strange adventure that befell him many years before the voyage of the Pequod when, during a visit with his late friend Tranquo, king of Tranque, an island of the Arsacides, he was taken inland to the king's retreat. There Ishmael's royal friend had collected a variety of barbaric rarities and distributed them "among whatever natural wonders, the wonder-freighted, tribute-rendering waves had cast upon his shores." Chief among the latter was the bleached skeleton of a great sperm whale which had been pulled up from the beach into the edge of the forest and in the course of time had become overgrown with foliage.

What meets Ishmael's eye, however, is no mere natural curiosity but a supernatural one. The whale's skeleton, now covered over by the forest, has been transformed into a chapel or temple whose floor appears "as a weaver's loom, with a gorgeous carpet on it, whereof the ground-vine tendrils formed the warp and woof, and the living flowers the figures," with the great sun above "a flying shuttle weaving the unwearied verdure." This spectacle immediately gives rise to a meditation on a kind of industrial weaver-god the sound of whose work drowns out human voices and also prevents human beings from hearing themselves in his presence. But Melville is not content to settle for this technological analogue and quickly extends the range of his image. He notes that this verdant deity, who, from another perspective, looks so like Moby Dick at the beginning of the great chase, as "a gigantic idler," is, in his entwined form, actually weaving death with life and life with death in an organic mosaic of incomparable beauty: "Life folded Death; Death trellised Life; the grim god wived with youthful Life, and begat him curly-headed glories." This is a god who embraces all ontic polarities and yet whose being cannot be identified with any of the polarities themselves but only with the mystery with which he unites them.

The fourth and final occasion when the image of weaving is introduced and is again changed comes in "The Gilder" (Chapter 114). The occasion is a meditation elicited by one of those endless days on the Japanese cruising grounds under a nurturing sun when Nature's soft brilliance and the Pacific's gentle rolls lead one to forget "the tiger heart that pants beneath it." Ishmael has been susceptible to such "ocean reveries" before, but this time he knows that such "blessed calms," whose effects are even measurable on Ahab himself, cannot last. Life is now depicted as a weaving whose warp and woof are calms and storms—"calms crossed by storms, a storm for every calm." Nor is there any progress to the pattern, any steady advance, to change the metaphor, to some "final harbor, when we unmoor no more." There is only the eternal cycle which keeps returning upon itself—"through infancy's unconscious spell, boyhood's thoughtless faith, adolescence's doubt (the common doom), then scepticism, then disbelief, resting at last in manhood's pondering repose of If." This final weaving or interpretation seems to be the most skeptical. Where we started with "fixities and definites" such as Chance, Free Will, and Necessity, which could be held in harmonious tension at least temporarily, we have moved through various stages to something as insubstantial as moods whose alternating rhythms lead in a circular fashion always back to the same subjunctive terminus and point of origin, a location midway between belief and unbelief. We are here very close to Ishmael's earlier position in "The Fountain" (Chapter 85), where he admits to "doubts of all things earthly, and intuitions of some things heavenly," and which make "neither believer nor infidel" but "a man who regards them both with equal eye." To this "The Gilder" simply adds that the secret to all such mysteries cannot be found this side of the grave, "and we must there to learn it."

What, then, it may be asked, do these various images tell us about the nature of reality itself, and how do they counterbalance the mind-annihilating, reason-shattering violence and destruction that are to follow on the last three days of the chase? The insights to be gained from these images obviously do nothing at all to deflect Ahab from his course because "the whole act," as Ahab calls it and now reasons, has been immutably decreed from the beginning. Having assumed himself at the end the Fates' lieutenant and now convinced that the path to his fixed purpose is grooved with iron rails, Ahab the theological determinist has eventually become Ahab the mechanical monist, and he will not even permit the memory of his young wife and child waiting for him back on Nantucket, or the image of mowers cutting hay in the Andes, to soften his heart or deflect his will. Submitting himself to the Parsee, Ahab has been transformed into diabolical agent of Necessity and rushes headlong upon what in the end, but only at the end, is, in both senses of the word, the equally determined brow of Moby Dick. By this time, however, we have achieved an entirely different perspective from which to view the ensuing catastrophe. Knowing that Ahab's conception of Moby Dick is partial at best and pathological at worst, we know that his quest is not only mad but blasphemous. The clues have been laid everywhere—in the dreams which have sent him screaming from his storm-tossed bed, in his asides about his own insanity, in her perverse manipulation of all reasonable arguments, in his deafness to the appeals of human sympathy and need, in his inability to cope with the plight represented by the hapless Pip, in his effect upon others such as Ishmael and the three mates as well as the rest of the crew, in the ritual machinery he employs to solidify his hold over the crew and consecrate his purpose, and, not least, in the negative comparisons one must make in connection with the numerous culture heroes with whom he is constantly compared.

But what, then, is Moby Dick, if not a symbol of all the evil "from Adam down," as Ahab believes ("Moby Dick"), or a symbol of life's horrible unknowability, as Ishmael sometimes suspects ("The Whiteness of the Whale," "Squid")? The most direct answer seems to be that he is a symbol of the entire created order in terms that simultaneously suggest everything that *can* be known about it and everything that *cannot*. R. P. Blackmur once remarked that "the artist is concerned with all the world of actual experience to which human response is possible, and he has therefore the impossible double task both of finding the means adequate to represent what experience he has had, and of finding, through the means he has, the experience he has not had." [60] As a symbol Moby Dick seems to serve this function for Melville. Capable of great destruction and invested with awesome power, he is nevertheless, like his fellow leviathans, also a victim of Nature's, and particularly of man's, sharkishness and the source of considerable natural good. Just as the whale's demise can be as brutal and poignant as that suffered by the helpless, blind, old whale who in his dying agony provides malicious sport for the barbaric Flask ("The Pequod Meets the Virgin"), so he is also the source of nourishment for man and

beast alike, his sperm oil provides light for the lamps of every nation, and the priceless ambergris extracted from his bowels serves
as a base for the world's most fragrant perfumes.

Calling Moby Dick a symbol of the ambiguity of creation itself is
perhaps to run perilously close to claiming that he is in fact a symbol of God. But Melville was much too deeply imbued with the
spirit of Calvinism ever to confuse a manifestation of God's power,
as Ahab does, with the very nature of God's essence, and he shared
sufficient affinities with the Transcendentalists to doubt that God,
if He exists, would ever become wholly and completely incarnate
in a single form. If there is a God in the universe of this book, then
Moby Dick is not that God himself but merely, as Daniel Hoffman
has argued, the greatest among His creatures and one who, in his
inscrutable but not entirely unknowable otherness, embodies as
much of the principle of divinity as Nature expresses.[61] Such a
God, if He exists, is best conceived in Paul Tillich's terms as the
"God beyond God," the God who subsumes all the other deities
men make in their own image—Father Mapple's Old Testament
Jehovah, Captain Bildad's Quaker Taskmaster, Gabriel's Shaker
God Incarnate, Pip's Divine Inert, Starbuck's reasonable Pantokra-
tor of the Quotidian, Queen Maachah of Judea's "grandissimus,"
Bulkington's "great God Absolute, the centre and circumference of
all democracy," Queequeg's Yojo, and even Ahab's clear spirit of
the fire of darkness—just as Moby Dick subsumes and transcends
all the partial interpretations he elicits. Immanent in Nature but
not identical with it, this ever-emergent creator God who in-
terweaves life with death in some larger pattern which is beyond
man's powers to discern and which is seemingly indifferent to
human desire, is, like Moby Dick himself, at once the sum of His
occasions and the remainder that is always left over. All one can
say of Him is what one can finally say of the natural world that
presumably is His handiwork. While in many of its spheres it
seems formed in fright, in certain others it seems formed in love
and, moreover, is beautiful to behold.

This insight is nowhere expressed more directly or vividly than in Ishmael's meditation on "The Tail" (Chapter 86). The tail is that point at which "the confluent measureless force of the whole whale" is most intensely concentrated. Yet the awesome, even terrifying, force with which it is invested in no way detracts from "the graceful flexion of its motions; where infantileness of ease undulates through a Titanism of power." "On the contrary," Ishmael continues, "those motions derive their most appalling beauty from it." But how is this combination of beauty and strength, of grace and power, possible, we ask? Melville's answer is neither equivocal nor evasive but merely frank. There is no explanation for this reconciliation of opposites, he avers; it is simply a fact of experience, of our experience of Nature, and must be accepted as such: "Real strength never impairs beauty . . . but often bestows it, and in everything imposingly beautiful, strength has much to do with the magic." And it is "the magic" that finally matters for Melville, that remains an essential and unalterable component of our experience—that magic unification of contrarities that constitutes the ultimate, impenetrable mystery.

In moving his reader toward this perception, it is evident that Melville availed himself of virtually every literary resource he could lay his hands on—techniques of dialogue reminiscent of Shakespeare and the Elizabethans, elements of the picaresque tradition from the history of the novel, a host of devices from the literature of romance, structural principles associated with the classical tradition of the epic, forms borrowed from seventeenth- and eighteenth-century traditions of metaphysical speculation, and a whole library of information on the subject of whales, whaling, seamanship, oceans, weather, and a variety of other scientific subjects. Yet he built his book out of the materials drawn from the common culture of his own time. To this degree his masterwork, albeit a classic, is made out of the stuff of everyday life. Hence it is no accident, as Richard Chase was the first to discern, that Melville's narrator and partial protagonist, Ishmael, in his many metamorphoses as school

teacher, raconteur, Yankee bumpkin, trickster, pedant, metaphysician, mystic, "sub-sub librarian," naif, punster, fabulator, and
bricoleur, is a distillation of virtually the whole gamut of American
folk experience.[62] Being so many things, however, one sometimes
wonders if Ishmael remains any one thing in particular, if through
all his changes and masks he retains any clear sense of identity. Do
his continued transformations deprive him of an essential self? Not
if we realize that they serve a thematic as well as narrative function. In addition to enlivening the textual surface and keeping the
full richness of the folk experience always before us, Ishmael's
great variety and diversity of reaction constitutes the sharpest possible contrast to Ahab's narrowness of response. In the teeth of
Ahab's rigidity and singlemindedness, Ishmael's plurality of being
helps dramatize the fact that experience is more multiple, more
plastic, and more unexpected than the human imagination can possibly conceive.

Yet if Ishmael can never fully perceive or articulate the most important lesson to be deduced from his experience, and if he winds
up in the "Epilogue" as no more than a fatherless orphan picked up
by "the devious-cruising Rachel" in "her retracing search for her
lost children," what authority is to be attached to his example?
Daniel Hoffman has answered this by noting that, "although Ishmael does not finally formulate the mystery he has experienced, his
experience is the knowledge, [and] his knowledge *is* the experience."[63] And Ishmael's experience, it bears repeating, draws from
and eventually reflects virtually every level of American life: "From
savagery to spindle-factories, from Old Testament Calvinism to the
gamecocks of the frontier, from demonology to capitalism, the imagery of American life on every level sinews the entire book."[64]
Thus Melville's classic does all the things a classic should do: expresses what is latent in the cultural metaphysic of its time, simultaneously challenges its underlying assumptions, and, in the process, alters our way of thinking about such things—not by
supplying us with new subjects to think about but by rearranging

the components of the thinkable into new patterns of meaning and significance.

In summary, then, our writers help form what can be called our mind insofar as they produce what can be called a classic. Our classics, in turn, create our mind and define it by shaping and coloring that luminous background against which we project all our experiences and from which we draw such interpretive resources as we have at our disposal for comprehending them. To do this, to be sure, is to do something not in a physical sense but in a symbolic one. Our classics create us, or, better, create a common mind among us, not because of anything they say about our experience but because of the light they cast it in. That light is the light shed by those interpretive paradigms we not only live by but live within. And we live within them only so long as we can see by them. Whatever their intent, their effect is to illumine our otherwise darkened and uncertain way through life by providing an "idea of order" which for the time being suffices.

5

American Literature and the Imagination of Otherness

The most profound theme that can occupy the mind of man—the problem on whose solution science, art, the bases and pursuits of nations, and everything else, including intelligent human happiness (here today, 1882, New York, Texas, California, the same as all times, all lands), subtly and finally resting, depends for competent outset and argument, is doubtless involved in the query: What is the fusing explanation and tie—what the relation between the (radical, democratic) Me, the human identity of understanding, emotions, spirit, etc., on the one side, of and with the (conservative) Not Me, the whole of the material objective universe and laws, with what is behind them in time and space, on the other side?

WALT WHITMAN
Specimen Days

In the title of an essay published several years ago called "America the Unimagining," Benjamin DeMott, one of our more observant cultural critics, drew attention to a problem which none of us can afford to take lightly. Noting the frequent public utterance of such slogans as "do your own thing" or "find your own bag" and the increased prestige, especially among the young, of the contrary tendency to seek engulfment by and complete mergence in the communal en-masse, DeMott claimed that Americans today suffer from a distinctive, though by no means exclusively American, form of myopia. Our national commitment to the ideal of personal self-fulfillment, together with our equally strong counterdesire to

175

achieve an ego-transcending oneness of identity with other people, are two sides of the same coin, he argued. Both represent a rejection of the idea that the realization of humanness, whether for oneself alone or for an entire group, "depends," as he put it, "upon my capacity and my desire to make real to myself the inward life, the subjective reality of the lives that are lived beyond me."[1] Instead, we either prate ourselves on rhetoric about the sanctity of the individual, or feed ourselves on fantasies of an undifferentiated sameness of feeling and response with other people, while remaining indifferent to, or uncomprehending of, modes of selfhood which take an expression other than our own. The problem is largely attributable to "obliviousness," he contended, "habitual refusal to harry private imaginations into constructing the innerness of other lives."[2]

In pointing to this failure of imagination, DeMott was hardly citing anything new. More than half a century earlier, William James had isolated the same problem in his essay entitled "On a Certain Blindness in Human Beings," when he noted our marked indifference to forms of existence other than our own, our habitual and pervasive intolerance of what is alien, in short, our characteristic inability through an act of the imagination to get outside of our own skins, to put ourselves in the place of others, to understand that the only hope of escaping from the prison of self-regarding egotism, without falling directly into the tranquilizing embrace of mobocracy, is by learning how to imagine, acknowledge, and value what is distinctively individual and other.

These modern jeremiads might prove less disconcerting if they were not confirmed by so much social and political fact. Unfortunately, the evidence of our imagination enervation and myopia is everywhere. Think only of the massive injustices which have been suffered by black people in this country, or the uncountable and unknown outrages we have committed against the native American, to say nothing of the discrimination we practice daily against everybody from women to homosexuals to Mexican-Americans.

Sociologists and historians are currently fond of employing an economic argument to explain these related phenomena, insisting that
they are motivated largely by greed and the concomitant desire for
political and social advantage; but surely the reasons run deeper. If
our inhumanity to minorities of all kinds in America is not to be
dismissed as simply another example of our bondage to the primal
curse, to something inherently perfidious in our nature as men and
women, then it derives rather from our inability to see, much less
feel, other people as real human beings. Anyone who deviates from
the official norm, whatever that is, anyone who fails to bear a like-
ness to the Standard Product, is simply not viewed as fully human,
and then becomes at best invisible, at worst a threat to the national
security.

James's prescription for this malady was slightly different from
DeMott's. With the optimism of a man reared in the middle of the
nineteenth century, James could still find Whitman's belief in the
plenitudinous variety of common life a bracing alternative, and was
thus inclined to exhort his audience to turn their attention to the
sublime human effulgence in the world about them. Failing the
possibility of this, he counseled remaining faithful to one's own opportunities and blessings "without presuming to regulate the rest of
the vast field," [3] hoping that a little modesty in such matters would
eventually dispose people to be more receptive to one another.

DeMott is not so sanguine. Because of his more vivid awareness
"of a general, culturewide dimming of the lights of inward life," [4]
he is much more pessimistic about our capacity through imaginative vision to renew our saving contact with all that lies outside the
perimeters of the self. Worse, he finds the past, and particularly
the more notable cultural and intellectual representatives of that
past, of little assistance in teaching us what it means "to grasp
another being's difference from within." [5] As D. H. Lawrence
demonstrated more than half a century ago in his *Studies in Classic
American Literature*, those of our writers, like Whitman and Poe,
who have meditated deeply on the stunted quality of American

lives, have usually proposed as an antidote, not the need for an imaginative, sympathetic fathoming of individual differences, but rather some illusory fantasy of engrossment with or complete submergence in the life of the "other." "And whenever the engrosser or merger disappears from American letters, an even more frightening figure—the self-bound man (Captain Ahab is the prince)—stands forth in his place."[6]

Thus when DeMott scans the American past for usable intellectual and spiritual resources, he comes away largely disappointed. The only "countervoices" he can find to our national Emersonian inclination either to withdraw back into the private sanctity of the self or to relinquish that sanctity in favor of fusing with the All, are few and far between. John Dewey is one, George Herbert Mead another, the sociologist Charles Horton Cooley a third, among that relatively small group of representative American thinkers who have at least understood what James was talking about and have thus tried, with varying degrees of success, to keep alive a sense of the importance of individual differences, of the distinction between the self and the other.

In his statement of the issue, DeMott is surely correct, but in his assessment of the cultural resources we possess for dealing with it, I think he is mistaken. If few of our classic writers and thinkers have provided us with any ready-made solutions to this problem— have shown us, for example, what it would be like to see, feel, and experience other selves as real and distinct—nonetheless a striking number of them have been obsessed with its consequences, and in their obsessive ways have realized, perhaps almost in spite of themselves, just what kind of problem it really is. By this I simply mean that many American writers have clearly perceived—though scarcely in always identical ways—that the problem of imagining and responding to that which is experienced as "other" is at once an ethical and a religious problem—ethical insofar as it involves a question of the "right relation" to that which is experienced as "other," religious insofar as it also involves a question about the nature of reality so experienced. That is to say, they have conceived of what might be called "the problem of otherness" as a problem pertaining not only to man's possible growth and fulfillment, to his capacities for imaginative self-transcendence, but also to the nature and meaning of life when it is perceived to be ingredient with just such possibilities. Hence their characteristic metaphysical preoccupation with what Emerson called in *Nature* the distinction—indeed, the transaction—between the "Me" and the "not-Me," and their consequent ethical interest in determining, under the widest variety of circumstances, the moral norms which might best govern and regulate this transaction. To explore this ethical and metaphysical impulse which determines the shape and substance of so much American writing is to penetrate to the very core of the American tradition. It is also to repossess many of the ways in which that tradition may still serve as a resource for helping us cope with one of our most crippling and destructive problems as a people.

Yet there is no blinking the distance which separates most contemporary Americans from all talk of "other" minds, "other" selves, indeed, of "otherness" itself. For in a world bounded on the one side by the agonies and atrocities of Vietnam or the American urban ghetto and on the other by televised moon landings and cloning experiments, it would appear that we wonder, if at all, only about what is left to wonder at or wonder about. The imaginative capacity for wonder—whether it takes the primitive form of awed and passive astonishment before the unexpected, or the more sophisticated form of active, imaginative penetration into modes of being other than our own—requires a special openness to the unanticipated, a certain susceptibility to surprise, and most of us can no longer allow ourselves to be so vulnerable. Instead of remaining receptive to novelty, we have become rotten-ripe with knowingness as the imagination's last defense in a world which, if experienced directly, might stun us back into the Stone Age. Having inured ourselves to strangeness with a surfeit of information, we have grown all but dead to those startling confrontations with otherness that have traditionally given shape and substance to the literature which has created as well as reflected so much of our national experience.

The reasons are not hard to find. In the shadows of a possible nuclear holocaust, where we have now lived for more than a quarter of a century, reality takes on proportions of enormity simply too vast, too horrific, for the imagination to grasp. What we have made, what in fact we have it in our power to do, is now beyond our capacity to dream. Suddenly there seem to be no "others" more monstrous than the ones which, if Marshall McLuhan is correct, are mere extensions of ourselves, and this is something beyond the compass of even our darkest "night thoughts." Yet when morning finally comes and the shadows of disaster lift at least high enough for us to see the landscape about us, all we are still likely to find is something we have put there ourselves, something which in the daylight may look more like a metropolis than a mushroom cloud but which, as Thomas Pynchon has suggested in *The Crying of Lot 49*, is less identifiable as a city "than [as] a grouping of concepts—census tracts, special purpose bond-issue districts, shopping nuclei, all overlaid with access roads to its own freeway."

To be sure, even in a world whose most discernible and meaningful patterns suggest nothing so much as the printed circuitry of a transistor radio, one may still, as with Pynchon's heroine, Oedipa Maas, discover what appears to be "a heiroglyphic sense of concealed meaning, . . . an intent to communicate." The problem is that when the environment has become but an extension of man himself, there is no way of telling the difference between what Robert Frost calls "counter-love, original response" and "our own voice back in copy speech." Thus one is left yearning, as Americans have always been, for "a world elsewhere"[7] beyond the self and independent and even other than the self, yet suspicious that whatever traces of it are left constitute evidence of nothing so much as our own delusion or paranoia. In such circumstances as these, wonder gives way all too easily either to cynicism or ecstatic frenzy, yearning to submission or resentment, and hope to the madness of boredom.

This is a prospect of which American writers, at least since the time of Jonathan Edwards, have been acutely conscious. Had they foreseen it with any less clarity, they would not have so consistently depicted life's greatest terrors in terms of the imagery of absolute abandonment. From Jonathan Edwards's Enfield sermon, where the self is faced with the appallingly modern prospect of being suspended over the abyss of non-being, through Walt Whitman's poignant image of the poet as "a noiseless, patient spider" sending out filament after filament "till the ductile anchor hold, Till the gossamer thread you fling catch somewhere," and on to John Berryman's Henry poems, where the self, reeling from his memory "of the vanished on their uncanny errands" and his own "need, need, need until he went to pieces," is compelled out of his own desperate loneliness to make the pieces sit up and write—in all these ways American writers have exhibited their horror at the thought of a world without others.

This obsession even infects our poetics. Herman Melville, though hardly the first, was surely the most famous of our writers to liken literature to religion on the grounds that each presents us with "another world" to which we can still feel the tie. And Wallace Stevens, a poet not otherwise noted for his receptivity to the numinous, went even further by arguing that, in a time of disbelief, when we have experienced the eclipse, if not the departure, of all the gods, literature must provide us with the satisfactions and consolations formerly guaranteed by faith, by mediating "for us a reality not ourselves," by revealing "something 'wholly other' by which the inexpressive loneliness of thinking is broken and enriched."[8] Poignant as these observations are, they reveal that we are Emerson's children still. Like him, we continue to interpret the "fall into existence" as a discovery of the disjunction between the self and all that stands outside it; and like him, even when circumstances have conspired to challenge our faith in the existence of both, we continue to assume that the secret of our destiny and the key to our deliverance is bound up with the relation the one bears to the other.

I

It must be conceded at the outset that Emerson's distinction between the "Me" and the "not-Me" has been formulated in very different terms by different writers in the American tradition. In Jonathan Edwards's theology, for example, this distinction is disclosed in what, at least from the human side of the equation, is the impassable experiential chasm between man's consciousness of himself as a wretched and unworthy sinner and God's absolute sovereignty and perfect love. In James Fenimore Cooper's fiction, on the other hand, it is expressed in the distinction between the ways of the world, of civilization, and the ways of the forest or Nature. In the poetry of Walt Whitman it manifests itself in the difference between the "simple, separate self" and the "democratic en-masse." In the fiction of Henry James it is epitomized by the contrast between American innocence and aspiration and European sophistication and decadence. In the novels of Theodore Dreiser it surfaces as the polarity between the unformed individual yearning to achieve social outline and the brute impersonality of the city. Yet, however the "other," the "not-Me," is conceived—whether as God or Being in Edwards, Nature in Emerson and Thoreau, Europe in Henry James, other selves in *Huck Finn*, the democratic mass in Whitman, or the city in Dreiser—it inevitably becomes that factor which, as Emerson said in "Experience," precipitates man's fall into existence and thus inaugurates his conscious life as an adult self. That fall can, of course, turn into a deadly plunge if the "other" exercises a governance over the self which is malevolent as well as pervasive, destructive as well as despotic; but without an experience of it, man never passes beyond the state of dreaming innocence, of blissful but infantile ignorance, which, as the authors of *Billy Budd* and *The Golden Bowl* both realized, possesses a potential for evil all its own.

This is not to say that American writers have projected but one manner of relating to the "other." Having defined it in a variety of ways, they have as surely portrayed a wide diversity of reactions to it. Melville's Ahab, for instance, experiences the "not-Me," that "other" epitomized so completely by Moby-Dick himself, as a personal outrage, a gigantic affront to his sense of "Me." Thus when the "not-Me," the "other," turns against him in a seeming act of vengeance, Ahab is driven into a fury of mind-annihilating hatred and rushes headlong to destroy it. Whitman, by contrast, views the "other" as comrade and thus seeks a relationship of reciprocal coequality with it. Robinson Jeffers plays still another variation on this theme by opting neither for the self in opposition to the "other," nor for a relationship of harmonious coexistence with it, but rather for the "other's" absolute dominion over the self. What is needed, as Jeffers declared in his book of 1948, *The Double Axe*, is a philosophy of "Inhumanism": "a shifting of emphasis and significance from man to not-man; the rejection of human solipsism and recognition of trans-human magnificence." [9]

A survey of such reactions tells us nothing in itself; it is important only to the extent that it demonstrates the view shared by so many of our writers, that man becomes fully human, or at least comes fully into possession of such opportunities as are afforded him to be human, only to the degree that he is willing to acknowledge the "other" and then respond to it. At the very most, as Melville knew, this can turn the life of the "meanest mariners, renegades and castaways" into a subject fit for great dramatic tragedy. At the very least, as the contemporary poet and novelist James Dickey has shown, it can shock us out of the boredom and complacency of the daily round, out of the grim banalities of everydayness, and thus retrieve for us some comprehension of what Alfred North Whitehead meant by the word *importance*, that root notion by which we distinguish between crude matter-of-fact and its significance. In either case, the object of all such experiences remains the same. As Dickey reminds us in the title of his first novel, the aim of all such experiences is nothing short of *Deliverance*.

Though I would hardly want to make any very large claims for Dickey's novel itself, it must be acknowledged that Dickey could scarcely have chosen a title for his novel better calculated to resonate with our deepest sense of ourselves, even our religious sense of ourselves, as a people. For in each one of its three meanings—as a state of being in which one is freed from restraint or captivity, as an act of transmitting or turning over something to an intended recipient, and as a form of authoritative self-expression—the word "deliverance" carries us all the way back to the motives which initially propelled the first colonists toward these shores in the beginning. As we now know after a generation of superb scholarship on the seventeenth century, deliverance is not only what the first Puritans thought they were seeking for themselves and their immediate posterity by, in Cotton Mather's words, "flying from the deprivations of Europe, to the American Strand"; it is also what they believed they could secure for all of Europe besides by erecting here a true theocratic society which might then serve as a model for the reformation of the rest of Western Christendom. Thus deliverance entailed not merely fleeing the restraints of the Old World for the freedom of the New, but also undertaking an experiment in theocracy truly expressive of the new faith to which they had been converted, which might then be perceived as an example worthy of universal, worldwide emulation.

Yet, as Perry Miller was the first to argue, the Puritans were largely deceived on all counts.[10] Not only were they unable to secure deliverance for the civilization they left behind, since Europeans generally failed to get the message; they had, in turn, no sooner gained a foothold on the edge of this new continent when for a variety of reasons the experiment itself began to turn sour. As so many Puritan historians have reconstructed it, this must have been a terrible moment in the history of New England. The Puritans' hopes for deliverance were inextricably tied to two propositions: first, that they could erect a civil state in the New World organized as strictly as possible according to theological principles derived from scripture and tradition; and second, that this new society could then serve as a redemptive beacon in the wilderness directing a fallen world back to the light of God's truth. But when European Christians failed to fix their attention upon any but the economic implications of this attempt to build, in John Winthrop's fine phrase, "a City upon a Hill," the American settlers were left alone with their theocratic experiment. And when by the second or third generation the experiment itself had begun to fail—for by then anyone could plainly see that the community was rife with dissension, backsliding, licentiousness, apostasy, or just plain apathy—the colonists were left alone, so to speak, with America herself, or, better, with the wilderness, since that was really all that the continent amounted to. The wilderness, in other words, together with European neglect, had taken its toll, and there was little choice but to come to terms with it or perish both physically and spiritually.

We know, of course, what happened. Rather than perish those early Americans decided to come to grips, but the price was larger than they first realized. Having undertaken "an errand into the wilderness," as Samuel Danforth described it, to secure deliverance both for themselves and for the rest of the world, the original Puritan theocrats discovered within several generations that the nature of their errand had been so drastically altered by the "otherness" of New World conditions that such deliverance as they had originally pursued could only be achieved by coming to terms with the American wilderness itself.[11] As the realm of the "other," of the "not-Me," the wilderness had begun to force upon them a redefinition of their consciousness as transplanted Europeans, a reconception of their sense of "Me." Whatever they had once been, they could no longer exactly remain. As with Kate Croy at the end of Henry James's *The Wings of the Dove*, they were compelled to admit: "We shall never be again as we once were!" [12]

The religious implications of this shift in theological perspective were enormous. Where in the beginning the wilderness or America had been but the location of an errand of the spirit run for other reasons altogether, by the end of the first century of settlement the wilderness or America itself had somehow become the chief reason for running spiritual errands at all. [13] The errand itself retained its theological impulse, the quest for deliverance, but the terms in which that aim was now formulated or could be realized had begun to change drastically. Deliverance, that is to say, was now conceived less as a problem of coming to grips with the Christian witness of faith or with the theocratic community than with the American strand itself. Or, to put it slightly differently, America— or at least that aspect of it that was most accessible to lived experience—had now begun to supplant both the Christian scriptures and the inherited faith of the fathers as the chief source of mediation for that encounter with "otherness," with the "not-Me," which, to the degree that Americans remained religious at all, continued to be both the origin and goal of their experience as *homo religiosus*.

2

In using this last phrase, I mean to suggest what historians of religion have taught us about man's experience as a religious being. According to Mircea Eliade, for instance, man becomes religious to the extent that he seeks reunification with those transmundane elements of his experience which are perceived to break through the profane dimensions of his existence and to confront him with a sense of "otherness" over which he has virtually no control. Yet since almost any object of existence both can and does serve to mediate this sense of "otherness" to man, the words *sacred* and *profane* apply not to different kinds of objects which confront us in experience but rather to different ways of perceiving and then relating ourselves to them. The clue to the distinction between these two differently perceived objects, then, derives from the power we impute to them and the point of origin we imagine for them. Even though sacred objects are accessible to us only within the world of profane existence, their liminal character and potency of expression make them appear to originate from beyond it. Man responds religiously to such objects, Eliade contends, only when he seeks through myth and ritual to repeat those acts *in illo tempore* by which their sacred character was first made manifest.

Joseph Bettis has illumined this distinction nicely when he writes that if man's purpose in relation to things perceived as profane is to shape them according to his needs, man's purpose in relation to things perceived as sacred is to bring himself into conformity with them.[14] This is chiefly effected through what Eliade and others call the *mode of repetition*, that religious strategy whereby primitive man, in imitation of the divine acts of creation through which the sacred discloses itself, attempts to conform himself to and remain within the sacred sphere, and to extend its dominion over the ephemeral world of the profane.[15]

For moderns, however, this strategy tends to require modification. Even if modern man can still acknowledge the distinction between the sacred and the profane, it is clear that he is much too conscious of the historicity of all experience to believe that the dimension of the sacred points to any realm of being which is stable and fixed for all eternity and to which he can simply attempt to conform. Though history may not exhaust for him what constitutes the realm of the Really Real, modern man knows—as the very terms of his identity as modern assume—that there is nothing real which does not change. Hence he is unable to conform himself to a model of the real which is fixed and timeless simply because he cannot believe that there is anything which is fixed, stable, and timeless. The result, in those cases where modern man retains, or strives to repossess, any trace of what might be called a religious orientation, is a marked alteration of his use of the *mode of repetition*, which is precipitated by an equally important alteration in his relation to what is experienced as "other."

Primitive man might be said to view the encounter with "otherness" as a mode of access to what Emerson called "a world elsewhere," a realm which, though revealing itself within the sphere of the profane, is nonetheless assumed to originate from beyond it. Just because of its stability and perdurance, this "other world" is assumed to be the "real" one and thus serves as model and norm for all that transpires in the unreal and haphazard realm of historical time. Modern man, on the other hand, just because he knows of no world untouched by the vicissitudes of temporality, tends to view the encounter with "otherness" instead as a mode of access to possibilities of change and development within the self and the self's relation to whatever is experienced as "other." To put it another way, reality for moderns, even religious moderns, is generally not identified with any worlds which exist, as it were, elsewhere, but is rather associated, insofar as we retain any imagination of other worlds, of "otherness" at all, with the process by which we respond to their imagined incursions from "beyond" and then attempt to readjust and redefine ourselves as a consequence.

When this brief excursion into the philosophy and history of religions is brought to bear upon the experience of those first American colonists, it becomes somewhat easier to understand how a shift in their perception of the location of "otherness," and the experience which precipitated and attended that shift, became an archetypal or paradigmatic one for subsequent Americans. Before the location of what was conceived to be "other" had shifted from scripture and tradition to the American wilderness, our forefathers had responded to the "Other" pretty much as archaic man always had. Their original encounters with "otherness" through scripture and tradition had convinced them that in order to reunite and conform themselves to its holy energies, they must repeat through myth (the rehearsal of the Word), ritual (the owning of the covenant), and, particularly, world-founding (the establishment of a theocracy) those divine acts by which life for the Puritan was revealed to be sacred both in origin and destiny. The keystone of the arch was the relation of the covenant, whereby God had originally called Israel to be His people in seeking to establish His reign in history. The Puritans saw themselves as belonging to the same continuity of election and considered the erection of a theocratic society as its inevitable expression. The establishment of a theocracy which united the civil and ecclesiastical realms was conceived to be as perfect an imitation as man could achieve here on earth of that model of the God-man relationship which was fixed for all eternity in Heaven. In patterning their life on earth after the very letter of the divine model, they intended to preserve themselves, as primitive man always has, in the realm of the sacred, and to extend its hegemony over the whole of the profane world.

When the sheer intractability of the wilderness caused their experiment to go awry, however, this not only precipitated a shift in their understanding of the nature and domain of the "Other," but also began to alter considerably their mode of relating to it. To foreshorten and radically simplify, it would seem as though the original colonists came to these shores with something like a primitive or archaic religious orientation but within a relatively few generations had acquired something closer to a modern one, perhaps the preeminently modern one. The existence of the wilderness had confronted them with a fact of "otherness" which profoundly threatened their identity as transplanted Europeans. In throwing their former identity into serious question, it thrust them into a situation where they could no longer repeat the saving formulas of the past and hope to survive, where they could no longer simply attempt to imitate, as it were, what they regarded as fixed models of reality and manage to cope. Faced with the constantly fluctuating, frequently novel, and often unexpected conditions of New World experience, it was therefore inevitable that an interest in discerning the order of being revealed by the "Other" and then attempting to accommodate oneself to it was slowly supplanted by a new interest in the actual process of response and redefinition itself.

The result, if I may borrow a phrase from Wallace Stevens, was nothing short of a revolution in the American "idea of order." Where the earliest Americans, say from the seventeenth century to the beginning of the nineteenth, tended to derive their ultimate ideas of order from the order of being they imputed to the "Other" revealed in scripture and vouchsafed to the tradition, later Americans, certainly from Emerson and Whitman onwards, tended to derive their ideas of order instead from their own innately human (though for some simultaneously divine) capacities to redefine and regenerate themselves in response to their experience of it. In either case, however, the incitement was, and remains, the same. Suddenly brought, in F. Scott Fitzgerald's words, "face to face for the last time in history with something commensurate to . . . [their] capacity for wonder,"[16] Americans could no longer look for salvation, for deliverance, in the theological formulations and injunctions of the past, but were compelled to find it, if at all, in what they could make of their New World situation. And thus was born what I believe Perry Miller was the first to describe as the essential paradigm of the American experience.

Parenthetically, it is important to add that it took years, even centuries, for a recurrent element in the actual experience of so small a group of Americans as the New England Puritans to become in time a unifying, interpretive thread in the experience of us all. And it did so only because the Puritans' experience of America as a disproving ground for what Daniel Boorstin calls utopias and what Perry Miller referred to as theocratic experiments was but the first in a series of jarring confrontations between the beliefs, dreams, and convictions of individual Americans (as well as American communities) and the "otherness" of the actual materials of reality in America. Furthermore, it was only as this recurrent pattern then worked its way down over the generations into our national consciousness and was there found and eventually given imaginative release by certain of our classic writers and thinkers that the experience itself took on the shape of a fully developed paradigm.

Though the paradigm to which I refer has been revised and elaborated by such various critics and scholars as R. W. B. Lewis, Leslie Fiedler, A. N. Kaul, Leo Marx, and Richard Poirier, its essential character remains pretty much as Miller initially described it.[17] Reduced to its fundamental components, that paradigm depicts a single, solitary self who is either characteristically transplanted from another culture (and hence unfinished), or essentially unformed and uncultivated (and hence innocent), falling, so to speak, into experience and encountering there that ideal "Other" in response to which he must, at the minimum, redefine himself and, at the maximum, virtually recreate himself. Whether the ideal "Other" confronts him in the form of God, the wilderness, Nature, other selves, history, the city, or the machine, man's chief aim in response to this "Other" is neither, at least initially, to try to define it nor, necessarily, to enter into a relationship with it. Though both of these things may follow as a consequence, the essential purpose of man's encounter with "otherness" is to compel him however he responds—whether with love, despair, submission, recoil, outrage, or awe—into some new understanding of and relationship to himself. The desired goal, whether successfully achieved or tragically frustrated, is deliverance and new life, and the method is always some form of *decreation*, a sloughing off of the old ways in response to the encounter with something astonishingly new.

3

To give this more concrete expression, I wish to examine in turn several short poems where some variant of the paradigm—indeed, what I shall later argue is in each case a historically significant variant of the paradigm—is presented in miniature. I have chosen poems rather than novels only because their brevity allows me to analyze in some depth the way the paradigm shapes their form and substance. But the paradigm itself, insofar as it constitutes our essential story, is no more restricted to the mode of poetry than it is, say, to the literary tradition which derives from our Puritan past. In point of fact, its chief exemplifications, as I shall presently indicate, are to be found in our longer fictions, where it has somewhat unexpectedly proven to be equally as useful in the ordering of Southern and Western experience as of New England, and of black experience as well as of white.

My first example is a relatively little-known poem by Emily Dickinson which, like those to follow, brilliantly exemplifies the *decreative* method. As will be quickly noted, the poem is concerned to describe a fundamental change in attitude, really a basic alteration of belief. The significance of that change, however, lies less in its specific nature and character than in the reasons for it, and their consequent impact upon the shaken speaker. The perceptive reader will immediately discern that the speaker's ironic tone at the beginning of the poem becomes tempered and grave at the end. In the beginning, the speaker is witty and knowing about the superficiality of conventional religious practice; by the end, however, her playful knowingness has been supplanted by an attitude that is more tentative and reserved. Where before she seemed at great remove from her subject, she now speaks from the immediacy of present experience. This alteration in attitude is caused by the sudden intrusion of the American landscape, whose striking images not only disrupt the poem but also transform the speaker's faith. Witty skepticism gives way to stunned belief as the American wilderness—but a trope for America herself—forces the speaker out of the complacency of diffident agnosticism and into a new attitude of religious wonder and awe. The poem is as follows:

> My period had come for Prayer—
> No other Art—would do—
> My Tactics missed a rudiment—
> Creator—Was it you?

God grows above—so those who pray
Horizons—must ascend—
And so I stepped upon the North
To see this Curious Friend—

His House was not—no sign had He—
By Chimney—nor by Door
Could I infer his Residence—
Vast Prairies of Air

Unbroken by a Settler—
Were all that I could see—
Infinitude—Had'st Thou no Face
That I might look on Thee?

The Silence condescended—
Creation stopped—for Me—
But awed beyond my errand—
I worshipped—but did not "pray"—

In the first two stanzas, the speaker is in complete control of the poem as she condescends to mock, however politely, the kind of civilized religion which approaches prayer as an exercise in spiritual artifice, requiring the proper tactics. God is merely one of the rudiments for a satisfactory performance, and if he is sensed somehow to be missing, one simply looks for him in the usual place where people have always located the God made in their own image. But once the speaker steps out of the protected enclosure of her own mocking contempt, once she steps "upon the North/To see this Curious Friend," she quickly discovers that the American landscape refuses to afford her the anticipated prospect: "His House was not—no sign had He—/By Chimney—nor by Door." The quaint "Residence" she had at least half expected to find, which would have kept matters comfortably domestic and therefore easy to ridicule, is suddenly swallowed up by "Vast Prairies of Air/Unbroken by a Settler." Although this marvelously native image, which conspires to fling open the doors of the poem onto the vacant and immense spaciousness of the American continent, is carefully prepared for by the speaker's ascent of horizons towards the American vista, it is still so striking that the third stanza needs the fourth to complete its thought, as though the speaker's rigid self-control were suddenly breaking down with the verse form. The "Creator" is no longer the familiar "Curious Friend" of stanza two but a featureless "Infinitude" who shatters the speaker's former self-assurance.

In the seemingly endless and unexplored open spaces of the American wilderness, none of the old names for the Diety nor the old rituals for domesticating Him any longer suffice. The traditional tactics of familiarity and the previous attitude of condescension, both of which came so easily and naturally at the beginning of the poem, have now been fundamentally altered by New World conditions. Contempt for the religion of domesticity and civility gives way to a recovery of the capacity for wonder and awe, as the formerly sophisticated and faintly cynical speaker is stunned into silence and veneration before certain of the sovereign and totally unaccommodating facts of the American experience. Whether these facts promise life or death, felicity or failure, we are not told. All we can do is measure their effects. Suddenly brought face to face with what is not the self, or even any possible projection of the self, the speaker confronts the "Other," the "not-Me," and is left in a profound state of shock, which is also a new state of being— "awed beyond my errand—/I worshipped—but did not pray."

This conclusion of the poem has a startling and unsettling quality about it, not only because it arrives so abruptly and unexpectedly, but also because it does and does not resolve the initial situation. Having originally set out to comment upon the termination of what is regarded as an odious kind of spiritual exercise, in this case prayer, the speaker is suddenly left at the end of the poem recalling the inexplicable commencement of a different and wholly unforeseen and unmanagable kind of spiritual experience called worship. In this, of course, the open-ended form of the poem bears striking affinities with many other American works. Whether one considers Hawthorne's *Scarlet Letter* or Mark Twain's *Huck Finn*, Fitzgerald's *Gatsby* or Hemingway's stories from *In Our Time*, Henry James's *Portrait of a Lady* or Ralph Ellison's *Invisible Man*, American writers display a penchant for bringing their characters to a state of sudden illumination and then leaving them, as it were, at the end of the book to work out their salvation in fear and trembling. The reason, I would submit, is a function of their interests and concerns as writers, and casts fresh light back upon the poem by Emily Dickinson.

Unlike their counterparts in English and European tradition, American writers often exhibit such interest as they have in human nature, not by inferring from the settled manners and morals of their characters the enduring qualities of their souls, but rather by submitting their characters to sudden, often violent, confrontations with "otherness" to see whether, and, if so, to what degree and with what effect, they can change. Hence, their concern, and the Emily Dickinson poem is but a single, striking example of this, is not with everyman in his humor but with everyman, as Whitman would have said, on the road.[18] The issue is whether man can be transformed along the way, and the incitement to such transformations always springs from those startling confrontations with "otherness" which simultaneously threaten and promise to astonish man into what Emerson called "an original relation to the universe."

"The Most of It" by Robert Frost offers both a vivid illustration of this desire for "an original relation to the universe" and also an ironic comment on it. In the beginning, the all-too-recognizable Emersonian figure standing solitary in the midst of the natural world is almost tempted into the illusion that he is the sole proprietor of the world he surveys. By crying out on life for a "voice in answer" which is more than "the mocking echo of his own," he would seek some reciprocal relation to the universe, in this case a relation of mutual coequality and comradeship—"not his own love back in copy speech,/But counter-love, original response." Yet

nothing ever comes of what he cries, unless it is "the embodiment"
that crashes "In the cliff's talus on the other side" and then, "instead of proving human when it near[s]/And someone else additional to him,/As a great buck it powerfully appear[s]." This, to be
sure, is a revelation of something and not nothing, and in the
words of Gerardus van der Leeuw's definition of the primordial
religious object, of something "that is a *highly exceptional* and *ex-*
tremely impressive 'Other.' "[19] At the same time, however, it is also a
revelation of something which in the very alienation of its "otherness" undercuts the initial presumption of the figure's expectation
even in the process of fulfilling it.

> He thought he kept the universe alone;
> For all the voice in answer he could wake
> Was but the mocking echo of his own
> From some tree-hidden cliff across the lake.
> Some morning from the boulder-broken beach
> He would cry out on life, that what it wants
> Is not its own love back in copy speech,
> But counter-love, original response.
> And nothing ever came of what he cried
> Unless it was the embodiment that crashed
> In the cliff's talus on the other side,
> And then in the far distant water splashed,
> But after a time allowed for it to swim,
> Instead of proving human when it neared
> And someone else additional to him,
> As a great buck it powerfully appeared,
> Pushing the crumpled water up ahead,
> And landed pouring like a waterfall,
> And stumbled through the rocks with horny tread,
> And forced the underbrush—and that was all.

At the end the ironic reversal of the protagonist's need and expectation, of an answering response which would signify recognition, community, even love, is doubled by virtue of the images
which the poet uses, remorselessly piling one on top of the next, to
dramatize the nature of that which is made manifest. The epiphany

which disrupts the protagonist's lonely vigil occurs in a natural setting, and yet the images employed to characterize its awesome, powerful movement through the water and then up onto land— "crashed," "splashed," "pushing the crumpled water up ahead," "landed pouring like a waterfall," "stumbled through the rocks with horny tread," and "forced the underbrush"—make us think less of the noisy approach of a large animal than of something like the beaching of an enormous landing craft or outer space machine. And this, as a consequence, only underscores the fearful strangeness of the apparition and the now even more terrible sense of isolation of the lonely and impotent witness.

An additional factor contributing to the protagonist's terrible sense of isolation and loneliness is the speaker's own absolute neutrality of tone. At no point does he intercede with a sympathetic aside or an interpretive comment, but instead allows the twofold irony of the protagonist's situation to work itself out to its merciless conclusion, a conclusion all the more merciless just because the final phrase, "And that was all," allows no margin of response either for the protagonist or for the speaker. What the protagonist wants is an "other" who is understanding and loving, a kind of comrade and friend; what he gets is a Something which is brutally indifferent and unfeeling. The only antidote to an encounter with this kind of "otherness," the poem seems to say, is the speaker's stoic neutrality of tone, a tone which refuses to sentimentalize the protagonist's situation because it would avail the protagonist nothing in the face of the harsh truth he must simply learn to accept.

Yet, in a sense, the speaker's stoic neutrality of tone *does represent* an intelligent and compassionate response, even if it comes from the poet rather than from something within the presented scene. The poet has put himself in the place of someone who neither gets what he wants from reality nor even what he could conceivably have expected; that someone, in turn, receives a sympathetic and original response even though it is ironically conveyed through the poet's reluctance to soften in any way the shock of the protagonist's discovery. The poet's discrete neutrality constitutes a kind of "counter-love" simply because it indicates the only way in which the awful finality of the protagonist's shuddering discovery may be borne.

William Carlos Williams's "By the road to the contagious hospital" begins almost where the Frost poem leaves off, in a world which refuses to offer any accommodation to the self's desire for an original and reciprocal relation with reality, but it then discovers through a new strategy of the imagination hidden resources in the unaccommodating landscape which bring new life both to the speaker and to the scene he surveys. One could say that this poem is built upon a cliché, the transition from winter to spring with its attendant emergence of new life out of death. But the power and vitality of Williams's poem derives from the way this process of rebirth is effected, from the way it precipitates a marriage between the details which are seen and the quickened power of perception through which they are given new visual life, a marriage which ultimately unites the emerging details themselves with the power that enables all things to be.

> By the road to the contagious hospital
> under the surge of the blue
> mottled clouds driven from the
> northeast—a cold wind. Beyond, the
> waste of broad, muddy fields
> brown with dried weeds, standing and fallen
>
> patches of standing water
> the scattering of tall trees
>
> All along the road the reddish
> purplish, forked, upstanding, twiggy
> stuff of bushes and small trees
> with dead, brown leaves under them
> leafless vines—
>
> Lifeless in appearance, sluggish
> dazed spring approaches—

They enter the new world naked,
cold, uncertain of all
save that they enter. All about them
the cold, familiar wind—

Now the grass, tomorrow
the stiff curl of wildcarrot leaf

One by one objects are defined—
It quickens: clarity, outline of leaf

But now the stark dignity of
entrance—Still, the profound change
has come upon them: rooted they
grip down and begin to awaken

Much of what the poem accomplishes results from what might be called an act of transcendence downward, where the eye of the observer is forced to make fresh contact with the actual and below that with whatever it is that pushes the actual, to reverse the spatial figure, back up both into being and into consciousness. Our eye, following the motions of the poem, moves from "the surge of . . . blue/mottled clouds driven from the/northeast" above the landscape, down across a "waste of broad, muddy fields/brown with dried weeds, standing and fallen," which is dotted with "patches of standing water," and then, finally, to the objects nearest to sight along the road—"the reddish,/purplish, forked, upstanding, twiggy/stuff of bushes and small trees." We know that there is evidence of waste and death here in this barren landscape even before we are told of the "dead, brown leaves" under those trees and the "leafless vines" presumably clinging to them. This is a scene out of the modern wasteland whose presiding institutional symbol is the contagious disease hospital, a scene we might simply accept without further thought if our attention had not already begun to be drawn to some of the idiosyncratic features of the details we had been compelled to observe along the way. But once having been obliged to notice those features, we cannot help taking a new interest in the otherwise ironic announcement, made almost as a kind of afterthought, that "sluggish,/dazed spring approaches." "Lifeless in appearance," spring's approach is nonetheless felt as a reality. As the apparently lifeless details of the natural scene become more vivid, they begin to stir with freshening vitality. Suddenly the eye finds itself in the process of witnessing the revivifying of those details which, more than announcing the arrival of spring, appears to define, to enable, to constitute spring's very existence—the naked bulbs on bare branches, the fragile blades of grass beginning to tuft the dark ridges of mud, both evoking the thought of "tomorrow" and "the stiff curl of wildcarrot leaf." As spring appears, objects "one by one" begin to be defined, or, what amounts to the same thing, perception starts to clarify. But by now the process of movement downward, far from slowing, has begun to hasten. The short, choppy phrases and flat, monochromatic rhythms at the beginning of the poem begin to give way toward the end to lines which are more emphatic, more tightly interwoven, more forcefully verbal and dynamic. The act of transcendence downward now enables the observer to see that within the new objects of his perception, as within his recovered powers of sight, bringing "clarity" and "outline of leaf," there exists an extraordinary Something—the only way to denominating what he sees is by reference to the impersonal pronoun "It"—which is known strictly because of *what it does*, an activity which can only be defined by the slightly archaic word *quickens*. Thus in the final stanza, with its heavy pauses and formal dignity, the eye actually permeates those objects, that scene, this vision, and discovers that which enables the whole landscape to root, to "grip down and begin to awaken"— an immanent Force which, though never visible as a thing in itself, now lends both to the objects themselves, and to the quickened capacities of perception through which they are seen, an unexpected, even numinous *hecceity*, or sheer thisness of being.

What the observer finally sees, then, and in his seeing for the first time knows, is not a wasteland at all but rather a fresh new world, which he discovers by releasing in himself, in the very act of transcending downward, that same power of life which at once quickens the vegetation into life and perception into vision. The experience itself finally takes on the character of a great pageant, a formal rite. What is being enacted is "the stark dignity of entrance" whereby spring is delivered from winter, insight from observation, life from death. The process, as always, is *decreative*; the result, in this case, is *restorative*. At the end, both the subject and its objects have become wholly transparent not only to each other but also to the power which holds both in Being itself. As J. Hillis Miller might well say, all exist in a new space of co-presence in which the light reflected from each is the light of All.[20]

The pattern which is here illustrated, and illustrated as well in our foregoing examples, is the one which R. P. Blackmur defined some years ago in his brilliant essay on "Religious Poetry in the United States." It is the pattern of what I have termed the essential paradigm of the American experience, the pattern of the self's, and by extension the work's, relation with what I would call the experience of the ideal "Other" and what Blackmur called, more forthrightly, perhaps, "the numinous force; the force within the self, other than the self, greater than the self, which, as one cultivates it, moves one beyond the self." "Poetry," Blackmur said, by which he meant all literary forms, "is one of the ways of cultivation; and the harvest is vision."[21]

The problem, however, is not to isolate the pattern, or to define the paradigm; examples of it abound everywhere in American literature, but by themselves tell us nothing more than that American writers, from time to time, have tended to order their experience in relation to a common set of terms, and beyond that in relation to a common set of premises about the possible relations between those terms which inevitably affects the variety of experiences which can be so ordered. To speak more plainly with the help of some formulations borrowed from John Lynen, the existence of something like a paradigm of the American experience tells us at most only that American writers, for a complicated set of reasons, have typically

organized their fictions, or at least some of their more representative fictions, in relation to what Lynen defines as a describable
"system of modes of experience which, though differing greatly,
are yet related as alternatives within a single range of possibilities."[22] The paradigm itself, then, simply describes the single
range or system of possibilities in relation to which individual
writers have created various and alternative modes of experience.
The question remains, what have they learned from their employment of this paradigm? What new knowledge have they acquired
from their utilization of this distinctively—though by no means
uniquely—American idea of order, knowledge that has something
to do with the lives we lead every day and that might make those
lives more livable, more valuable, more humane? More particularly, how does their work prove a resource for overcoming that
curious form of spiritual myopia which seems to afflict us as Americans, what William James and Benjamin DeMott referred to as our
insensibility to forms of life, of being, other than our own?

4

The answer, which can only be outlined in cursory fashion here, is
closely allied with the ideal ways which American writers have
proposed for responding to the "Other," and these in turn are to a
large degree dependent upon the mode in terms of which the
"Other" is experienced. The three poems by Dickinson, Frost, and
Williams illustrate, respectively those three modes, and thus serve
to indicate the three ideal ways which our writers have devised for
responding to one of the several, more representative modes in
which the "Other" or "otherness" has been experienced in
America.

To put this all in the form of a proposition, I would argue that
American writers have tended to imagine the experience of "otherness" or the "Other" in three characteristic modes, which turn out
on closer inspection to be distinctive of, but by no means confined

to, three successive periods in the history of American culture. Having imagined the experience of "otherness" in three different modes, I would contend that they have also proposed, respectively, three different ways of responding to it, have proposed, if you will, three very nearly generic definitions of what might be called "the nature of true virtue." In saying this, I mean to suggest that an examination of the various modes in terms of which many of our more representative writers and thinkers have imagined and responded to that which is experienced as "other" affords significant insight into what Lionel Trilling has recently described as "the moral life in process of revising itself, perhaps by reducing the emphasis it formerly placed upon one or another of its elements, perhaps by inventing and adding to itself a new element, some mode of conduct or of feeling which hitherto it had not regarded as essential to virtue."[23]

Among those writers and thinkers who have experienced "otherness" in the transcendental mode, as the expression of a God, Power, or Being who is reputed to dwell, so to speak, above and beyond, it is either tacitly or overtly assumed, as Jonathan Edwards indicated in *The Nature of True Virtue*, that the appropriate form of response is some manifestation of "the consent of being to Being." This is the mode of experience and resultant ethical orientation which typifies most American writing from the Puritan period through the first half of the nineteenth century, and which finds representative expression in such diverse figures as John Winthrop, John Cotton, Anne Bradstreet, Jonathan Edwards, Benjamin Franklin, James Fenimore Cooper, and Ralph Waldo Emerson, though variations of the mode itself can also be seen in such later figures as Emily Dickinson, Edwin Arlington Robinson, and Robinson Jeffers. Whether their experience of it is a source of joy and renewal, like Edwards's and Emerson's, or more often a source of anguish and despair, like Dickinson's and Robinson's, most of the writers who imagine "otherness" in this mode comprehend the experience itself as some form of what M. H. Abrams, echoing

Carlyle, has aptly named "Natural Supernaturalism."[24] And the
exercise of consent in this case, or the withholding of it when the
experience of "otherness" in this mode proves either too hostile or
too empty, is viewed as affording the possibility, or destroying the
possibility, of a kind of *transcendence upward.*

By the mid-nineteenth century, however, a subtle shift in theological emphasis began to occur in America, which was accom-
panied by an equally subtle alteration in our idea of the nature of
true virtue. One can discern intimations of this shift in the writings
of Nathaniel Hawthorne, where a marked skepticism toward all
forms of traditional belief and worship is coupled with an equally
fervid conviction about the sanctity of the human heart, but it
achieved its first full articulation in the writings of the elder Henry
James. This was the shift in emphasis from allegiance to the God,
Power, or Being who dwells above and beyond to belief in, or at
least greater curiosity about, the God, Power, or Being who dwells
both within and without, the ideal "Other" who meets one, if anywhere, in the form of what the elder James called, borrowing a
phrase from Emmanuel Swedenborg, our "Divine Natural Humanity." Most of the writers who imagine "otherness" in this newer
mode inevitably tend to reconceive the ideal way of relating and
responding to it. Where those who imagine "otherness" in the transcendental mode define virtue as a form of consent, those who
imagine "otherness" in what may be described as the social mode
redefine virtue as a form of sympathy. The ethical ideal, in other
words, is not to consent to others, nor even to feel for them, but
rather to feel with them, to project ourselves so completely into the
interiority of their own distinctive inwardness that, as D. H.
Lawrence once said, we "feel with them as they feel with themselves."[25] And, correspondingly, the aim of all such efforts is not
to effect a kind of transcendence upward but rather a kind of *transcendence outward.*

This is the ethical ideal or notion of true virtue which first begins
to show itself in Hester Prynne's relation to the townspeople of

Salem at the end of *The Scarlet Letter*, is explored more leisurely in Ishmael's developing experience of brotherhood with Queequeg in *Moby-Dick*, becomes the great controlling theme of *Leaves of Grass*, attains temporary consummation in the idyllic pastoral interlude which Huck and Jim enjoy together floating down the river in *The Adventures of Huckleberry Finn*, and then, finally, is realized both as an achievement of character and as an achievement of form in the great novels of Henry James's major phase. But, again, this notion of virtue is recalled and partially retrieved as an ethical norm long after the mode in which it serves as the ideal response begins to lose its hold over the American imagination. One finds variations of the idea of sympathy cropping up as the moral touchstone in such different works, for example, as Sherwood Anderson's *Winesburg, Ohio*, Robert Frost's dramatic monologues, Willa Cather's tales of frontier life, Ernest Hemingway's stories of love and marriage, Nathaniel West's *Miss Lonelyhearts*, Bernard Malamud's novels about the meaning of suffering, and, above all, in the Yoknapatawpha saga of William Faulkner.

In the second quarter of the twentieth century, however, a second shift in ethical and religious orientation began to occur in America, one which I believe we are still very much in the throes of. This new alteration in what deserves to be called, after R. P. Blackmur's famous *Anni Mirabiles* lectures of 1956, the "irregular metaphysics" of the American experience, involves a discovery which many of the great modern writers made close to the end of their careers, but which many of our best contemporary writers have accepted as a working assumption almost from the very outset. This is the discovery of the astonishing numinousness of things as they are, of the rich liminality, in Denis Donoghue's phrase, of "the ordinary universe." [26] Whether, like the late Eliot, they have made this discovery through the repossession of a traditional myth which puts greatest emphasis upon the mysterious incarnate union of Word and flesh, spirit and matter, or, like the later Stevens, through the employment of a "later reason" raised to the level of

metaphysical speculation, or, like the later Williams, through a
fresh plunge into "the filthy Passaic" of crude fact, all are engaged
in "the act of finding what will suffice,"[27] and all must follow
Theodore Roethke in "The Abyss" past the surfeit of too much reality and the exhaustion of too close an immediacy until they reach,
"beyond the fearful instant," "A sunlit silence," where

> Knowing slows for a moment,
> And not-knowing enters, silent,
> Bearing being itself,
> And the fire dances
> To the stream's
> Flowing.

Is this moving "toward God," the poet asks, "or merely another
condition?" The only answer is the one found in the poet's images
as they rise dreamlike but clear from the fusion of his own inner
ambivalence:

> By the salt waves I hear a river's undersong,
> In a place of mottled clouds, a thin mist morning and evening.
> I rock between dark and dark
> My soul nearly my own,
> My dear selves singing.
> And I embrace this calm—
> Such quiet under the small leaves![28]

"Such quiet under the small leaves"; that "luminous stillness" "in
the eyeless seeking" of the fragile tendrils of young plants; the envi-
able, innocent delicacy of "the child's hand reaching into the coiled
smilax"[29]—all these phrases, and the gestures of spirit they represent, signify the mysterious recovery of a sense of Presence which
each of these poets achieves through an imaginative encounter with
a form of the "Other" which is experienced as wholly immanent.
The ideal response to all such encounters with "otherness" in the
immanental mode is neither consent nor sympathy but rather
transparency, a kind of reversal, as Geoffrey Hartman suggests in
reference to Stevens, where we "become what we see instead of

seeing what we are."[30] This is the strategy adopted by such disparate characters as Stevens's Canon Aspirin, Saul Bellow's Herzog, and Robert Lowell's skunk-watcher, each of whom strives, however imperfectly, to become utterly transparent to the "other," to take their energy, courage, even identity from the "other's" luminous reality, and each of whom achieves, as a result, a kind of transcendence which is neither upward nor outward but rather a *transcendence downward.*

Such acts of transcendence, whether upward, outward, or downward, comprise the three strategies, to use Kenneth Burke's language, by which American writers have attempted to encompass the situation confronting them, what Stevens calls "the man-locked set." Taken together, they represent the way in which our writers have kept alive a sense of "otherness," an imagination of "worlds elsewhere" beyond the perimeters of the self, by which the self, through an act of recognition and reaction, has been able, as a consequence, to learn how to transcend its own perimeters. Such knowledge may never save us, but it can at least make us a little more human by teaching us how to respond both to the Me we are not—to modify Emerson's formulation—and to the Me that we are.

In the remainder of this chapter, I wish to examine in greater detail a single text which explicitly sets out to delineate this precarious distinction. F. Scott Fitzgerald's *The Great Gatsby* is the more remarkable because it hazards such an experiment with materials so meretricious as almost to ensure its failure. Nonetheless, Fitzgerald knew what he was about. What was at stake for him, of course, was not the survival of Gatsby himself or even the importance of his vision; the one is fatally vulnerable, the other hopelessly naive and corrupt. The novel is rather devoted to the energy and quality of imagination which propels both Gatsby *and* his vision, and which endures if at all only in the narrative designs of Fitzgerald's art. Viewed as a story about Gatsby and his dream, the novel is simply an elegy, or, more precisely, a threnody, sung over the death of one of American literature's most affecting but flawed innocents. Viewed instead as a story about Gatsby's poetry of desire, his imagination of wonder, the novel is an act of historical repossession which lays bare what is common to all three strategies of self-transcendence and constitutes the source of each.

5

As Fitzgerald makes clear on the very last page of his novel, Gatsby's dream belongs to a historical order which has long since ceased to exist, to a vision of possibility which almost died on the eyes of those first Dutch sailors to these shores who were paradoxically the last to look out upon the American landscape in comparative innocence: "for a transitory enchanted moment," Fitzgerald writes, "man must have held his breath in the presence of this continent, compelled into an aesthetic contemplation he neither understood nor desired, face to face for the last time in history with something commensurate with his 'capacity for wonder'." Fitzgerald describes this "capacity for wonder" as an "aesthetic contemplation," but for Jay Gatsby, in whom Fitzgerald invests it to such an extraordinary degree, it is clearly something more. "Out of the corner of his eye," Fitzgerald tells us at one point in the novel, "Gatsby saw that the blocks of the sidewalk really formed a ladder and mounted to a secret place above the trees—he could climb to it, if he climbed alone, and once there he could suck the pap of life, gulp down the incomparable milk of wonder."

There is, it scarcely needs saying, an incredible garishness involved in Gatsby's capacity for wonder, precisely because he attempts to make so transparent and gauche a religion out of it. What with all his gorgeous sacramental shirts, his splended gestures of supplication, and his ornate West Egg mansion which functions throughout the novel as a kind of sacred shrine, Gatsby seems a grotesque parody of some high priest or shaman who is continually dispensing holy waters, consecrated food, and other elements of the sanctified life to whatever aspirants he can gather around him.

Walt Whitman or in Hart Crane, to a new American imagination of wonder. The "fresh, green breast of the new world," which first presented itself to those unsuspecting Dutch sailors, has now diminished to the tiny, green light which burns all night on Daisy Buchanan's pier, and which illumines little more than the desolate Valley of Ashes, that wasteland of frustrated desire and shattered hopes existing, so Fitzgerald would have us believe, at the end of every contemporary American rainbow.

Thus Jay Gatsby, "born of his Platonic conception of himself," as Nick tells us, and "elected to be about his Father's business" is left from the beginning without anything in twentieth-century America but "a vast, vulgar and meretricious beauty for him to serve." Yet the tragedy is not his alone but also his society's, for both seemed doomed by what they lack—Gatsby by his lack of any critical ability to differentiate his spiritual ideals from the material conditions in and through which he must realize them; American society by its lack of either substance or form commensurate with Gatsby's belief in them.[32] But if Gatsby's destruction by "the foul dust" which "floats in the wake of his illusions" is inevitable, his inexhaustible store of wonder and good will still confer upon the very actuality which eventually extinguish them whatever truth, beauty, or goodness that American actuality ever fully attains. Fitzgerald is thus able to celebrate Gatsby's veritable religion of wonder, while at the same time exposing its pathetic vulnerability and ultimate defilement. His tribute is part of his critique, a single act of judgment and love which proves how truly Fitzgerald spoke when he remarked that "the test of a first-rate intelligence is the ability to hold two opposed ideas in the mind, at the same time, and still retain the ability to function."

6

Nick Carraway's first glimpse of Gatsby outlined in all his elemental loneliness against the sky, as he makes his trembling gesture of

And the fact that Gatsby's friends inevitably turn out to be [worth]less" in the end only heightens the parody: it was never in[tended] that he serve their illusions but rather that they serve his. [But] Gatsby remains ridiculously sentimental to the very end, a foo[l of,] and ultimately a victim of, the faith he has made out of his own unquenchable thirst for wonder.[31]

Part of the triumph of the novel is that Fitzgerald refuses to [dis]count the vulgarity of it all and instead confronts it directly, e[m]ploying as his narrator and chief spokesman a character who, li[ke] one side of Fitzgerald himself, possesses an "unaffected scorn" f[or] everything that Gatsby represents. During the course of the novel, however, Nick Carraway undergoes what Melville would have called a "sea-change" as he is himself brought slowly face to face with something at once intransigently American and also universal which by the end of the novel somehow transcends and, to a point, even redeems the crude and sordid materials in terms of which it is expressed. I refer to Gatsby's marvelous capacity for wonder when it is viewed not as an inborn trait of character so much as a reflex response to life, and which issues in what Nick describes as his "extraordinary gift for hope," his "romantic readiness." If Gatsby's personality is no more than "an unbroken series of successful gestures," as Nick muses at the beginning, still there is what can only be described as "something gorgeous about him, some heightened sensitivity to the promises of life, as if he were related to one of those intricate machines that register earthquakes ten thousand miles away."

By the end of the novel, Nick is able to identify this responsive capacity with something the American continent once might have elicited in all men, but neither he nor Fitzgerald is under any illusions about what America offers now. Contemporary American society presents itself in *The Great Gatsby* as utterly devoid of any of those fresh and unexpected images which once astonished man into a new and original relation with the universe, and which thus gave rise, whether in Jonathan Edwards or in Ralph Waldo Emerson, in acknowledgment and supplication to the green light which beckons to him from across the bay, contains nearly the entire meaning of Gatsby's story. For, like Melville's Captain Ahab before him and Faulkner's Thomas Sutpen after him, Gatsby has committed his life to a pursuit in the future of what has already become a symbol of his own reinterpreted and idealized past. As a symbol, the green light is most clearly associated in Gatsby's mind with Daisy Buchanan (the former Daisy Faye of Louisville), but it represents much more than Daisy herself. As Gatsby's appropriately sexual substitute for "the fresh, green breast of the new world," the green light symbolizes to Gatsby all that Daisy once meant to him during their very brief but poignant love affair five years before, some idea of himself which went into his loving of her but which he irretrievably lost the moment he "forever wed his unutterable visions to her perishable breath." Once the incarnation was complete, the vision began to wither, and Gatsby would henceforth be condemned to live in that country of American fantasy which is located in the spiritual as well as historical wilderness between the "no longer" and the "not yet," or, to recall Klipspringer's song, "In the meantime, In between time," where all one asks is, "Ain't we got fun?"

From the very beginning, Gatsby's "unutterable visions" had served to convince him "that the rock of the world was founded securely on a fairy's wing," but they had remained inchoate and unformed until the day Dan Cody's yacht dropped anchor in the shallows of Lake Superior and the young Jimmie Gatz rowed out to take a look. To young James Gatz—soon to become Jay Gatsby, but now only a recent drop-out from St. Olaf College—the appearance of Cody's yacht seemed as momentous as the arrival of the Nina, the Pinta, and the Santa Maria, and so he signed on to serve Cody in some vague personal capacity for what eventually turned out to be five years. When Cody died at the end of that time, Jimmie Gatz was cheated out of the $25,000 his mentor had left him, but Jay Gatsby had acquired something much more valuable— what Nick describes, with not a little irony, as an "appropriate ed-

ucation" from a man who was the "product of the Nevada silver
fields, of the Yukon," and "of every rush for the metal since sev-
enty-five." The historical allusion is perfect. At Gatsby's point of
time in history, who but one of the fallen Sons of Leatherstocking
could have transmitted to him what was left of that earlier American vision which now lives on only in the body of his corruption?
Yet it was not until the now hardened but still adolescent Jay
Gatsby of Minnesota met Daisy Faye, the beautiful but unstable
young socialite from the Blue Grass country around Louisville
during the Great War, that his education began to be filled out. The
myth of the Northern Yankee forever seeking the paradise of his
dreams in the ever-vanishing world of the West had to be joined to
what was left of the legend of the Southern Cavalier discovering a
salvation of refinement in the gossamer world of midnight balls and
late afternoon teas before Gatsby's vividly American identity could
be firmly fixed.

If Cody's world, as Nick speculates, is the world of "the pioneer
debauchee, who during one phase of American life brought back to
the Eastern seaboard the savage violence of the frontier brothel and
saloon," Daisy's is the artificial, vapid, and completely brittle
world of the teenage socialite whose only real aim in life is to
remain "gleaming, like silver, safe and proud above the hot strug-
gles of the poor." Like so many before him, Gatsby was compelled
into an attitude of absolute enchantment by the sense of "ripe mystery," of throbbing expectation, which seemed so much a part of
Daisy's person, her house, her culture, and, particularly, her voice.
There was "a singing compulsion" to it, "a whispered 'Listen,' a
promise that she had done gay, exciting things just a while since
and that there were gay, exciting things hovering in the next hour."
It was a voice which held out to him the possibility of every promise's fulfillment, a future of unlimited beatitude and sexual felicity
which was, to quote Howard Mumford Jones, "if not the kingdom
of Prester John, the empire of the Great Kahn, or Asia heavy with

the wealth of Ormuz and of Ind, then next door to it, or a passage toward it. . . ."[33] Only years later, in telling Nick of his poignant affair with Daisy five years before, Gatsby would be able to perceive that "the inexhaustible charm that rose and fell in it, the jingle of it, the cymbals' song of it" was simply the sound of money. Gatsby and Daisy had, of course, fully intended to marry after the war, but before Gatsby could cut through the red tape delaying his return, Daisy's febrile will had collapsed and her letter had arrived announcing her marriage to a midwesterner named Tom Buchanan.

As so many critics have noted,[34] Tom exists in the novel as a kind of double to Gatsby, thus permitting Fitzgerald to point up by contrast Gatsby's incomparably greater stature. Tom strikes Nick from the moment he meets him as "one of those men who reach such an acute limited excellence at twenty-one that everything afterward savors of anti-climax." A Chicago boy from an enormously wealthy family, Tom had played end at Yale and ever after gave the impression that he "would drift on forever seeking, a little wistfully, for the dramatic turbulence of some irrecoverable football game." If Daisy's most striking attribute is the sound of her tinkling voice, Tom's is his "cruel body," "a body," Nick surmises, "capable of enormous leverage." Gatsby, by contrast, is all spirit. Far from creating the impression of power, Gatsby conveys the impression of desire. Nick acquires this impression the first time he meets Gatsby when he catches a glimpse of it in Gatsby's most characteristic attribute, his smile:

> It was one of those rare smiles with a quality of eternal reassurance in it, that you may come across four or five times in life. It faced—or seemed to face—the whole eternal world for an instant, and then concentrated on *you* with an irresistible prejudice in your favour. It understood you just as far as you wanted to be understood, believed in you just as you would like to believe in yourself, and assured you that it had precisely the impression of

you that, at your best, you hoped to convey. Precisely at that
point it vanished—and I was looking at an elegant young rough-
neck a year or two over thirty, whose elaborate formality of
speech just missed being absurd.

This passage is so brilliantly executed because, as Marius Bewley
has suggested, "it presents Gatsby to us less as an individual than
as a projection, or mirror of our ideal selves."[35] In truth Gatsby's
youthful impression has nothing to do with age at all: It is a quality
of good will, of total willingness, which neither time can stale nor
age wither—a prejudice, to paraphrase part of Alfred North Whitehead's definition of religion, that the facts of existence shall find
their justification in the nature of existence. As a prejudice which
has no concern for the facts as they are, it can, of course, become
absurdly sentimental; but even here Gatsby is to be contrasted
with Tom. For whereas Tom's sentimentality is decadent and
wholly self-serving, Gatsby's is ebullient and wholly self-effacing.
Tom is never more revealing than when he is brought to tears over
the sight of a box of half-finished dog biscuits which constitute the
final remains of a day of drunken philandering with his now dead
mistress, a day which was finally brought to a close only after
Tom, in a fit of adolescent pique, had broken her nose with his
open hand in one "short, deft movement." Gatsby's sentimentality,
on the other hand, is revealed in his constant temptation to confer
his essentially heroic capacity for faith and wonder upon objects
which are decidedly unworthy of them, objects ultimately as dangerous as style, money, and class. The latter points only to a deficiency of mind, the former to a deficiency of heart. What Gatsby
lacks is the critical ability to temper his generous, if also innocent,
feelings, which are in turn responsible for the splendor and naiveté
of his illusions. What Tom lacks is the affective power to feel truly
anything but pity for himself, which renders him depraved and
inhuman.

In this, as in other ways, Tom and Gatsby reflect related but different strains in the development of American history and culture.

Tom is a scion of the great robber barons of the Gilded Age who "seized the land, gutted the forests, laid the railroads,"[36] and turned the cities into vast urban fortresses for the purpose of protecting their own moneyed interests. Descendants of those early pioneers, frontiersman, and later settlers who attempted to transform the Virgin Land into a New World Garden, these later empire-builders of the post-Civil War period, who wanted to replace crops with machines, farms with factories, and villages with cities, set aside morality as easily and quickly as they attempted to buy up culture. Men of single-minded purpose who were at once daring and perseverant, they, like their literary forbear, Captain Ahab, allowed nothing to stand in their "iron way," and they assured themselves of Heaven's blessing—as Tom would if he could but remember the right words—by convincing themselves that they were doing Heaven's will.

Gatsby, by contrast, recalls an earlier generation of American worthies who originally journeyed to these shores in the hopes of establishing a kingdom on earth which might more nearly conform to the Kingdom of Heaven. But in the century and a half intervening between first settlement and the establishment of the Republic, the dreams of the one had become intertangled with the success of the other. The original theocratic impulse to found a City upon a Hill to the greater glory of God had been displaced by the more secular desire to build a nation in the wilderness which testified instead to the inalienable rights and achievements of man. The seventeenth-century propulsion to know why had been reduced to the eighteenth- and nineteenth-century preoccupation with know-how. The Calvinist belief in God as the maker of man's destiny had been supplanted by Benjamin Franklin's doctrine of self-help. To be sure, there were still traces of that earlier Puritan dream in its later, more utilitarian expression. As Perry Miller has noted, Benjamin Franklin pursued worldly success every bit as disinterestedly as Jonathan Edwards pursued "the nature of true virtue," and both shared a similar conviction "that the universe is its own excuse for being."[37] But by the time Gatsby appeared, American society, but for an hour on Sunday mornings, had long since abandoned the view Franklin strangely shared with Edwards, the view that life on earth could and should be, as it were, lifted up to Heaven. Instead, for a century or more America had been telling the Jimmie Gatz's of this world that the Kingdom of God could be established right here in America, perhaps even on somebody's rented estate, and that, further, one could get away with populating this New World paradise with Daisy Fayes, Tom Buchanans, and Meyer Wolfsheims, the latter being reputed to have fixed the World Series in 1919.

This is absurd, and Fitzgerald knew it was. Thus he is at pains to show that the elaborate and pathetic plan Gatsby concocted to express it was doomed from the beginning, and he does not mince words as to the reason why. Gatsby's proposal to rectify what he considers the mistake of Daisy's marriage to Tom, by asking her to request a divorce so that she can marry him instead, is based upon his incredible belief that history doesn't matter, that the past can be repeated. This is the ultimate flaw at the heart of Gatsby's dream, and, with the dream itself, it shatters like glass against Tom and Daisy's brutal indifference.

That indifference is nowhere more apparent than when Daisy accidentally kills Myrtle Wilson, Tom's mistress, with Gatsby's car. The accident merely fulfills and completes that earlier act of violence which Tom committed against Myrtle himself, and thus serves as a perfect expression of the reliance upon brute force, at once physical and material, which holds Tom and Daisy and their kind together. Hence when Gatsby magnanimously offers to protect Daisy from any possible recriminations from Tom, Tom and Daisy repay his generosity by insinuating to Myrtle's grief-crazed husband, George, that Gatsby was responsible instead. In deflecting George Wilson's certain vengeance away from themselves out of a habit of self-protection it took their forbears several generations to perfect, Tom and Daisy make Gatsby the scapegoat of their own irresponsible pasts. Yet this is in character, Nick later surmises, for in spite of their wealth and glamor, perhaps even because of it, Tom and Daisy were simply "careless people" who "smashed up things and creatures and then retreated back into their money or their vast carelessness, or whatever it was that kept them together, and let other people clean up the mess they made."

Thus when George kills Gatsby and then himself, a strange circle of significance is finally closed. If Gatsby represents that irrepressible reaction of wonder and hope which once gave motive force to the vision of what the American reality might one day be, Wilson represents that spiritless desperation and hopelessness at the center of what the American reality, in this novel at least, has actually become. The only people who escape are ironically those who have done most to create the one out of the other, people like Tom and Daisy who have acquired enough money and shrewdness in the process to buy their way out of trouble.

7

But Gatsby's destruction at the end in no sense indicates a complete triumph of the forces, both from within and without, which have conspired against him. For Fitzgerald has so constructed his novel that Gatsby's true stature and significance can only be finally measured by his impact upon the narrator, and to Nick Carraway Gatsby's ultimate victory is absolutely assured.

As narrator, Nick seems perfectly suited to his task. He describes himself on the very first page of the novel as one of those people who is "inclined to reserve all judgments, a habit that has opened up many curious natures to me and also made me the victim of not a few veteran bores. . . ." But Nick's tolerance is not without its limits; for he is concerned to live as he has been raised, according to "a sense of the fundamental decencies." And having returned from the East to tell his story, he confesses, "I felt that I wanted the world to be in uniform and at a moral attention forever;

I wanted no more riotous excursions with privileged glimpses into the human heart."

Yet much as Nick tries to remain ambivalent and uninvolved throughout the book, "simultaneously enchanted and repelled by the variety of life," he cannot maintain the distance of a neutral observer as he becomes progressively more involved in Gatsby's incredible scheme to recapture Daisy. For if Nick is contemptuous of everything Gatsby represents, he still cannot resist admiring the intensity with which Gatsby represents it. And the more Nick uncovers the cynicism and corruption beneath Tom and Daisy's glamor, the more he grows to respect Gatsby's optimism and the essential incorruptibility not of his vision but of the desire it incarnates. Hence by the time Gatsby is murdered by the demented Wilson, Nick has come to think that Gatsby was "worth the whole damn bunch put together." But he also finds that, like Gatsby before him, he must pay the price of loneliness for his conviction. For it readily becomes apparent at the time of Gatsby's death that Gatsby's friends no longer have any use for him. And then it is that Nick realizes the nature of his own relationship to Gatsby: "it grew upon me that I was responsible, because no-one else was interested—interested, I mean, with that intense personal interest to which everyone has a vague right in the end."

This feeling of genuine concern and sympathy for another human being emerges as one of the most important positive values of Gatsby's tragedy. If it does not seem capable of mitigating the pathos of Gatsby's destruction, much less preventing it, Nick's capacity for concern and love nonetheless enables him to see in the tragedy of Gatsby's own idealism a symbol for the tragedy of all human aspiration. Before Nick leaves the East permanently after Gatsby's death, he crosses his front yard to take one last look at Gatsby's house:

> . . . as the moon rose higher the inessential houses began to melt away until gradually I became aware of the old island here, that flowered once for Dutch sailors' eyes—a fresh, green breast of the

new world. Its vanished trees, the trees that had made way for
Gatsby's house, had once pandered in whispers to the last and
greatest of all human dreams; for a transitory enchanted moment
man must have held his breath in the presence of this continent,
. . . face to face for the last time in history with something commensurate to his capacity for wonder.

Nick is able to give his words such a beautiful, haunting, evocative quality because he had himself been partially seduced by
Gatsby's dream. Not only had he once felt the mysterious attraction in Daisy's voice; he had also fallen half in love with someone
who suggested its rich ring of promise. But Nick had been able to
discern the note of cynicism and emptiness behind the magic
suggestiveness of Daisy's voice, just as he had also been able to perceive that Jordan Baker, his temporary lover, was basically a liar
and a cheat.

At the end Nick can only surmise as to whether Gatsby was ever
able to acknowledge the terrible disparity between his magnificent
illusions and the coarse actuality which finally betrayed them. Nick
can scarcely believe that Gatsby remained ignorant to the very end
of "what a grotesque thing a rose is," but as for himself there is no
question. The culture of the East, which once held out to him, as it
always did to Gatsby, the promise of beginning all over again in a
New World in the very next hour—the culture of the East now appears to Nick as a night scene from El Greco:

> In the foreground four solemn men in dress suits are walking
> along the sidewalk with a stretcher on which lies a drunken
> woman in a white evening dress. Her hand, which dangles over
> the side, sparkles cold with jewels. Gravely the men turn in at
> the house—the wrong house. But no one knows the woman's
> name, and no one cares.

The only illumination which relieves Nick's otherwise dark and
ferral tableau is the absurd little green light at the end of Daisy's
pier which Gatsby so fervently believed in, "the orgiastic future
that year by year recedes before us. . . ." ". . . But that's no

matter," Nick assures us—"tomorrow we will run faster, stretch out our arms farther. . . . And one fine morning—"

"So we beat on," Nick concludes, "boats against the current, borne ceaselessly back into the past."

This image, with its perfect union of sexual and spiritual promise, arrests us with its terrible poignancy. Gatsby's capacity for wonder was doomed from the beginning. "He had come a long way to this blue lawn, and his dream must have seemed so close that he could hardly fail to grasp it," Nick muses. "He did not know that it was already behind him, somewhere back in that vast obscurity beyond the city, where the dark fields of the republic rolled on under the night." Yearning always forward to secure a future that was already lost to the past, Gatsby is borne ceaselessly backward in time until he becomes a sacrificial victim of the pasts of others, indeed, of the American Dream itself.

The pathos of the final image thus seems definitive: Gatsby's beautiful circuit of belief and desire is broken on the rack of America's cruel indifference; his generous "willingness of heart" is simply no match for Tom and Daisy's "hard malice." Committed to pure spirit in a world almost exclusively composed of mere matter, Gatsby is defeated by his inability to understand that the things of the spirit can only exist amidst the unavoidable conditions which the actual and the material make for them.[38]

Yet this is not the whole truth, either for Nick as narrator or for us as readers. Because if the coarse materials of Gatsby's world have refused to yield to the impulses of his spirit, if, indeed, Gatsby himself at the end "must have felt that he had lost the old warm world, paid a high price for living too long with a single dream," still the very intensity of his commitment to spirit has nonetheless transfigured, for however brief a time, the otherwise drab materials of existence. That Gatsby's imagination of wonder can never overcome the current, cannot even resist the current, is nothing to the point: It is the poetry of beating on that counts! As a reflex response to that most elemental, though not most profound, intimation of the sacred both within and beyond us, Gatsby's spontaneous act of resistance constitutes here, as in life generally, what might be described, in R. W. B. Lewis's fine phrase, as "the tug of the Transcendent."[39] Without it, life loses all of its energy and interest, all of its color and originality. With it, we recover a sense of that radiance which temporarily redeems life even as the flow of life itself bears it away.

But we do not have to settle for Fitzgerald's word alone on this subject. Robert Frost once used an image almost identical to Fitzgerald's boats beating on against the current and gave that image of primitive spiritual resistance one of its most enduring religious expressions. Frost's image occurs in the poem "West-Running Brook." Fred and his wife have been speaking of the meaning of contraries when suddenly an illuminating example presents itself: ". . . see how the brook," he remarks to his wife,

> In that white wave runs counter to itself.
> It is from that in water we were from
> Long, long before we were from any creature.
> Here we, in our impatience of the steps,
> Get back to the beginning of beginnings,
> The stream of everything that runs away.
> . . . .
> The universal cataract of death
> That spends to nothingness—and unresisted,
> Save by some strange resistance in itself,
> Not just a swerving, but a throwing back,
> As if regret were in it and were sacred.
> It has this throwing backward on itself
> So that the fall of most of it is always
> Raising a little, sending up a little.
> It is this backward motion toward the source.
> Against the stream, that most we see ourselves in,
> The tribute of the current to the source.
> It is from this in nature we are from.
> It is most us.

Gatsby's abundant store of wonder, with its reflexive capacity to generate and sustain such marvelously radiant, if also deeply flawed, visions *is* "a throwing back,/ As if regret were in it and were sacred." So is Nick's narrative attempt to understand its meaning. Taken together, then, Nick's and Gatsby's "backward motion toward the source,/ Against the stream" constitute Fitzgerald's "tribute of the current to the source." We are thus left at the end of the novel where we are left at the end of so many of our classic books, believing without belief, as Wallace Stevens says, "beyond belief."[40] What we believe "beyond belief" has to do with our capacity as men and women to be quickened and renewed through such sacred acts of resistance, or, as Frost would say, to be made "whole again beyond confusion." We are forced to transcend our various beliefs in this or that so that we may recover by way of the imagination our ability to believe as such. In other words, we are driven back to that in both literature and religion which is prior to creed or conviction, to felt possibility and the imagination of desire. Rather than arriving at something like an expressed article of faith or principle of doctrine, we have been drawn into a mode of experience where, in all our unexpectedness, the act of belief suddenly becomes again an authentic form of response.

Postscript

In a recent essay on "Literary Criticism and Its Discontents," Geoffrey Hartman has offered an interesting emendation of Matthew Arnold's prediction that in the modern period religion would survive solely in its poetry. "If what remains of religion is its poetry, what remains of poetry is its heterodox theology, or myth-making." To "revisionists" like Hartman, this does not mean that all literature is implicitly or incipiently religious, only that the more intensely literature is scrutinized in a disinterested and critical spirit, the "more evidence of archaic and sacred residues comes to light . . . A Presence which is not to be put by." Despite Hartman's ambivalence about this fact—"it would be a great relief to break with the idea of the sacred, and especially with institutions that claim to mediate it"—he concedes that there is no getting around it. The sacred has inscribed itself too deeply into our language, if not into the very forms of our discourse, to be neglected or dismissed: "while it must be interpreted, it cannot be removed."[1]

In a militantly secular age such as our own, this is a hard saying. We have been brought up on too many tales of deracination and spiritual disinheritance not to wonder if the postulation of sacred traces in a literature so aggressively profane isn't self-contradictory, or worse, symptomatic of a failure of mind. Yet the "traces," the "residues," the "Presence" is there. Gabriel Josipovici points in a different way to the same phenomenon when, at the end of *The World and the Book*, he refers to "the paradox of solipsism and communion" that lies at the heart of all modern literature.[2] As modern writing draws the net of self-consciousness ever more tightly around us, transforming everything into a projection of the observant ego, it produces the ironic effect of simultaneously making us

aware of all that is not included within the horizon of consciousness, all that remains outside the parameters of the self, and con-
sequently affords us an indirect opportunity to participate in it.
"The encyclopedia of fragments which makes up 'Gerontion' or
Robbe-Grillet's *Le Voyeur* allows us to experience the limits of our
world and so to sense what lies beyond, the absolutely other, distinct from me and my desires. And this momentary and silent experience, as Proust knew, is worth all the deep thoughts and beautiful phrases that were ever penned."[3]

We are here in the presence of formulations that are at the further remove from any form of theological or religious imperialism—either of the sort that applies religious terminology descrip-
tively to individual works of literature that are consciously or
unconsciously designed to challenge and discredit such language,
or of the sort that searches for analogues and parallels between systems of belief and whole literary movements or traditions that arose
directly as a result of the collapse of such systems. Here the critic's
interest in exploring the relations between literature and religion
derives from his or her assumption that the provenance and hegemony of both have become problematic, but that fresh inquiry into
their curious patterns of attraction and repulsion, of linkage and au-
tonomy, of congeniality and aversion, may help make them seem
less so. The goal of their inquiry is the discernment of a fresh spiritual, or at least a fresh discernment of things spiritual, which
very nearly comes to the same thing.

It was R. P. Blackmur, in that extraordinary series of lectures he
delivered at the invitation of the Library of Congress in 1956 and
published under the title *Anni Mirabiles, 1921–1925,* who established the paradigm for this revisionary criticism of the spiritual
dimensions of literature, when he defined the modern literary situation in terms of the new problems man has invented for himself
with his new knowledge and then went on to describe the achievement of the modern writer as the adumbration of a new and "irregular metaphysics" to cope with them. To some in Blackmur's audi-

ence, this may have sounded like only another variation on the old Arnoldian prophecy. But Blackmur was not so much referring to the process of religion's displacement by literature as to a process where literature takes upon itself the authentic spiritual task, of leading us back "to that in religion which is not dogma but imagined idea."[4] If this image of the writer as a kind of irregular metaphysician who undertakes the authentic spiritual task by addressing those problems man keeps inventing for himself through the creation in his art of a world in which those problems may be comprehended and even encompassed—if this image of the writer strikes us as too mechanical and self-possessed, this is still what writers have been doing from the earliest ages of literacy, and one measure of their success is our continued ability to prevail over the obstacles we place in our own way.

But there is a danger in overstating the case. As most critics agree, literature will not save us but only increase our chances of survival. And the view of art as a form of covert and irregular metaphysics can be misleading if it encourages the notion, still widespread among critics of all theoretical persuasions, that the chief justification of the study of literature in its relation to religion must be the discovery of a better or a truer metaphysics. If we have learned anything at all from such study in the past, we have surely been forced to recognize that men and women have produced almost as many metaphysics as they have literatures. To the skeptic, this merely confirms the suspicion that the religious impulse is quixotic and unstable, and hence constitutes further proof, if any is needed, of the futility and irrelevance of examining literature in light of its religious aspects. To an agnostic like Schopenhauer, however, this same evidence could be used to prove just the opposite: if there are no constants in man's experience of the sacred, man's quest for the sacred may still be the one constant in his experience. For no matter how much variation there is in what men and women take to be ultimately real and significant, Schopenhauer perceived, they seem surprisingly consistent in their desire to search out and lay claim to some version of it. Thus Schopenhauer was inexorably driven back to a definition of man as the *animal metaphysicum*—not because all human beings believe in one and the same "idea of order," but because the universality of their need for such an "idea" seems to be the one attribute they all share in common as human beings.

As any sort of intellectual foundation on which to justify further study of the spiritual dimensions and ramifications of literature and culture, Schopenhauer's position will scarcely satisfy those who think that religion is concerned solely with what an earlier age conceived of as "fixities and definites" and with what our own age views as absolutes. In this case, their problem lies in the inability to distinguish between what has universally been experienced as a need and what has historically been achieved in experience. But on this there will never be agreement, and that is as it should be. Advances in humanistic scholarship, to paraphrase something Clifford Geertz once said of the interpretive sciences generally, are not measured by the spread of consensus but by the refinement of the debate. "What gets better is the precision with which we vex each other."[5]

Notes

Introduction

1. *The Life of the Drama* (New York: Atheneum, 1967).
2. *The Secular Scripture* (Cambridge: Harvard University Press, 1976).
3. *Elements of Tragedy* (New Haven: Yale University Press, 1969).
4. *The Barbarian Within and Other Fugitive Essays and Studies* (New York: Macmillan Company, 1962); *The Presence of the Word* (New Haven: Yale University Press, 1967).
5. *A Rhetoric of Irony* (Chicago: University of Chicago Press, 1974); *Modern Dogma and the Rhetoric of Assent* (Notre Dame: University of Notre Dame Press, 1974).
6. *The Sense of an Ending* (New York: Oxford University Press, 1967).
7. *Beginnings, Intention and Method* (New York: Basic Books, 1975).
8. See, for example, John T. Frederick, *The Darkened Sky: Nineteenth-Century American Novelists and Religion* (Notre Dame: University of Notre Dame Press, 1969); Howard Mumford Jones, *Belief and Disbelief in American Literature* (Chicago: University of Chicago Press, 1967); Cleanth Brooks, *The Hidden God* (New Haven: Yale University Press, 1963).
9. Kenneth S. Murdock, *Literature and Theology in New England* (Cambridge: Harvard University Press, 1949); Warner Berthoff, *The Ferment of Realism* (New York: The Free Press, 1967); Hyatt S. Waggoner, *The Heel of Elohim* (Norman: University of Oklahoma Press, 1950).
10. Perry Miller, *The New England Mind*, 2 vols. (1939; 1953; Boston: Beacon Press, 1961).
11. Richard Chase, *The American Novel and Its Tradition* (Garden City, N.Y.: Doubleday & Company, 1967).
12. Roy Harvey Pearce, *The Continuity of American Poetry* (Princeton: Princeton University Press, 1961).
13. William C. Spengemann, *The Adventurous Muse* (New Haven: Yale University Press, 1977).
14. A. D. Van Nostrand, *Everyman His Own Poet* (New York: McGraw-Hill Book Company, 1968).
15. "The Recovery of American Religious History," *American Historical Review* 7 (1964): 79–92. It is by no means irrelevant that Professor May considered the recovery of American religious history to be quite possibly the most important achievement of the last thirty years "for the study and understanding of American culture."
16. Charles Feidelson, Jr., *Symbolism and American Literature* (Chicago: University of Chicago Press, 1953).

17. Ursula Brumm, *American Thought and Religious Typology* (New Brunswick: Rutgers University Press, 1970).

18. Philip Rahv, *Image and Idea* (Norfolk, Conn.: New Directions, 1947), pp. 6–21.

19. Sacvan Bercovitch, *The Puritan Origins of the American Self* (New Haven: Yale University Press, 1975).

20. Tony Tanner, *The Reign of Wonder* (Cambridge: Cambridge University Press, 1965).

21. John F. Lynen, *The Design of the Present* (New Haven: Yale University Press, 1969).

22. A. N. Kaul, *The American Vision* (New Haven: Yale University Press, 1963).

23. R. W. B. Lewis, *The American Adam* (Chicago: University of Chicago Press, 1955).

24. Leslie Fiedler, *Love and Death in the American Novel* (New York: Criterion Books, 1960).

25. Henry Nash Smith, *Virgin Land* (Cambridge: Harvard University Press, 1950).

26. James E. Miller, Jr., *Quest Surd and Absurd* (Chicago: University of Chicago Press, 1965).

27. Roderick Nash, *Wilderness and the American Mind* (New Haven: Yale University Press, 1967).

28. Frederick I. Carpenter, *American Literature and the Dream* (New York: Philosophical Library, 1955).

29. Leo Marx, *The Machine and the Garden* (New York: Oxford University Press, 1964).

30. Tony Tanner, *The City of Words* (New York: Harper & Row, 1971).

31. Richard Poirier, *A World Elsewhere* (New York: Oxford University Press, 1966); Quentin Anderson, *The Imperial Self* (New York: Alfred A. Knopf, 1971).

32. Charles L. Sanford, *The Quest for Paradise* (Urbana: University of Illinois Press, 1961).

33. Sidney E. Ahlstrom, *A Religious History of the American People* (New Haven: Yale University Press, 1972), p. xiv.

34. John Dewey, *Experience and Nature* (1929; LaSalle, Ill.: Open Court Publishing Company, 1971), p. 323.

35. Ibid., p. 326.

Chapter 1   The Religious Use and Abuse of Literature

1. Walter Jackson Bate, *The Burden of the Past and the English Poet* (1970; New York: W. W. Norton and Co., 1972), p. 129.

2. *Christianity and Liberalism* (New York: Macmillan Company, 1923), p. 7.

3. *Contemporary American Literature and Religion* (Chicago: Willett, Clark and Co., 1934), p. 9.

4. T. S. Eliot, *Selected Essays* (New York: Harcourt, Brace & Company, 1950), p. 343.

5. *The Dyer's Hand and Other Essays* (New York: Vintage Books, 1968), p. 458.
6. "The Uses of a Theological Criticism," in *Literature and Religion*, ed. Giles Gunn (New York: Harper & Row, 1971), p. 41.
6. "The Uses of a Theological Criticism," in *Literature and Religion*, ed. Giles Gunn (New York: Harper & Row, 1971), p. 41.
7. Sidney E. Ahlstrom, *A Religious History of the American People* (New Haven: Yale University Press, 1972), p. 948.
8. An excellent short treatment of Tillich's method of correlation, and one that deserves to be better known, is Bernard Loomer, "Tillich's Theology of Correlation," *Journal of Religion* 36 (July, 1956): 150–56.
9. *The Broken Center* (New Haven: Yale University Press, 1966), p. lx.
10. Epigraph to *Rescue the Dead* (Middletown, Conn.: Wesleyan University Press, 1968).
11. See Langdon Gilkey, *Naming the Whirlwind* (Indianapolis: Bobbs-Merrill, 1969), pp. 85–115.
12. *The Wild Prayer of Longing* (New Haven: Yale University Press, 1971), p. 53.
13. E. D. Hirsch, *The Aims of Interpretation* (Chicago: University of Chicago Press, 1976), pp. 140–44.
14. Examples of such work, by scholars whose association with any "field" of religion and letters ranges from considerable to none at all, would include Wallace Fowlie's *Rimbaud* (1947) and *Mallarmé* (1953); Erich Heller's *The Ironic German* (1953) and *The Artist's Journey into the Interior and Other Essays* (1965); R. W. B. Lewis's *The American Adam* (1955), *The Picaresque Saint* (1959), *Trials of the Word* (1965), and *The Poetry of Hart Crane* (1967); R. P. Blackmur's *Anni Mirabiles, 1921–1925* (1956); J. Hillis Miller's *Charles Dickens* (1958), *The Disappearance of God* (1963), *Poets of Reality* (1965), *The Form of Victorian Fiction* (1968), and *Thomas Hardy* (1970); Murray Krieger's *The Tragic Vision* (1960) and *The Classic Vision* (1971); Marjorie Hope Nicolson's *Mountain Gloom and Mountain Glory* (1963); Edward Wasiolek's *Dostoevsky* (1964); Albert Gelpi's *Emily Dickinson* (1965); Joseph N. Riddel's *The Clairvoyant Eye* (1965) and *The Inverted Bell* (1974); Denis Donoghue's *Connoisseurs of Chaos* (1965) and *The Ordinary Universe* (1968); Tom F. Driver's *Romantic Quest and Modern Query* (1968); Hyatt Waggoner's *American Poets* (1968); Vincent Buckley's *Poetry and the Sacred* (1968); Gabriel Josipovici's *The World and the Book* (1971); Theodore Ziolkowski's *Fictional Transfigurations of Jesus* (1972); Herbert Schneidau's *Sacred Discontent* (1976); John Seelye's *Prophetic Waters* (1977); and many others.
15. Early instances of this can be seen in Philip Wheelwright's *The Burning Fountain* (1954), Northrop Frye's *Anatomy of Criticism* (1957), Kenneth Burke's *The Rhetoric of Religion* (1961), and Cleanth Brooks's and William K. Wimsatt's *Literary Criticism: A Short History* (1962); but more recent examples would include Ray L. Hart's *Unfinished Man and the Imagination* (1968), Richard Palmer's *Hermeneutic* (1969), Geoffrey Hartman's *Beyond Formalism* (1970) and *The Fate of Reading* (1975), Helen Gardner's *Religion and Literature* (1971), Paul de Man's *Blindness and Insight* (1971), Harold Bloom's tetralogy beginning with *The Anxiety of Influ-*

ence (1973) and ending with *Poetry and Repression* (1976), Robert Scholes's *Structuralism in Literature* (1974), Wayne Booth's *Modern Dogma and the Rhetoric of Assent* (1974), and Denis Donoghue's *The Sovereign Ghost* (1976), together with the translation of such important works as Georges Poulet's *Studies in Human Time* (1956) and *The Interior Distance* (1959), Vladimir Propp's *Morphology of the Folktale* (1958), Ferdinand de Sassure's *Course on General Linguistics* (1959), Maurice Merleu-Ponty's *Phenomenology of Perception* (1962) and *Signs* (1964), Claude Lévi-Strauss's *Tristes Tropiques* (1964), *The Savage Mind* (1966), and *Structural Anthropology* (1967), Roland Barthes's *Writing Degree Zero* (1967) and *Elements of Semiology* (1970), Paul Ricoeur's *The Symbolism of Evil* (1967) and *The Conflict of Interpretations* (1974), Jacques Lacan's *The Language of the Self* (1968), Michel Foucault's *The Order of Things* (1970) and *The Archeology of Knowledge* (1972), Jean Piaget's *Structuralism* (1970), Roman Ingarden's *The Literary Work of Art* (1974), Hans-Georg Gadamer's *Truth and Method* (1976), and Jacques Derrida's *Of Grammatology* (1976).

Chapter 2   Forms of Religious Meaning in Literature

1. See *Relations of Literary Study: Essays on Interdisciplinary Contributions*, ed. James Thorpe (New York: Modern Language Association of America, 1967).
2. *Language and Silence: Essays on Language, Literature and the Inhuman* (New York: Atheneum, 1967).
3. Henry Nash Smith, "Can American Studies Develop a Method?" *American Quarterly* IX, Pt. 2 (Summer, 1957): 203. For a somewhat contrary view of the New Critics, see Gerald Graff, "What Was New Criticism? Literary Interpretation and Scientific Objectivity," *Salmagundi*, No. 27 (Summer–Fall, 1974): 72–93.
4. For a representative sampling, see the bibliography in *The New Orpheus: Essays Toward a Christian Poetic*, ed. Nathan A. Scott, Jr. (New York: Sheed & Ward, 1964), pp. 420–31.
5. Stanley Edgar Hyman, *The Armed Vision: A Study of the Methods of Modern Literary Criticism* (rev. and abr. ed.; New York: Vintage Books, 1955), p. 3.
6. *Trials of the Word: Essays in American Literature and the Humanistic Tradition* (New Haven and London: Yale University Press, 1965), p. 110.
7. *The Transcendentalists: An Anthology* (Cambridge: Harvard University Press, 1960), pp. 8–9.
8. For alternative analyses of the various approaches critics have taken to the study of religion and literature, see Sallie TeSelle, *Literature and the Christian Life* (New Haven and London: Yale University Press, 1966), pp. 7–59; J. Hillis Miller, "Literature and Religion" in *Relations of Literary Study: Essays on Interdisciplinary Contributions* pp. 111–26; Vernon Ruland, *Horizons of Criticism: An Assessment of Religious-Literary Options* (Chicago: American Library Association, 1975).

9. See *The Mirror and the Lamp: Romantic Theory and Critical Tradition* (New York: The Norton Library, W. W. Norton and Co., 1958), pp. 3–29. The utility of Abrams's typology can be seen in the fact that Lionel Trilling has also employed it in his "Introduction" to *Literary Criticism: An Introductory Reader*, ed. Lionel Trilling (New York: Holt, Rinehart and Winston, 1970), pp. 5–11.

10. See R. S. Crane *et al.*, *Critics and Criticism: Ancient and Modern* (Chicago: University of Chicago Press, 1952).

11. *The Poetics*, trans. S. H. Butcher, *Aristotle's Theory of Poetry and Fine Art* (London: Macmillan & Co., 1895), pp. 21–23.

12. *Biographia Literaria* (London, 1817), reproduced in *Criticism: The Major Texts*, ed. Walter Jackson Bate (New York: Harcourt, Brace & World, 1952), p. 379.

13. Ibid.

14. Ibid., p. 387.

15. See Abrams, *The Mirror and the Lamp*, p. 119.

16. See Murray Krieger, *The New Apologists for Poetry* (Minneapolis: University of Minnesota Press, 1956), pp. 33 ff.

17. For this description of the general characteristics of modern semantic criticism, I am chiefly indebted to R. S. Crane, *The Language of Criticism and the Structures of Poetry* (Toronto: University of Toronto Press, 1953), pp. 80–115.

18. Crane's distinction between the two major tendencies in modern semantic criticism is reiterated in different terms by Lee T. Lemon, in his *The Partial Critics* (New York: Oxford University Press, 1965). Lemon reduces the numerous examples of modern critical theory to formalistic theories that conceive of literature, in Crane's terms, as a special kind of meaningful expression, and mimetic theories that conceive of literature as the expression of a special kind of meaning. Lemon's categories have the advantage of greater specificity because he has broken down each classification, suggesting three variations of formalistic theory (closed form theories, open form theories, and symbolic form theories) and six variations of mimetic theory (personality and experience theories, edification theories, social theories, tradition theories, psychological theories, and perception theories). Lemon is careful to insist that any given critic may be classified under any of several of these categories. His purpose, however, is not so much to classify critics but, as any typology should, to help systemize critical discussion, and his method works admirably.

19. See William K. Wimsatt, Jr., and Cleanth Brooks, *Literary Criticism: A Short History* (New York: Alfred A. Knopf, 1962), pp. 724 ff.

20. See Philip Wheelwright, *The Burning Fountain: A Study in the Language of Symbolism* (new and rev. ed.,; Bloomington and London: Indiana University Press, 1968).

21. See Walter J. Ong, S. J., "A Dialectic of Aural and Objective Correlatives," *The Barbarian Within* (New York: Macmillan Company, 1962), pp. 26–40.

22. See Paul Ricoeur, *The Symbolism of Evil* (New York: Harper & Row, 1967).

23. See R. W. B. Lewis, *The American Adam: Innocence, Tragedy and Tradition in the Nineteenth Century* (Chicago: University of Chicago Press, 1955).

24. See, for example, Vincent Buckley, *Poetry and the Sacred* (London: Chatto & Windus, 1968); J. Hillis Miller, *Poets of Reality* (Cambridge: Harvard University Press, Belknap Press, 1965); and R. W. B. Lewis, *Trials of the Word: Essays in American Literature and the Humanistic Tradition* (New Haven and London: Yale University Press, 1965).

25. See Amos N. Wilder, *Theology and Modern Literature* (Cambridge: Harvard University Press, 1958).

26. See Nathan A. Scott, Jr., *The Broken Center: Studies in the Theolgical Horizon of Modern Literature (New Haven and London: Yale University Press*, 1966), and *Negative Capability: Studies in the New Literature and the Religious Situation* (New Haven and London: Yale University Press, 1969); and William F. Lynch, S. J., *Christ and Apollo: The Dimensions of the Literary Imagination* (New York: Sheed & Ward, 1960).

27. William F. Lynch, S. J., "Theology and the Imagination," *Thought* XXIX (Spring, 1954): 61–86.

28. Denis de Rougemont, "Religion and the Mission of the Artist," *Spiritual Problems in Contemporary Literature*, ed. Stanley Romaine Hopper (New York: Harper Torchbooks, 1957), pp. 173–86.

29. Stanley Romaine Hopper, "Introduction," *Interpretation: The Poetry of Meaning*, ed. Stanley Romaine Hopper and David L. Miller (New York: Harcourt, Brace & World, 1967), pp. ix–xxii.

30. F. O. Matthiessen, *The Achievement of T. S. Eliot: An Essay on the Nature of Poetry* (New York: Oxford University Press, 1935); and Lionel Trilling, "Freud and Literature," *The Liberal Imagination: Essays on Literature and Society* (Garden City, N.Y.: Doubleday Anchor Books, 1957), pp. 32–54.

31. The phrase is Howard Mumford Jones's, which he uses to describe the theory of literature Bacon adumbrated in the *De Augmentis Scientiarum*, in *The Theory of American Literature* (rev. ed.; Ithaca, N.Y.: Cornell University Press, 1965), p. 14.

32. See Roy Harvey Pearce, *The Continuity of American Poetry* (Princeton: Princeton University Press, 1961).

33. Erich Heller, *The Disinherited Mind: Essays in Modern German Litertature and Thought* (New York: Farrar, Straus & Cudahy, 1957), p. 268.

34. *The Collected Poems of Wallace Stevens* (New York: Alfred A. Knopf, 1964), p.239.

35. *Coleridge on Imagination* (Bloomington: Indiana University Press, 1960), p. 230.

36. *The Burning Fountain: A Study in the Language of Symbolism*, p. 205.

37. *Creation and Discovery* (New York: The Noonday Press, 1955), p. 87.

38. "Between the Numen and the Moha," *The Lion and the Honeycomb* (New York: Harcourt, Brace & Co., 1954), p. 297.

39. *The New Romantics* (Bloomington: Indiana University Press, 1962), p. 32.

40. Ibid., p. 42.

41. Ibid.

42. Ibid.

43. *Essays in Criticism*, Second Series (London: Macmillan & Co., 1891), pp. 1–2.
44. Ibid., p. 3.
45. Ibid., p. 2.
46. See Abrams, *The Mirror and the Lamp*, p. 15.
47. See Preston T. Roberts, Jr., "A Christian Theory of Dramatic Tragedy," *Journal of Religion* XXXI (January, 1951): 1–20.
48. See Louis L. Martz, "Introduction" to *The Meditative Poem: An Anthology of Seventeenth-Century Verse*, ed. Louis L. Martz (Garden City, N.Y.: Doubleday Anchor Books, 1963), pp. xvii–xxxi.
49. Henry Rago, "Faith and the Literary Imagination—The Vocation of Poetry," *Adversity and Grace: Studies in Recent American Literature*, ed. Nathan A. Scott, Jr. (Chicago: University of Chicago Press, 1968), p. 240.
50. Ibid., p. 248.
51. See R. W. B. Lewis, *Trials of the Word*, p. 110.
52. Henry Rago, "Faith and the Literary Imagination," p. 241.
53. Dorothy Van Ghent, *The English Novel: Form and Function* (New York: Harper Torchbooks, 1961), p. 3. Miss Van Ghent's references are to fiction, but we may as easily apply her remarks to poetry and drama as well.
54. "Historicism Once More," *The Kenyon Review* XX (Autumn, 1958): 566.
55. Ibid.
56. Ibid.
57. Ibid.
58. For this insight, and several others which follow, I am indebted to Dorothy Van Ghent, *The English Novel*. See particularly pp. 3–7.
59. *Art as Experience* (New York: Minton, Balch and Company, 1934), p. 325.
60. *The Collected Poems of Wallace Stevens*, p. 382.
61. *The English Novel*, p. 3.
62. Ibid., pp. 3–4.
63. *Tradition and Poetic Structure* (Denver: Alan Swallow, 1960), p. 141.
64. "Historicism Once More," p. 567.
65. *Anatomy of Criticism* (Princeton: Princeton University Press, 1957), p. 94.
66. George Steiner, *Language and Silence: Essays on Language, Literature and the Inhuman* (New York: Atheneum, 1967), p. 6.
67. *Types of Religious Experience Christian and Non-Christian* (Chicago: University of Chicago Press, 1951), p. 32.
68. I am indebted to an unpublished paper by Professor Edward Wasiolek for illumination of what I mean by a work's metaphysic. Wasiolek employs this concept himself in *Dostoevsky: The Major Fiction* (Cambridge: The M.I.T. Press, 1964), pp. 36, 55–59, 72, 77.
69. "Historicism Once More," p. 567.
70. Paul Ricoeur, *The Symbolism of Evil* (New York: Harper & Row, 1967), p. 354.
71. Ibid., pp. 351–52.
72. Roy Harvey Pearce, "Historicism Once More," p. 546.

73. "Preface" to *The Nigger of the "Narcissus"* (1897; London: J. M. Dent & Sons, 1950), p. viii.
74. Ibid., p. x.

Chapter 3   The Place of the Literary Critic
in Religious Studies

1. Gordon D. Kaufman, *An Essay on Theological Method* (Missoula, Mont.: Scholars Press, 1975), p. 30.
2. See E. D. Hirsch, Jr., *The Aims of Interpretation* (Chicago: University of Chicago Press, 1976), pp. 156–58.
3. See especially Tillich's *Theology of Culture* (New York: Oxford University Press, 1959), p. 42.
4. See Niebuhr, *The Kingdom of God in America* (1939; New York: Harper Torchbooks, 1959), p. ix.
5. Stevens, *Opus Posthumous* (London: Faber & Faber, 1957), p. 198.
6. The phrase is invoked by Clifford Geertz in *The Interpretation of Cultures* (New York: Basic Books, 1973), p. 6, to define the mode of analysis appropriate to what he calls "an interpretive theory of culture."
7. Hartman, *Beyond Formalism* (New Haven: Yale University Press, 1970), p. 56.
8. Ibid., p. 57.
9. For these two distinctions I am indebted to Clifford Geertz, *Islam Observed* (New Haven: Yale University Press, 1968), p. 98.
10. See Burke, *The Philosophy of Literary Form* (New York: Vintage Books, 1957), pp. 3–117.
11. Trilling, *Sincerity and Authenticity* (Cambridge: Harvard University Press, 1972), p. 135.
12. Ibid., pp. 135–36.
13. Ibid., p. 136.
14. Ibid.
15. Frank Kermode, *The Sense of an Ending* (New York: Oxford University Press, 1967), p. 39.
16. Northrop Frye, *Fables of Identity* (New York: Harcourt, Brace & World, 1963), p. 30.
17. Berthoff, *Fictions and Events* (New York: E. P. Dutton & Co., 1971), p. 50.
18. It should be noted that Lévi-Strauss sees a basic opposition between art and myth. As he puts it (*The Savage Mind*, p. 16, 21, 22, 25–26), "The creative act which gives rise to myths is in fact exactly the reverse of that which gives rise to works of art. In the case of works of art, the starting point is a set of one or more objects and one or more events which aesthetic creation unifies by revealing a common structure. Myths travel the same road but start from the other end. They use a structure to produce what is itself an object consisting of a set of events (for all myths tell a story). Art thus proceeds from a set (object &

event) to the *discovery* of its structure. Myth starts from a structure by means of which it *constructs* a set (object & event)." In the formulation to be later developed in this chapter, the relation between art and structure is seen somewhat differently. Rather than merely revealing the common structure that unites a set of "objects" or "events" in Lévi-Strauss's sense, art seeks to test, probe, and even revise "structure." As Herbert N. Schneidau has pointed out, "Lévi-Strauss's description really applies only to medieval or other mythologized arts, for he has missed [E. H.] Gombrich's points about the sacred discontent that dismantles the schema" (*Sacred Discontent: The Bible and Western Tradition* [Berkeley: University of California Press, 1976], p. 294).

19. Berthoff, *Fictions and Events*, p. 46.

20. Victor Turner, *The Ritual Process* (Ithaca, N.Y.: Cornell University Press, 1977), p. 43.

21. For the description of a literary theory that provides general explanation of this process, see my "Creation and Discovery: The Literary Theory of Eliseo Vivas," *Renascence* 22 (Summer, 1970): 196–206.

22. The argument in question is to be found in Peter L. Berger, "Some Second Thoughts on Substantive versus Functional Definitions of Religion," *Journal for the Scientific Study of Religion* (June, 1974): 125–33.

23. For the three-fold differentiation of kinds of theory which follows, I am indebted to Joseph Bettis, ed., *Phenomenology of Religion* (New York: Harper & Row, 1969), pp. 1–4.

24. van der Leuuw, *Religion in Essence and Manifestation* (London: George Allen & Unwin, 1938), p. 23.

25. See Geertz, *Islam Observed*, pp. 96–97.

26. Whitehead, *Religion in the Making* (1926; Cleveland: Meridian Books, 1960), p. 83.

27. Geertz, *Islam Observed*, p. 97.

28. See Toulmin, *An Examination of the Place of Reason in Ethics* (Cambridge: Cambridge University Press, 1950), pp. 204–20.

29. See Ogden, *The Reality of God* (New York: Harper & Row, 1966), pp. 25–43.

30. See Stevens, *Opus Posthumous*, pp. 199, 205–16.

31. Scott, "Eliot and the Orphic Way," *Journal of the American Academy of Religion* 42 (June, 1974): 227. Professor Scott seems to speak for them all when he writes, "the act of religious reflection is the act that all men are performing at whatever point they begin to search their experience, at the level of *theos* or of ultimate meaning, for the guaranty or sanction that finally gives warrant to human existence. Yet, in speaking of what authentic religious inquiry intends, to use a language (of 'warrant' and 'guaranty') whose flavor is moderately forensic is already somewhat to have falsified the case, since what is at issue is not matters of formal assurance but the question as to the possibility of a kind of Pascalian wager, that the world of our habitance is so constituted as to be, in its basic tendency, supportive rather than spendthrift of the human enterprise. It is, indeed, the felt need for assurance of the possibility of such a wager being made that is

deeply a part of the hopes and expectancies that men bring to the world, even when their cultural environment is one representing radical secularization."

32. Geertz, *Islam Observed*, p. 97.
33. Ibid., p. 97.
34. Nathan A. Scott, Jr., for example, speaks for a good many critics in noting how "the literary imagination vitalizes matters of ultimate concern by making concrete before the immediate gaze of the mind the real cost of a given life-orientation," not, of course, by lining up arguments in dialectical opposition to one another, "but rather—in terms of drama and symbolic action"—by "danc[ing] out (as Kenneth Burke would say) the real entailments of 'religiousness A' and "religiousness B'. . . ." From "Theology and the Literary Imagination" in *Adversity and Grace*, ed. Nathan A. Scott, Jr. (Chicago: University of Chicago Press, 1968), p. 22.
35. Lynen, *The Design of the Present* (New Haven: Yale University Press, 1969), p. 18.
36. Ibid., p. 25.
37. This last phrase is frequently mistaken to connote something abstract and readily paraphrasable. As employed by Wallace Stevens, from whom I borrow it, the notion of an "idea of order" is as much a formal as an ideational designation and, far from being wholly intellectual, is in most works of literature equally affective.
38. See Miller, *Errand Into the Wilderness* (1956; New York: Harper Torchbooks, 1964), pp. 184–85.
39. Ralph Barton Perry, *The Thought and Character of William James* (Boston: Atlantic, Little, Brown & Company, 1935), vol. 1 p. 71.
40. See Geertz, *Islam Observed*, p. 96.
41. Abrams, *Natural Supernaturalism* (New York: W. W. Norton and Co., 1971), p. 68.
42. Ibid., p. 13.
43. Ibid., p. 65.
44. Heller, *The Disinherited Mind* (Cleveland: Meridian Books, 1959), p. 263.
45. Ibid., pp. 262–63.
46. Ibid., p. 264.
47. Ibid., p. 268.
48. Ibid., p. 268.
49. Ibid., p. 46.
50. Marcel, *Homo Viator* (1951; New York: Harper Torchbooks, 1962), p. 100.
51. Ibid., p. 101.
52. I am paraphrasing an idea of Roy Harvey Pearce's, in which he explains the nature of the new historiography which he deems one of the main achievements of the American Studies movement. " 'The American Adam' and the State of American Studies," *Journal of Higher Education* 27 (February, 1956): 106.
53. Lynen, *The Design of the Present*, p. 35.
54. Trilling, *Beyond Culture* (New York: The Viking Press, 1965), p. 13.

55. John Dewey, *Art as Experience* (New York: Capricorn Books, 1958), p. 346.

56. Kazin, *Contemporaries* (Boston: Little, Brown & Company, 1962), p. 497.

57. *The Design of the Present*, pp. 25, 28.

58. This observation, which Ricoeur has made on several occasions, is most recently expressed in "Metaphor and the Main Problem of Hermeneutics," *New Literary History* 6 (Autumn, 1974): 106; and *Interpretation Theory: Discourse and the Surplus of Meaning* (Fort Worth: The Texas Christian University Press, 1976), pp. 87–88.

59. MacLeish, "Crisis and Poetry," an address delivered before the Yale Alumni Convocation in the Arts and Sciences, 7 October 1960; quoted by Maynard Mack, "To See It Feelingly," *PMLA* 86 (May, 1971): 373.

60. Ricoeur, *Interpretation Theory*, p. 94.

61. Ibid., p. 95.

62. Walter Slatoff has a particularly good discussion of this aspect of literature in *With Respect to Readers* (Ithaca, N.Y.: Cornell University Press, 1970), pp. 1–27.

63. A. N. Kaul, *The American Vision* (New Haven: Yale University Press, 1963), p. 46.

64. Erich Heller, *The Disinherited Mind*, p. 268.

65. Clifford Geertz, with Paul Ricoeur among others in mind, says something like this in *The Interpretation of Cultures*, pp. 19–20, 30.

66. By this phrase I mean the sort of thing Robert Langbaum refers to in his essay, "The Function of Criticism Once More." See his *The Modern Spirit* (New York: Oxford University Press, 1970), pp. 16–17.

67. Blackmur, *Anni Mirabiles, 1921–1925* (Washington, D.C.: The Library of Congress, 1956), p. 54.

Chapter 4   The American Writer and the Formation of an American Mind

1. "Literature and Culture: An Interview with Saul Bellow," *Salmagundi*, No. 30 (Summer, 1975): 6.

2. Ibid.

3. Ibid., p. 7.

4. Ibid., p. 8.

5. Ibid.

6. Henry Steele Commager, *The American Mind: An Interpretation of American Thought and Character Since the 1880s* (New York: Yale University Press, 1950), p. vii.

7. Perry Miller, *Nature's Nation* (Cambridge: Harvard University Press, Belknap Press, 1967), p. 13.

8. Henry Nash Smith, *Virgin Land: The American West as Symbol and Myth* (Cambridge: Harvard University Press, 1950), p. v.

9. See Gilbert Ryle, *Theory of Mind* (London: Hutchinson's University Library, 1949).

10. John Dewey, *Art as Experience* (1934; New York: Capricorn Books, 1958), p. 264.

11. Ibid.

12. Ibid.

13. *Experience and Nature* (1929; LaSalle, Ill.: Open Court Publishing Company, 1971), p. 247.

14. *Art as Experience*, p. 266.

15. *Experience and Nature*, p. 251.

16. Ibid.

17. Ibid., p. 248.

18. *Art as Experience*, p. 266.

19. Ibid., p. 264.

20. Susanne K. Langer, *Philosophy in a New Key* (Cambridge: Harvard University Press, 1959), p. 42.

21. Ibid., p. 29.

22. Some of the most important evidence for this view that mind and culture represent a compensation for genetic deficiency comes from recent anthropological studies concerning the origins of man's development from the lower animals. See Clifford Geertz, *The Interpretation of Cultures* (New York: Basic Books, 1973), pp. 46–47, to whom I am largely indebted for my remarks on the symbolic character of culture.

23. Ibid., pp. 55–83.

24. Ibid., p. 145.

25. These terms are those of Pitirim Sorokin. See Geertz, ibid., p. 145.

26. Quoted by Karl J. Weintraub, *Visions of Culture* (Chicago: University of Chicago Press, 1966), p. 261–62. My discussion of Ortega, and particularly his notion of *creencias*, is indebted to Weintraub's excellent exposition of Ortega's general theory of reality and culture, pp. 247–87.

27. This helps explain why, and in what ways, there is a considerable degree of continuity among the culture patterns of different peoples. As Geertz puts it, "The problems, being existential, are universal; their solutions, being human, are diverse." Ibid., p. 363.

28. This formulation was suggested to me by John F. Lynen, *The Design of the Present: Essays on Time and Form in American Literature* (New Haven: Yale University Press, 1969), p. 26.

29. See Edmund Wilson, *Patriotic Gore* (New York: Oxford University Press, 1962), pp. 5–11.

30. Quoted by Cushing Strout, "*Uncle Tom's Cabin* and the Portent of Millennium," *Yale Review* 57 (Spring, 1968): 378.

31. Strout is arguing that these elements not only explain much of the book's contemporary appeal but also suggest its irrelevance to the context in which responsible thinking about race relations in America must occur today.

32. This view of the novel owes much to Henry Nash Smith's interpretation in *Mark Twain: The Development of a Writer* (1962; New York: Atheneum, 1967), pp. 113–37.

33. See Stuart Hampshire, *Modern Writers and Other Essays* (London: Chatto & Windus, 1969), pp. x–xvii.
34. Hayden White, "The Point of It All," *New Literary History* II((Autumn, 1970): 180.
35. E. H. Gombrich, *Art and Illusion* (New York: Pantheon Books, 1960), p. 60.
36. Ibid., p. 88.
37. Ibid., p. 86.
38. Hans Robert Jauss, "Literary History as a Challenge to Literary Theory," *New Literary History* II (Autumn, 1970): 23. This essay is a translation of chapters 5–12 of the author's *Literaturegeschichte als Provokation der Literaturwissenschaft*, Konstanz, 1967.
39. Gadamer would, up to a point, reverse Collingwood's procedure of ferreting out the question to which the text is an answer by claiming that the relation of question and answer is just the reverse: "The voice that speaks to us from the past—be it text, work, trace—itself poses a question and places our meaning in openness. In order to answer this question, we, of whom the question is asked, must ourselves begin to ask questions. We must attempt to reconstruct the question to which the transmitted text is the answer. But we shall not be able to do this without going beyond the historical horizon it presents us with. The reconstruction of the question to which the text is presumed to be the answer takes places itself within a process of questioning through which we seek the answer to the question that the text ask us" *(Truth and Method* [New York: The Seabury Press, 1975], p. 337).
40. White, ibid., 179–80.
41. Gadamer, ibid., pp. 333–41.
42. See Leo Marx, "American Studies—Defense of an Unscientific Method," *New Literary History* I (October, 1969): 89.
43. See Lee T. Lemon and Marion J. Reis, eds. and trans., *Russian Formalist Criticism: Four Essays* (Lincoln: University of Nebraska Press, 1965), pp. 4, 11–13.
44. For Shklovsky defamiliarization, as the very essence of literariness, accentuates that in literature all the weight is on the particular way of seeing something, not on the thing seen. This is parallel to Gombrich's point that representational art is not the portrayal of an object but of its representation in an image, which is a new reality in its own right. See Herbert N. Schneidau, *Sacred Discontent: The Bible and Western Tradition* (Berkeley: University of California Press, 1977), p. 269. It is also consistent with Paul Ricoeur's view of art as an augmentation of reality whose aim is not reproduction but metamorphosis. See Ricoeur, *Interpretation Theory: Discourse and the Surplus of Meaning* (Fort Worth: The Texas Christian University Press, 1976), pp. 40–43.
45. John Dewey, *Experience and Nature*, p. 253.
46. Frank Kermode, *The Classic: Literary Images of Permanence and Change* (New York: The Viking Press, 1975), pp. 113–41.
47. Kermode sees this change as a religious transformation best understood in terms of the process of secularization. "Secularization multiplies the world's structures of probability, as the sociologists of religion tell us, and 'this plurality of re-

ligious legitimations is internalized in consciousness as a plurality of possibilities between which one may choose.' It is this pluralism that, on the long view, denies the authoritative or authoritarian reading that insists on its identity with the intention of the author, or on its agreement with the readings of his contemporaries; or rather, it has opened up the possibilities, exploited most aggressively by the structuralists and semiologists, of regarding the text as the permanent locus of change; as something of which the permanence no longer legitimately suggests the presence and permanence of what it appears to designate" (ibid., pp. 138–39).

48. Ibid., p. 113.
49. Marx, "American Studies—Defense of an Unscientific Method," p. 89.
50. White, "The Meaning of It All," p. 181.
51. White, "The Meaning of It All," p. 180.
52. Gadamer, *Truth and Method*, p. 255.
53. See E. H. Gombrich, *Art and Illusion*, p. 90.
54. There is currently a growing awareness on the part of literary historians concerning the wide spectrum of relationships that all literary texts, and not just classics, can have to the prevailing value or belief system of their age. While I am here arguing that the classic typically does more than simply affirm the mental set of its age, I am not unmindful of the fact that certain traditional classics seem to do little more than this, and that if one were in a position to pursue this issue more closely, it would be possible to come up with a fairly complex set of ratios describing the relationships even classic texts bear to the conscious or unconscious metaphysic of their time. Taking a hint from Wolfgang Iser's article on "The Reality of Fiction" A Functionalist Approach to Literature" (*New Literary History* VII [Autumn, 1975]: 7–38), Quentin Skinner has presented one such schematization of the range of polemical relations a text can possess to the surrounding matrix of cultural attitudes and assumptions as follows: "The dominant end of the spectrum would be filled by works in which the author has it as part of his aim to affirm a prevailing set of values or attitudes. This might, as in Hooker's *Laws*, be a matter of defensively upholding, maintaining, and reminding people of certain beliefs; or it might, as in Spenser's *Fairie Queene*, be a matter of celebrating or extolling certain values or attitudes. The middle part of the spectrum would be filled by works in which the author had it as part of his aim to submit the ideas or the events of the age to discussion and debate. This might take the form of challenging, questioning, or criticizing certain prevailing beliefs, as in the case of much Augustan satire; or it might take the form in a similarly oblique style, of pleading, advising, or warning about certain current policies, as in most early stage allegories from the time of *Gorboduc*. Finally, the negative end of the spectrum would include all those works in which the author's aim is fundamentally to reject some cherished value or assumption of the age. The chosen method might be sheer invective, as in some of Dickens; or ridicule and parody, as in much of Cervantes; or it might more straightforwardly take the form of discursive argument, as in the work of a moralist (Machiavelli is

a good example) whose aim is to challenge some of the basic moral assumptions of his age" (*New Literary History* VII [Autumn, 1975]: 221–22).

55. Henry Nash Smith, "The Scribbling Women and the Cosmic Success Story," *Critical Inquiry* I (September, 1974): 47–70.
56. See John Seelye, *Melville: The Ironic Diagram* (Evanston, Ill.: Northwestern University Press, 1970).
57. Daniel Hoffman, *Form and Fable in American Fiction* (New York: Oxford University Press, 1965), pp. 233–78; Newton Arvin, *Herman Melville* (New York: William Sloan Associates, 1950), pp. 182–93.
58. Northrop Frye, *Anatomy of Criticism* (Princeton: Princeton University Press, 1957), pp. 308–14. The following discussion is essentially a summary of Frye's ideas.
59. Ibid., p. 306.
60. Quoted by Denis Donoghue, *The Sovereign Ghost: Studies in Imagination* (Berkeley: University of California Press, 1976), p. 27.
61. Hoffman, *Form and Fable in American Fiction*, p. 274.
62. Richard Chase, *Herman Melville, A Critical Study* (New York: Macmillan Company, 1949), p. 73.
63. Hoffman, *Form and Fable in American Fiction*, p. 263.
64. Ibid., p. 278.

Chapter 5   American Literature and the Imagination of Otherness

1. Benjamin DeMott, *Supergrow: Essays and Reports on Imagination in America* (New York: E. P. Dutton & Co., 1969), p. 93.
2. Ibid., p. 12.
3. William James, *Essays in Faith and Morals*, ed. Ralph Barton Perry (1899; Cleveland: World Publishing Company, 1962), p. 284.
4. DeMott, *Supergrow*, p. 99.
5. Ibid., p. 93.
6. Ibid., p. 94.
7. The phrase is Ralph Waldo Emerson's, which Richard Poirier uses as the title of his fine study, *A World Elsewhere: The Place of Style in American Literature* (New York: Oxford University Press, 1966).
8. Wallace Stevens, *Opus Posthumous* (London: Faber & Faber, 1957), p. 237.
9. Robinson Jeffers, *The Double Axe* (New York: Random House, 1948), p. vii.
10. See Perry Miller, *Errand Into the Wilderness* (Cambridge: Harvard University Press, 1956), pp. 1–15.
11. The best account of the impact of the wilderness on American Puritanism, which treats, among other things, of the variety of metamorphoses the New World underwent in Puritan thinking, is to be found in Peter N. Carroll, *Puritanism and the Wilderness: The Intellectual Significance of the New England Frontier,*

1629–1700 (New York: Columbia University Press, 1969). The fullest account, which is heavily weighted down with a mythic superstructure borrowed from Joseph Campbell's *Hero with a Thousand Faces* and which tends to oversimplify the relationship by polarizing it as a contest between the Christian myth of the American Puritans and the natural myth based on "blood-knowledge" of the native Americans, is Richard Slotkin, *Regeneration Through Violence: The Mythology of the American Frontier, 1600–1860* (Middletown, Conn.: Wesleyan University Press, 1974), pp. 3–222.

12. Henry James, *The Wings of the Dove* (1902; New York: Charles Scribner's Sons, 1939), II, p. 439.

13. Miller, *Errand Into the Wilderness*, pp. 1–15.

14. Joseph Bettis, ed., *Phenomenology of Religion* (New York: Harper & Row, 1969), p. 203.

15. For the description of Eliade's understanding of religion, I am indebted to an extremely helpful and illuminating essay by Jonathan Z. Smith, "The Wobbling Pivot," *Journal of Religion* 52 (April, 1972): 134–49.

16. F. Scott Fitzgerald, *The Great Gatsby* (1925; New York: Charles Scribner's Sons, 1953), p. 182.

17. In the large body of material which constitutes his vast corpus, there is no single passage where Miller defines the paradigm exactly as I have formulated it. Nor is there any moment in the work of the aforementioned critics where the paradigm is explicitly described in terms parallel to my own. The definition I have provided is a personal reconstruction of various elements that I have found threaded throughout the work of many critics and can therefore, if found wanting, be held against no one but myself.

18. This is a variation on an observation of F. O. Matthiessen's in which he remarks that American writers in the nineteenth century, in contrast to such English contemporaries as Jane Austen, Dickens, or Thackeray, "were more concerned with human destiny than with every man in his humor" (*American Renaissance* [New York: Oxford University Press, 1941] p. 271).

19. Gerardus van der Leeuw, *Religion in Essence and Manifestation* (London: George Allen & Unwin, 1938), p. 23.

20. See J. Hillis Miller, *Poets of Reality* (Cambridge: Harvard University Press, 1965), pp. 10–11.

21. R. P. Blackmur, "Religious Poetry in the United States," *Religious Perspectives in American Culture*, ed. James Ward Smith and A. Leland Jamison (Princeton: Princeton University Press, 1961), p. 286.

22. John F. Lynen, *The Design of the Present* (New Haven: Yale University Press, 1969), p. 26.

23. Lionel Trilling, *Sincerity and Authenticity* (Cambridge: Harvard University Press, 1972), p. 1.

24. See especially M. H. Abrams, *Natural Supernaturalism* (New York: W. W. Norton and Co., 1971), pp. 65–70.

25. D. H. Lawrence, *Studies in Classic American Literature* (1923; Garden City, N.Y.: Doubleday Anchor Books, 1951), p. 185.

NOTES

43

26. *The Ordinary Universe: Soundings in Modern Literature* (London: Faber & Faber, 1968).

27. The phrase is Wallace Stevens's from "Of Modern Poetry," *The Collected Poems of Wallace Stevens* (New York: Alfred A. Knopf, 1954), p. 239.

28. Theodore Roethke, *The Far Field* (New York: Doubleday & Company, 1971), p. 53.

29. Ibid.

30. Geoffrey Hartman, *Beyond Formalism* (New Haven: Yale University Press, 1971), p. 257.

31. In this there is, to be sure, a marked parallel between Gatsby and all those other devotees and avatars of something like an American "religion of wonder"— Emerson, Thoreau, Whitman, Twain, a certain side of Henry James, Gertrude Stein, Sherwood Anderson, Hemingway, Salinger, and Walker Percy—whose idealization of an unencumbered simplicity of response Tony Tanner discusses in *The Reign of Wonder: Naivete and Reality in American Literature* (Cambridge: Cambridge University Press, 1965). But where Tanner is interested in wonder chiefly as a way of seeing, as "the cultivation of a naive eye," I am more interested, as I think Fitzgerald was as well, in wonder as a mode of being, as something intrinsic to the very nature of life itself.

32. For this and several other insights in this discussion, I am indebted to Marius Bewley's excellent chapter on the novel entitled "Scott Fitzgerald and the Collapse of the American Dream" in *The Eccentric Design: Form in the Classic American Novel* (New York: Columbia University Press, 1963), pp. 159–87.

33. Howard Mumford Jones, *O Strange New World* (New York: The Viking Press, 1964), p. 41.

34. See, in particular, Bewley, pp. 283–85.

35. Ibid., p. 284.

36. F. O. Matthiessen, *American Rennaissance*, p. 459. The reference is to Captain Ahab's descendants.

37. See Perry Miller, "Benjamin Franklin—Jonathan Edwards," in *Major Writers of America*, Vol. I, ed. Perry Miller (New York: Harcourt, Brace & World, 1962), p. 96.

38. I am here paraphrasing an idea expressed in Lionel Trilling's essay "Anna Karenina," which is reprinted in his *The Opposing Self* (Compass Books Edition; New York: The Viking Press, 1959), p. 75.

39. R. W. B. Lewis, *Trials of the Word: Essays in American Literature and the Humanistic Tradition* (New Haven: Yale University Press, 1965), p. vii.

40. *Opus Posthumus*, p. 202.

Postscript

1. Geoffrey Hartman, "Literary Criticism and Its Discontents," *Critical Inquiry* III (Winter, 1976): 219.

2. Gabriel Josipovici, *The World and the Book: A Study of Modern Fiction* (Stanford: Stanford University Press, 1971), p. 302.

3. Ibid., p. 307.

4. Stephen Spender, *The Struggle of the Modern* (Berkeley: University of California Press, 1963), p. 15.

5. Clifford Geertz, *The Interpretation of Cultures* (New York: Basic Books, 1973), p. 29.

Index

Stevens, Wallace, 22, 51, 52, 70, 83, 84,
    92, 98, 108, 117, 181, 190, 205–7, 222
Stewart, Randall, 21
Stowe, Harriet Beecher, 144–47, 152, 153
Strout, Cushing, 145, 146
Studies in Classic American Literature, 177
"Study of Poetry, The," 72
Swedenborg, Emmanuel, 204
Swift, Jonathan, 162
Symbolism of Evil, The, 45

Tate, Allen, 35, 64, 71, 86
Taylor, Edward, 109
Themis, 40
Theology and Modern Literature, 30
Theopoetic, 30
Thoreau, Henry David, 22, 36, 56, 126,
    182
Thought (journal), 34
Three American Moralists, 32
Tillich, Paul, 22, 23, 26–29, 35, 41, 96,
    105, 171
Tillyard, E. M. W., 38
Tocqueville, Alexis de, 127
Toulmin, Stephen, 93, 108
Tracy, David, 43
Trilling, Lionel, 33, 65, 101, 117, 203
Tristes Tropiques, 45
Trollope, Anthony, 97
Trotsky, Leon, 99
Turner, Victor, 40, 103
Twain, Mark, 146–48, 152–53, 195

Uncle Tom's Cabin, 144, 152–53
Underground Man, The, 77
Use and Abuse of History, The, 49

Vahanian, Gabriel, 30
van der Leeuw, Gerardus, 104, 196
Van Ghent, Dorothy, 80, 83, 120
Vico, Giovanni, 151
Virgil, 157

Vivas, Eliseo, 71
Voltaire, 162
Voyeur, Le, 224

Wach, Joachim, 40, 86
Wait Without Idols, 30
Walden, 126
Walton, Izaak, 162
Warren, Robert Penn, 22, 54
Waste Land, The, 40, 121, 154
Weber, Max, 40
West, Nathaniel, 205
Weston, Jessie L., 40
Wharf, Benjamin Lee, 156
Wheelwright, Philip, 40, 71
White, Hayden, 149, 151, 156
Whitehead, Alfred North, 42, 106, 183,
    214
Whitman, Walt, 109, 133, 175, 177, 181–
    83, 190, 195, 210
Wieman, Henry Nelson, 14
Wilder, Amos, 22, 30
Wild Prayer of Longing, The, 32
Willey, Basil, 38
Williams, William Carlos, 198, 202, 206
Will To Believe, The, 9
Wilson, Edmund, 20, 38, 40, 64, 65, 118,
    145
Wimsatt, William, 86
Winesburg, Ohio, 127, 205
Wings of the Dove, 126, 186
Winters, Yvor, 55, 64
Winthrop, John, 185, 203
Wittgenstein, Ludwig, 37, 43
Word of God and the Word of Man, The, 15
Wordsworth, William, 12, 61, 68, 113
World and the Book, The, 223

Yeats, William Butler, 90, 130

Zeus, 40
Zwingli, Ulrich, 114